Introduction to Crime Scene Photography

Please visit the Companion Website to
Introduction to Crime Scene Photography

www.elsevierdirect.com/companions/9780123865434

The Companion Website contains hundreds of color images from the book arranged as PowerPoint™ slideshows that demonstrate key concepts in the text. These additional images are meant to aid students in their own practical experience by showing examples of successes and failures in crime scene photography.

Introduction to Crime Scene Photography

Edward M. Robinson

The George Washington University
Forensic Science Department
Washington, DC, USA

AMSTERDAM ● BOSTON ● HEIDELBERG ● LONDON NEW YORK ● OXFORD ● PARIS
● SAN DIEGO SAN FRANCISCO ● SINGAPORE ● SYDNEY ● TOKYO

Academic Press is an imprint of Elsevier

Academic Press is an imprint of Elsevier
The Boulevard, Langford Lane, Kidlington, Oxford, OX5 1GB, UK
225 Wyman Street, Waltham, MA 02451, USA

First published 2013

Notices
Knowledge and best practice in this field are constantly changing. As new research and experience broaden our
understanding, changes in research methods, professional practices, or medical treatment may become necessary.

Practitioners and researchers must always rely on their own experience and knowledge in evaluating and using
any information, methods, compounds, or experiments described herein. In using such information or methods
they should be mindful of their own safety and the safety of others, including parties for whom they have
a professional responsibility.

To the fullest extent of the law, neither the Publisher nor the authors, contributors, or editors, assume any
liability for any injury and/or damage to persons or property as a matter of products liability, negligence or
otherwise, or from any use or operation of any methods, products, instructions, or ideas contained in the
material herein.

British Library Cataloguing in Publication Data
A catalogue record for this book is available from the British Library

Library of Congress Control Number: 2012938245

ISBN: 978-0-12-386543-4

For information on all Academic Press publications
visit our website at **store.elsevier.com**

Printed and bound in China

12 13 14 15 10 9 8 7 6 5 4 3 2 1

Dedication

To my wife, Sue. Words are not enough to express my appreciation of you.

Contents

Acknowledgments

I must begin by thanking Norm Tiller, the photography instructor at the Virginia Forensic Science Academy in Richmond, Virginia, in 1988. He first kindled my interest in crime scene photography. Because of Norm's ability to explain complex photography concepts in ways I could understand, my love of photography grew and I began collecting photography books and subscribing to multiple photography magazines. This book began back then.

It is also a pleasure to acknowledge my two friends and collaborators in this book, Gerald B. Richards and David ("Ski") Witzke. I've known both for ages and invited them to participate in this book because of their love of photography and digital imaging. They have both probably forgotten more about photography than I'll ever know.

Jerry was an FBI Special Agent; he held the position of Chief of the Document Operations and Research Units and retired from the FBI as the Chief of the Special Photographic Unit, FBI Laboratory. For ten years, Jerry taught Forensic Photography at The George Washington University, Washington DC. When his consulting business demanded more of his time, I was fortunate enough to take over his course. I was thrilled when Jerry offered to write the chapter on ultraviolet, visible, and near infrared imaging.

Ski is currently Vice President, Program Management, at Foray Technologies and is generally considered to be one of the foremost experts in forensic digital image processing and AFIS technologies. He has taught Digital Imaging of Evidentiary Photography at the FBI Academy in Quantico, Virginia, and spends a good portion of his time training and speaking at regional and international forensic science conferences. There is no one else I would consider to write the chapter on digital imaging.

Throughout this text, you will find images captured by my past and current students in my Forensic Photography course taught at The George Washington University, Washington, DC. Their images make the verbal explanations of the photographic concepts and principal come alive. I am indebted to all of them and to others who have contributed images for this text: J. Wreh, I. Walker, M. Simms, S. Dickson, K. Kinsie, D. Schweizer, S. Reeve, J. Buffington, L. Larsen, L. Etheridge, Melinda and Melody Hashemi, M. Blake, M. Hur, M. Towers, B. Pridgen, S. Keppel, S. Lingsch, M. Halter, D. Sedig, T. Nelson, Major Stutzman; J. Sinex, J. Polangcus, and S. Kingsbury.

I had to slip two images of my niece, Jenna Stanners, into this book somehow. When you see her photos, you'll know why. How photogenic! Thanks, Jenna, for giving me permission to use your images.

Bill Pekala and Ron Taniwaki, with Nikon Professional Services, provided many images and the Nikon cameras, lenses, and flash units to take some of my own images. A special thanks goes out to them for their help with this text.

Many individuals have helped me in innumerable ways as I developed this book. My thanks go out to all of them. There are undoubtedly typos and errors, despite their help. Those are my fault entirely.

Introduction

I joined the Arlington County Police Department (ACPD) in Virginia in 1971 and first became interested in crime scene photography in 1978, as I was preparing for the promotional process for new Police Agents, our agency's name for crime scene investigators. There was no text adequate for us to study, so we learned photography from our senior Police Agents, who taught us all their photography tricks and the techniques that worked for them and what they had in turn learned when they had first studied for the promotional process. It did not seem very organized, but we all eventually learned how to take some very good crime scene photographs.

Because I loved photography, I began reading as many general photography books as I could find, trying to learn photography techniques that I could apply to my crime scene photography. Naturally, many of these books had common elements, but every now and again one of the books would explain a technique in a way that made more sense to me or mentioned a different aspect about why one technique was better than another for creating a particular effect. I started to collect a scrapbook of these tips and tricks. At crime scenes I was working, I would frequently encounter a particular photographic problem, and I could often find the solution among the notes I had collected. I wondered why no one had thrown all these good ideas into a single book specifically targeting crime scene photographers.

In 1988, I learned I would be sent to the Virginia Forensic Science Academy (VFSA) in Richmond, Virginia, for a ten-week residential program in which police officers from all over the state were taught by professional trainers and the lab examiners from the Central Laboratory of the state's regional lab system. We were taught state-of-the-art methods to locate, document, process, package, and preserve physical evidence so that once the evidence eventually arrived at one of the forensic laboratories, its full value as physical evidence would be maintained.

At the VFSA, photography was taught by Norm Tiller, a training professional who had previously been a police officer. Not only did he seem to know more than all the previous books on photography that I had read, but he also had the special ability to express these complex matters in ways that made them easy to understand. Photographic concepts with which I had previously had difficulty now made sense.

When I returned from the VFSA, it was understood that I would begin teaching photography to all the newer officers now preparing for the Police Agent exams. I was asked what book I would recommend to help them prepare for the exam process, and I had to report that there was no comprehensive text that contained all the photography techniques a crime scene investigator would need. I then asked if I could write a police photography manual for our department and was given the go-ahead. In 1990, I wrote the 59-page Arlington County Police Department Basic Police Photography for Police Agents Handbook, which included no photographic examples. It was produced for use only within the ACPD. However, I still kept collecting tips and tricks on photography from every general book on photography I read.

After retiring from the ACPD, I became a full-time associate professor with the Forensic Science Department of The George Washington University in Washington DC in 2000. One of the regular courses I have taught since then is Photography in the Forensic Sciences. Besides my Police Photography Handbook from 1990, my collection of photography notes had doubled in size. I kept promising my departmental chair that I would eventually publish everything as one complete text on crime scene photography. In 2006, an Acquisitions Editor with Academic Press named Jennifer Soucy knocked on my office door out of the blue and asked if I had ever considered writing a book. It seemed that all the stars had aligned perfectly, and I had no more excuses; I agreed to write Crime Scene Photography, which was first printed in 2007. This text was specifically written for working crime scene photographers all over the country and for advanced undergraduate- or graduate-level crime scene photography courses. The second edition came out in 2010. This text is currently required reading for all crime scene investigators preparing for the exam to become certified by the International Association for Identification (IAI) Crime Scene Certification Board.

Last year, my current Academic Press Editor, Elizabeth Brown, mentioned the increasing need for a scaled-down version of Crime Scene Photography. Community colleges, junior colleges, and even many high schools across the country are now teaching Introduction to Forensic Science courses. Their students do not need a text the size of Crime Scene Photography because photography is just one of multiple aspects covered in these courses. Could I edit my current text, keeping as much of the content necessary to make it worthwhile to this new market? I decided to accept this challenge, and this text is the result. This is also the first crime scene photography text, I believe, to use as its basis the guidelines set out in the recommendations of SWGIT, SWGTREAD, and SWGFAST, the three Scientific Working Groups developing the best photographic practices related to Imaging Technology, Shoe Prints, Tire Tracks and Fingerprints, respectively. Invariably, if an agency wants to assure themselves that they are capturing crime scene images in ways that will be able to withstand challenges in court, following the guidelines recommended by the SWGs is advised. Regardless of the perceived quality of an image, the crime scene photographer has wasted their time by capturing any images that are ultimately held to be inadmissible in court.

Another benefit of this book is that if you can assimilate the crime scene photographic techniques taught in this text, all of your other photographs will improve as well. Many of these skills will easily translate to your other, non-crime scene photos. I actually felt so comfortable in my photographic skills that I briefly ventured into wedding photography. That proved to be just a brief part-time job. I could take the images necessary as a wedding photographer, but dealing with brides-to-be was my undoing. Dealing with criminals and crime scenes was much less stressful!

As you can tell by a brief paging-through of this text, it is loaded with many, many images. I am constantly looking for good examples of crime scene images, as well as photographs showing how the techniques are to be done. If you have some great shots you'd like to share with me, I'd love to see them. If I really like them, I may ask you for permission to use them in one of my future editions, with your name mentioned as well. How many other times has reading a book opened up the possibility of having your images being published in a text on crime scene photography? I look forward to seeing your talents. After all, that is what this book is about: teaching you the skills you need to be a great crime scene photographer.

Edward M. Robinson
erobinso@gwu.edu

CHAPTER 1

An Overview of Crime Scene Photography and Composition

KEY TERMS

Cardinal Rule I: Fill the Frame
Cardinal Rule II: Keep the Film Plane Parallel
Cardinal Rule III: Maximize the Depth of Field (DOF)
Close-up photographs
Composition
Depth of field (DOF)
Examination-quality photographs
Exterior overalls

Full-body panorama
Full field of view responsibility
Hard shadows
Interior overalls
Isosceles triangle
Labeled scale
Lens distortion
Lens flare
Midrange photographs
Natural perspective
Overall photographs
Perspective distortion

Photo identifier
Photographic
Photo memo form
Scales on the same plane
Shadow control
Soft shadows
SWGs
SWGIT
SWGFAST
SWGTREAD
Wagon wheel ellipse

CONTENTS

LEARNING OBJECTIVES

Upon completion of this lesson, you will be able to:
- Explain the three cardinal rules of good photography
- Explain how the same subject can be composed differently in various images
- Explain why "fill the frame" has two aspects: both a positive and a negative connotation
- Explain why good composition partly depends on the point of view of the photographer
- Explain why the careful written documentation of each photograph is necessary
- Explain three techniques by which photographs are documented
- Explain how overall photographs relate to the general crime scene area
- Explain how exterior overall photographs are to be taken
- Explain how interior overall photographs are to be taken

- Explain how midrange photographs are best taken
- Explain the four types of close-up photographs
- Explain additional types of photographic concerns related to documenting the wounds of suspects and victims
- Explain the complete photographic documentation of a homicide victim

Crime scene photography is very different from many other types of photography. Creative and artistic photography often follow very different rules, which is perfectly fine. But crime scene photography differs from other variations of photography because the crime scene photographers usually have a very specific purpose for capturing each image. There is a specific job to be done and specific types of images that have to be captured. Nevertheless, the crime scene photographer, at times, has to be very creative to successfully get the shot. But instead of the creativity being the purpose of the shot, the creativity necessary to capture a crime scene image should almost be unnoticed.

Crime scene photography serves several purposes. For those who were at the original crime scene, these images will help refresh their memory after a period of time has gone by. For those who could not be present at the original crime scene, it provides them with the opportunity to see the crime scene and the evidence within the crime scene. This purpose can apply to other law enforcement professionals who will become involved with the case and will later apply when the case goes to trial. The judge, jury, attorneys, and witnesses can all benefit from seeing the original crime scene images. And sometimes the images captured at the crime scene may be one way to actually walk away from the crime scene with the evidence. Often, photography is the only way to actually collect the evidence. Therefore, crime scene photography is a method to:

- Document the crime scene and the evidence within the crime scene,
- Collect the evidence. These images can then be later used as examination-quality photographs by experts/analysts from the forensic laboratory.

This book will help the reader not only to understand what images should be taken but will also explain how a digital SLR (single-lens reflex) camera system should be used to optimally capture these required images.

The authors have extensive experience with crime scene photography. We will, of course, use our experience to convey to the reader both the photographic principals and techniques we have successfully used in the field. Perhaps even more important, this text will base much of its information on the recommendations of the various Scientific Working Groups (SWGs) as they apply to crime scene photography. In particular, we will rely on the Scientific Working Group on Imaging Technology (SWGIT[1]), the Scientific Working Group on Shoeprints and Tire Tracks (SWGTREAD[2]), and the Scientific Working Group on Friction Ridge Analysis, Standards, and Technology (SWGFAST[3])—latent print examiners. These SWGs maintain their recommendation on their websites, which can be updated and revised as necessary.

The authors will rely on the SWG documents that were current as this text was written. Therefore, you need not rely on the experience of just the three authors; you will be able to also rely on all the professionals involved with the SWGs, whose members include working crime scene photographers, researchers, and academics.

PHOTO DOCUMENTATION FORMS

Because crime scene images can be offered in court as evidence, they are subject to normal chain-of-custody rules and eventually must be offered to the court as evidence by an individual who will have to swear that they are a "fair and accurate representation of the scene." In order to establish that individual images meet these standards, three types of documentation have traditionally been used.

The Photo Identifier

At the beginning of every series of photographs of a crime scene, the very first image captured is usually of the photo identifier after it has been filled out. Although some variations of photo identifiers are used by different agencies, four elements are frequently included on this form:

- The case number
- The date and time
- The address/location
- The photographer

The case number is used rather than the incident type because the incident type can change over time but the case number usually does not. For instance, what was originally dispatched as a malicious wounding may be upgraded to a homicide if the victim dies. Or an initial report of a sexual assault may be upgraded to a rape when more information is obtained. The original incident type may also be downgraded for a multitude of reasons.

---

[1] http://www.theiai.org/guidelines/swgit/
[2] http://www.swgtread.org
[3] http://www.swgfast.org

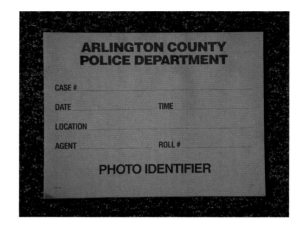

FIGURE 1-1
Photo identifier

The date and time of the incident, at least with regard to the images of the crime scene, are usually the date and time the photographs first begun.

The address of the incident is frequently listed, but the name of the location can be used as well. A bank robbery can be documented as 123 Main Street, but the bank's branch name can also be included along with the street address.

Of course, the photographer's name must be indicated in some way. Depending on the agency, photographers can list either their name or initials, or perhaps their badge number or some other identification (ID) number that their agency provides its employees.

 RULE OF THUMB 1-1

*It is recommended to photograph a new Photo Identifier any time one of these four variables change. (This note is the first **rule of thumb** in this text. Rules of Thumb are key points and fundamental concepts emphasized in this book. Remember them! When in doubt about a particular photographic technique, referring to them will help you.)*

Each new case requires its own photo identifier. If the location of one case changes, a new photo identifier is suggested. For instance, for a bank robbery, one photo identifier will cover the images taken within the bank lobby, but a new identifier should be created for a suspect's residence if that's where a search warrant will be served related to the bank robbery. Many agencies also want a new photo identifier when the clock ticks past midnight. And if you loan your camera to another person who will use it briefly, the fact that a new photographer is using the camera should be documented with a new photo identifier. When you receive your camera back, before continuing your photographs, photograph a new photo identifier. As always, comply with your agency's standard operating procedure (SOP) on this matter.

When film cameras were used, the number of film rolls used at an incident is also recorded. If your agency is using digital cameras, just insert the word "digital."

Why is the photo identifier shown above a midtoned gray? That convention is a remnant of film days, when automatic film processing machines frequently set the exposure for the entire roll of film based on the first image on the roll. As will be explained further in the next chapter, light meters in an SLR camera body are designed to recommend proper exposures for scenes that reflect 18 percent of the light striking them back toward the camera. This shade of gray is similar to an 18 percent gray card, which is used by many photographers to determine proper exposures in tricky lighting situations.

The Photo Memo Form

As each image is captured, it should be logged on a photo memo form. This step is best done immediately after each image is taken. This step was critical when film cameras were used because film cameras frequently did not record all the photographic variables, the way that current digital cameras do. Even though today's digital cameras frequently retain these camera variables in the metadata of the image's file, this data can sometimes be lost for various reasons. Again, comply with your agency's SOP.

This example photo memo form is actually a synthesis of several agencies' individual forms merged for a forensic photography course taught by one of the authors. Feel free to use it or modify it to suit your needs.

The photo memo form can be used to refresh your memory months or even years after you originally took the images being offered in court as evidence. Many readers might ask why this form is necessary when today's digital cameras capture much of the same information in an image's metadata. Each image becomes a file on the digital camera's memory card, and this file will eventually be transferred to a computer's hard drive. The file contains more than just the image. It also contains many of the camera's settings when the images were captured: date and time, camera type, lens focal length, aperture, shutter speed, ISO setting, focal length, whether the flash was used, white balance selection, and so on. Why duplicate this information on a redundant written form? Although the metadata is supposed to be a permanent addition to an image's file, the authors have found that at times, once the image has been transferred from the camera to a computer or transferred from one computer to another,

Case Number   **Date/ Time**   **Address/ Location**   **Lens:** Indicate specific mm used, or Macro = M

Photographer   **Camera**   **Light:** Available: **A;**   Flashlight: **FL**
M Flash: **M, M/2, M/4, M/8, M/16, etc.;**
Ded/TTL: **D-Full, D-½, D-¼, D-1/8, D-1/16**, etc.

(With Close-Up filters, indicate either M+1 through M+7 in the lens column.)   (Indicate GuideNumber of Flash) :

#	Lens	Light	SS	F-#	ISO	Description
1						
2						
3						
4						
5						
6						
7						
8						
9						
10						
11						
12						
13						
14						
15						
16						
17						
18						
19						
20						
21						
22						
23						
24						

Notes:

FIGURE 1-2
Photo memo form

the metadata can be lost. Though this can happen, the best advice is to follow your own agencies' SOP regarding use of photo memo forms.

Another use for the photo memo form is as a training aid. Inevitably, there will be some images that were not up to your expectations. You might examine them and decide that they could have been better. Sometimes this issue is not evident when just quickly viewing the last captured image on the camera's LED screen. Many times, a problem will not be noticeable until you view a full-sized image on a computer monitor. So, if it isn't as good as it could have been, how could it have been better? Knowing precisely the settings used to capture the original, you now can make a judgment regarding what would have been a better set of exposure variables. Without knowing how the original was captured, correcting mistakes would be more difficult. Also, in an academic situation, requiring that a photo memo form accompany required images captured as part of a course or training exercise can provide the instructor with much of the information necessary when evaluating a student's images.

It goes without saying that the first image documented on the photo memo form should be the one of the photo identifier!

It is always asked if accidental images (as when one accidentally presses the shutter button all the way down when trying to determine a proper exposure by depressing the shutter button just half way down) or poor images (overexposed, underexposed, out of focus, etc.) can be deleted. SWGIT does not specifically forbid deleting accidental or poor images. SWGIT does frequently suggest adhering to your agency's SOPs. If your agency does allow the deletion of these kinds of images, the guidelines for doing so should be clearly indicated in your department's SOPs. However, because occasionally a defense attorney will complain in court that deleted images might possibly have contained content that was exculpatory for their client, law enforcement agencies seem to be leaning towards policies dictating that all images must be retained, regardless of quality. One justification for retaining all digital images is that it takes time and effort to delete poor images. So, why bother? Why run the risk of appearing to be hiding or deleting exculpatory details in images? Avoid the risk. Don't do it.

The Labeled Scale

A scale is often used to provide an indication of the size of a particular item of evidence. But why not have the scale do more than just this one job? By adding a label to the scale, the scale can be made more useful. For an image to be offered in court as evidence, an individual will have to testify that the image is "a fair and accurate representation of the scene." However, the more the image itself can provide information about the conditions under which the image was taken, the more "trustworthy" the image will be. What information should be included on such a label? The answer may vary with the jurisdiction you work for, but many agencies include these elements. They are the same elements found on the photo identifier:

- The case number
- The date and time
- The address/location
- Photographer's name/initials/badge number/ID number

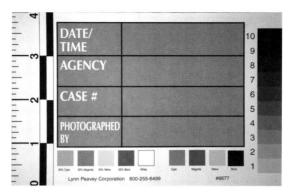

FIGURE 1-3
Commercially available labeled scale

In addition to the listed information, the labeled scale will frequently include some additional information, depending on agency SOPs. As each item of evidence is captured in images, the chronological sequence of the evidence encountered can also be indicated on the labeled scale by using a series of hash marks as each item of evidence is photographed. These hash marks can be additive, like a series of four vertical hashes and then a diagonal through them to indicate the fifth item encountered.

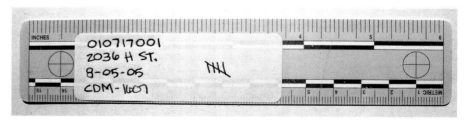

FIGURE 1-4
Labeled scale

When the image is of a subject or certain aspects of a subject such as wounds, clothing, or similar, some agencies recommend placing the name of the subject on the labeled scale. Of course, once these images are completed, the labeled scale will have to be replaced with a new one without the subject's name on it. Or an additional label can be added near the original label, with just the subject's name on it, which can be removed when no longer needed.

In addition to the information placed on the labeled scale, the placement of the labeled scale must be addressed next. The recurring phrase that will be encountered time and time again is, "Place the labeled scale *on the same plane* as the evidence." The labeled scale should not simply sit next to the evidence. If not "next" to the evidence, where should it be placed? What does "on the same plane" mean?

 ## RULE OF THUMB 1-2

Whenever scales are used, they should be positioned on the same plane as the evidence they are associated with.

Of course, some evidence that is already lying on a surface may actually be on the same plane as the surface it is on. For instance, a bank robbery demand note might have been left on the bank counter. If just a sheet of paper, the demand note will actually sit on the bank counter and be at the same plane as the bank counter. Then, when it's about to be photographed, focusing on the paper and focusing on the bank counter would be virtually the same thing. In this situation, the labeled scale could correctly be placed "next" to the demand note, on the bank counter.

However, many types of evidence fall into one of two very different situations. These are:

1. When the evidence is thicker than a sheet of paper, when focusing on the top of the item of evidence is different than focusing on the surface the evidence is lying on.
2. When the evidence has been depressed into a substrate and focusing on the detail at the bottom of the depression is different than focusing on the substrate into which the depression was placed.

Two examples will make this point nicely. A .45 caliber cartridge casing is found on a hardwood floor. The casing has mass and thickness. The top of the casing is approximately half an inch (0.45 inches, to be precise) above the floor. Focusing on the top of the casing is very different than focusing on the floor the casing is lying on. Or a shoeprint in dirt can be depressed approximately half an inch into the dirt's surface. Focusing at the depth of the shoeprint is very different than focusing on the top of the dirt the shoeprint has been depressed into.

Why does this issue matter? There are two reasons. The scale is being used in order to indicate the size of the evidence being photographed. The scale itself will appear as different sizes if placed at different distances from the camera. You might say, "Excuse me! Won't an inch segment always be an inch? Won't six inches always be six inches?" No!

If two scales are placed in a scene—one as high as the casing is high and one on the surface the casing is lying on—each scale still shows inch increments.

FIGURE 1-5A
Focused on the top of the casing *(courtesy of J. Wreh, GWU MS student)*

FIGURE 1-5B
Focused on the carpet *(courtesy of J. Wreh, GWU MS student)*

However, the relative sizes of the two scales are now different when viewed from the perspective of the camera! The scale closest to the camera has inch segments larger than the inch segment on the lower scale. See Figures 1-6A and 1-6B.

FIGURE 1-6A
Relative heights of the scales *(courtesy of J. Wreh, GWU MS student)*

FIGURE 1-6B
An inch on the left scale appears longer *(courtesy of J. Wreh, GWU MS student)*

The scale on the carpet has inch segments that appear shorter than inch segments of the other scale. If it becomes necessary to enlarge the image of the casing with a scale included, which scale can be used to do this job? Only the scale on the same plane: at the top surface of the casing. Using the other scale to enlarge the image will result in a photo of a casing smaller than the actual casing! Would this be a "fair and accurate representation of the evidence"? No!

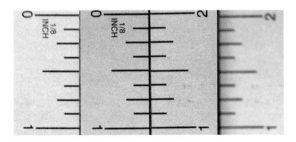

FIGURE 1-7
Focus changes

There is a second reason for placing the labeled scale on the same plane as the evidence. In addition to the inch segments on the scale being different sizes, take a close look at crops from each of these scales positioned at different heights. The two middle scales are at the same height, and they are the point of focus. The far left scale is ¼ inch lower than the middle two scales, and it appears to be a bit out of focus. The far right scale is ½ inch lower than the two middle scales, and it is obviously out of focus. Why are the left and right scales out of focus? Often the area of an image that is critically sharp or in focus does not include everything in the image. Especially when doing close-up photography and filling the frame with just one small item of evidence, when getting very close to an item of evidence, the area of the image that is perceived to be critically sharp is severely restricted. This topic will be addressed later in the book, in Chapter 3, where depth of field is fully explained. But for now, just notice this variance in scale sharpness in these images of scales placed at different heights.

Each of the images offered in court as evidence will eventually have to be offered to the court by someone who was present when the image was captured; this person does not actually have to be the photographer, although it usually is. However, with a labeled scale included in the image, all viewers are more willing to accept this testimony because the image, to a large extent, is also providing the same information.

COMPOSITION AND FULL FIELD OF VIEW RESPONSIBILITY

Many images are captured on a daily basis that have little thought devoted to an awareness of everything within each photograph. As long as the primary subject is in the field of view, most photographers are satisfied and depress the shutter button. Crime scene photographs should be composed with more thought put into each shot. Crime scene photographs are not the same as photos of family and friends, pets, and vacation memories. Crime scene photographs can be responsible for having someone incarcerated or having someone sentenced to death. This is a great responsibility. Therefore, more care than usual should be put into capturing crime scene images.

Properly composing an image means more than just making sure the primary subject is within the field of view. Composition should also include the intentional selection of the details surrounding the primary subject so that they contribute to, rather than distract from, the success of the image. Even the primary subject can be viewed from different angles or points of view. One particular point of view may be noticeably better than other points of view. Composition is not just acknowledging what appears in the field of view: it is the conscious selection of everything in the field of view.

A crime scene photographer is responsible for everything that appears in his or her captured images. Crime scene photographers have a full field of view responsibility. What appears in their images should be there because the photographers wanted it to be included in their images. There are many aspects of this responsibility. This first chapter will explain the various concepts that are the foundation of this idea.

CARDINAL RULE I: FILL THE FRAME

This is the first cardinal rule of good crime scene photography. If something is important enough to photograph, fill the frame with it.

Make the Primary Subject as Large as Possible: Get Closer to It!

The primary subject of a photograph can be just one item, such as the revolver in Figures 1-8A and 1-8B

FIGURE 1-8A
Not filling the frame *(courtesy of I. Walker, GWU MS student)*

FIGURE 1-8B
Filling the frame *(courtesy of I. Walker, GWU MS student)*

Why include a lot of carpeting in the image when the purpose of the photograph is to show the viewer the pistol? When Figure 1-8B is possible, don't settle for capturing Figure 1-8B.

The primary subject does not just have to be one item. The primary subject can also be a relatively small area. As will later be explained in depth, a midrange photograph shows one item of evidence in relation to a fixed feature of the scene. Once the photographer has this task in mind, he or she should try to fill the frame with just these two items and the area between them. Figure 1-9 is a midrange photo of a black talon bullet in its relation to a sidewalk line, where it contacts a painted brick wall. To properly photograph these two features, the photographer stood close enough to them that they almost entirely filled the frame of the image.

FIGURE 1-9
Proper midrange

One way to fill the frame with the primary subject is to decide whether a horizontal or vertical camera position is best for it. The camera's viewfinder and digital sensor are both rectangles. Because many objects are longer than they are wide, they can better fill the frame by aligning the length of the object on the horizontal plane of the viewfinder and sensor. This concept is easily understood by thinking about photographing a knife. The knife is long; therefore it will better fill the frame of the image if the length of the knife is positioned horizontally rather than vertically.

Which image fills the frame better? Which image makes the knife bigger while at the same time reducing the amount of carpeting in view? Figure 1-10B does the job better. This framing concept applies to many images in crime scenes.

FIGURE 1-10A
Knife vertical in a horizontal format *(courtesy of M. Simms, GWU MS student)*

FIGURE 1-10B
Knife vertical in a vertical format *(courtesy of M. Simms, GWU MS student)*

A body viewed from the head to the feet is best composed vertically. If composing a photo to capture the right or left sides of the body, the horizontal viewpoint is best.

Try to Eliminate Anything that Is Not the Primary Subject

To the extent possible, crime scene photographers should intentionally include in an image the primary subject of the photograph while minimizing or eliminating as much as possible from the field of view that does not contribute to the photographer's purpose for capturing that image. Most images look best

FIGURE 1-11A
Head-to-toe shot *(courtesy of S. Dickson, GWU MFS student)*

FIGURE 1-11B
Right side

when there is one purpose for taking that photograph, and eliminating distractions or unnecessary elements from view usually increases the success of an image. This approach makes the photographer responsible for what is included within an image. The best compositions are those that contain only the elements the photographer chose to be in that image. Composition should therefore mean not just noticing what happened to have been around the primary subject; composition should be the active inclusion of what the photographer wanted to be included in the image as well as an intentional elimination of any elements not wanted to be included in the image. Composition includes:

- The choice of included elements
- The choice of excluded elements
- The selection of the viewpoint

If there is clutter or unnecessary detail in the area to be photographed, one possible solution is to adjust your viewpoint.

Distracting Foreground Elements: Tilt the Camera Up

When the initial composition includes unnecessary details in the foreground, one simple solution is to tilt the camera up just a bit until the unnecessary details are no longer in view.

FIGURE 1-12A
Unnecessary details in foreground

FIGURE 1-12B
Tilting the camera up: a better composition

Distracting Background Elements: Tilt the Camera Down

When the initial composition includes unnecessary details in the background, one simple solution is to tilt the camera down just a bit until the unnecessary details are no longer in view.

FIGURE 1-13A
Unnecessary details in background

FIGURE 1-13B
Tilting the camera down: a better composition

Left and Right: Wide versus Narrow Scene

At times, the camera's normal horizontal view of a scene may include irrelevant details to the left or right of what is considered the primary subject. In these cases, consider switching to a vertical view of the scene. Figure 1-14A shows a shoe in relation to a school building, but the horizontal viewpoint includes more than is needed to establish this relationship. Figure 1-14B, with the camera held vertically, is a cleaner, less busy image of the area needed to make this point.

The point to be remembered is that once the photographer has determined the primary subject for a particular photograph, he or she should compose that shot and then, before depressing the shutter button, should quickly scan the entire perimeter of the composed image, making sure there are no unnecessary or irrelevant details within the field of view.

FIGURE 1-14A
Horizontal viewpoint includes unnecessary detail *(courtesy of K. Kinsie, GWU MS student)*

FIGURE 1-14B
Vertical viewpoint includes just the necessary detail *(courtesy of K. Kinsie, GWU MS student)*

Shadow Control

The photographer's full field of view responsibility sometimes also includes controlling the shadows present at the crime scene. Obviously, one cannot do anything about a tree's shadow over a portion of an exterior overall photo. However, when the composition of a particular image is a smaller area, the photographer does have control over those shadows.

Sun Shadows: Block When Possible

If you are composing a particular image and notice that the shadows present in your field of view are distracting and do not contribute to the success of that image, then position yourself so that you own body blocks the sun in the area of interest. If there is another person available, they can block the sun also.

FIGURE 1-15A
Sun shadows *(courtesy of M. Simms, GWU MS student)*

FIGURE 1-15B
Sun shadows blocked *(courtesy of M. Simms, GWU MS student)*

Then, with the entire area now in shadow, merely expose for the shade and the image will not be underexposed.

Your Own Shadow: Eliminate or Minimize It

There will be times when the sun also throws your own shadow across the area in view. To the extent possible, try not to let this happen. You will often have to reposition yourself on another side of what is being photographed. This repositioning may totally prevent your own shadow from appearing in the field of view. If you cannot totally eliminate your own shadow from the field of view, minimizing it is the next best thing.

FIGURE 1-16A
Photographer's shadow

FIGURE 1-16B
Photographer's shadow minimized

Flash Shadows

When using an electronic flash, you often create flash shadows in your own images. The problem is that you cannot see the flash shadow until after the image is captured. With some experience, however, one can learn to anticipate the creation of shadows.

Previsualize Them. The shadows that are a result of your own flash going off are at times very distracting. They occur when you position the flash unit before taking the shot. When using a flash unit, try to previsualize the shadow that will be created with your current flash head position.

Minimize or Eliminate Them. Because you usually have the option of repositioning the flash head wherever you desire, the flash shadow can often be minimized or eliminated. Just before you depress the shutter and capture an image, ask yourself whether the resulting flash shadow will be a welcome addition to the composed image or a distraction. Of course, if you are using a digital camera, you will get to see the flash shadow on your LED screen immediately after taking the shot. But the experienced crime scene photographer does not have to follow up a bad shot with an improved shot. Bad shot; improved shot. Bad shot; improved shot. Why double all the photos you will have to take? Learn how to take them correctly the first time. In Figure 1-17B, the distracting shadow in Figure 1-17A is eliminated by correctly positioning a bounce flash shot off of the ceiling.

FIGURE 1-17A
Flash shadow *(courtesy of M. Simms, GWU MS student)*

FIGURE 1-17B
Flash shadow eliminated *(courtesy of M. Simms, GWU MS student)*

Hard versus Soft shadows

One final aspect about shadows must be mentioned at this point. An electronic flash produces shadows that are often so dark that details cannot be seen in the shadow area. These are called **hard shadows**. This issue is especially important when capturing examination-quality images. For instance, when capturing images of shoe prints or tire tracks, an oblique flash technique is the best practice; however, it produces hard shadows within the areas of the shoe print pattern or tire track pattern. If our own flash technique is responsible for hiding part of the shoe pattern or tire track pattern in hard shadows, then the photographer may be to blame for the examiner not being able to see the details necessary for making an identification. This result would be counterproductive.

The series of images in Figure 1-18A through 1-18F make this point. They are images of a .410 shot shell casing. In the series, the first four images show the hard shadows produced by moving the flash unit to different positions around the casing. These hard shadows make it impossible to see the carpet detail within the shadow areas. With the casing shots, it is completely irrelevant if part of the carpeting is hidden from view. But when the shadows fall over areas of shoe print pattern or tire tread pattern, then creating a hard shadow may be a critical flaw in the photographic technique. In Figure 1-18E there is a **soft**

shadow on the right side of the casing. The shadow is still present, but now details can be seen within the shadow. Creating soft shadows in areas of shoe print pattern and tire tread pattern is critical so that the examiner can see details in all areas of the evidence. Figure 1-18F demonstrates how soft shadows are produced: a bounce card or reflector is positioned on the opposite side of the evidence. The light from the oblique flash strikes the evidence, moves beyond the evidence, and then strikes the bounce card. Some of the light is reflected back towards the evidence, adding enough light to the shadow areas to lighten them somewhat without overexposing the evidence. Now details can be seen in the shadow areas.

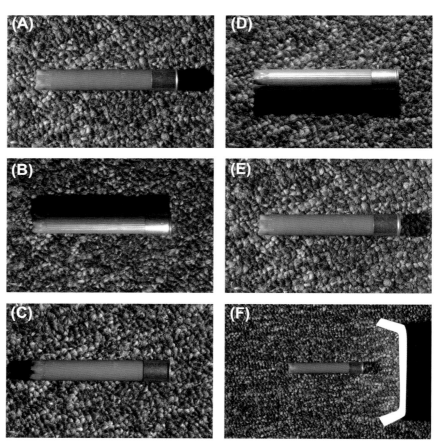

FIGURE 1-18A–F
Hard and soft shadows

Lens Flare (Sun in Front of the Photographer)

There will be times when the crime scene photographer must compose an image with the sun in front of the photographer. When there is a choice, it is usually recommended that the composition be arranged so that the sun is behind or at least to the side of the photographer. But sometimes the sun will be unavoidable.

The Flare Itself

Lens flare is frequently produced when the sun is in front of the photographer. This effect is caused by the sun's light coming directly into the lens and reflecting off of the different lens elements, frequently causing multicolored geometric shapes or bright streaks. The problem is that most of the time the photographer cannot see the lens flare in the viewfinder before the shot is captured. This flare is particularly a problem when one is taking a series of exterior overalls of buildings, but it can occur whenever the sun is in front of the photographer.

FIGURE 1-19
Lens flare

Lens Hood

Many lens manufacturers provide a lens hood with their lenses to be used when the sun is in front of the camera. The lens hood is a plastic extension of the lens that is designed to block the sun's rays so they don't come directly into the lens.

Photographer's Hand

Unfortunately, not every lens comes with a lens hood. If one is caught without a lens hood when one is needed, every photographer still has the

FIGURE 1-20A
Camera and lens *(courtesy of D. Schweizer, GWU MFS student)*

FIGURE 1-20B
Lens hood *(courtesy of D. Schweizer, GWU MFS student)*

ability to avoid lens flare. We can use the "poor man's lens hood.": simply hold your free hand so that it is positioned to block the sun coming directly into the lens. All that is necessary is to block the light coming straight from the sun.

 ## *CARDINAL RULE II: KEEP THE FILM PLANE PARALLEL*

We'll explain this cardinal rule in relation to the various classic images captured at crime scenes. These are overall photographs, midrange photos, and close-ups.

FIGURE 1-21A
Lens flare *(courtesy of S. Reeve, GWU MFS student)*

FIGURE 1-21B
No lens flare *(courtesy of S. Reeve, GWU MFS student)*

FIGURE 1-22A
Lens hood used to avoid flare *(courtesy of S. Reeve, GWU MFS student)*

FIGURE 1-22B
Hand used to avoid flare *(courtesy of S. Reeve, GWU MFS student)*

Overall Photographs

The judge and jury, and other investigators involved with the case, frequently cannot go back to the original scene of the crime. It is up to the crime scene photographer to take a sufficient number of images so the subsequent viewers of these images can get a good feel for:

1. The area or neighborhood in which the crime occurred
2. The actual crime scene itself
3. The relationship of each item of evidence to fixed features in the crime scene
4. The actual items of evidence

To do each of these sets of images, the crime scene photographer usually begins by taking what are called overall photographs.

Natural Perspective

Overall photographs are normally taken from what is referred to as a **natural perspective**. Basically, that means the photographer is standing at his or her full natural height, viewing the scene or area as anyone would have seen it had they been standing right next to the photographer when the image was captured. To the extent possible, other viewpoints are avoided. Of course, there is a specialized type of crime scene photography called **aerial photography**, in which images are captured while standing on bridges or buildings while looking down at the crime scene below. Included in this kind of photography are images taken from balconies, from the top of cherry pickers or fire department ladder trucks, and even from planes and helicopters (whether manned or unmanned). However, the overall photographs taken as part of normal crime scene photography are usually taken from a natural perspective. When viewing these types of photographs, the assumption is that the photographer took these images while standing at their full height, not standing on a chair or kneeling on the ground. These kinds of images can be taken later on, for other purposes, and are not usually included as overall photographs.

One problem associated with photos that are not taken from a natural perspective is that they frequently show too much background, including elements that are not required for any particular photo. See the following two images of body shots. When taking the image for Figure 1-23B, had the photographer stood at his or her full height, the background details—including the building—would not have appeared in the shot.

FIGURE 1-23A
Natural perspective *(courtesy of S. Dickson, GWU MFS student)*

FIGURE 1-23B
Not from a natural perspective *(courtesy of J. Buffington, GWU MS student)*

Of course, there will be times when standing at your full height cannot be done to take a particular shot. If a gun is under a bed and you want to photograph it as it was originally found, you'll have to get lower to do so. However, whenever possible, try to stand at your full natural height when taking most photographs.

Overall photographs are usually broken down into two general categories: exterior overalls and interior overalls.

Exterior Overalls

One of the purposes of exterior overall photographs is to lead the viewer into the crime scene from some distance away. When considered all together, the photographs should tell a pretty comprehensive story about the crime in question. This story is usually best told by gradually leading the viewer into the crime scene by beginning just outside the scene. Every crime has a context; every crime scene is surrounded by an area immediately around it, which is not technically part of the crime scene. Documenting this area is usually the crime scene photographer's first priority.

There may be times, of course, when this approach is inappropriate, including crime scenes that are considered **active crime scenes**, such as:

- A barricade situation in which a suspect will not immediately surrender when an arrest warrant is being served
- A bank robbery gone bad in which hostages have been taken for negotiation purposes
- Any crime in which suspects flee and are chased by law enforcement, whether on foot or in vehicles
- Victims have been injured in some way and are still present at the scene

And there are many other similar situations. But once the crime has been committed, the suspects are gone, law enforcement has been notified, they have secured the crime scene, and they have determined that there are no suspects present or victims requiring treatment, the normal course of our crime scene photography begins with exterior overalls.

One of the easiest ways to do this task, if in an urban area, is to begin at the closest intersection and photograph the street sign there.

This is the perfect time to remind yourself to fill the frame! Recall that the concept of filling the frame has two aspects to it. We should emphasize the primary subject by making it as large as we can in the composed image. If the current job is to document the street sign at the nearest intersection to the crime scene, then fill the frame with the street signs. The signpole is not necessary to do this job correctly—just the signs themselves.

The other meaning of filling the frame is eliminating from the composition, to the extent possible, everything that is not considered your primary subject. While composing the image with the street signs, try to eliminate all the trees, buildings, power lines, and any other objects in the background. Try to keep the background clean, if possible. Sometimes this is impossible, but to the extent you can, try to compose the image with just the street signs in the viewfinder.

Many street signs show the names of both streets at the intersection. If the crime occurred on just one of these streets, then the photographer should somehow let the viewer know which of these two streets the crime occurred on. The best way to do this is to try to place a bit more emphasis on the street of interest. Make this street name a bit more prominent in the field of view. If both streets are viewed from a 45-degree angle, then the viewer won't know which one is related to the crime scene address.

FIGURE 1-24A
Intersection signs not filling the frame *(courtesy of L. Larson, GWU MFS student)*

FIGURE 1-24B
Street signs filling the frame *(courtesy of L. Larson, GWU MFS student)*

FIGURE 1-25A
Emphasis on Pergate La.

FIGURE 1-25B
Emphasis on Poplar Tree Rd.

In the next photograph, try to show this intersection with the actual street on which the crime occurred in the background leading to the crime scene. In the attempt to lead the viewers into the crime scene, you may also capture one or more additional images of the street as you get nearer to the actual crime scene. When you are 100 feet or so away from the crime scene and it can clearly be seen in the background, take another photo. Then it may be a good idea to stand across the street and photograph the crime scene building, with portions of both neighboring buildings in the field of view also.

At this point, you will begin photographing the entire building, showing all the sides, trying to capture every door and window the suspect may have used. Early in an investigation, this level of detail may not be known. Even when it is thought to be known, the subsequent investigation may reveal that the original

FIGURE 1-26A
Crime scene intersection and street *(courtesy of K. Kinsie, GWU MS student)*

FIGURE 1-26B
Crime scene street *(courtesy of K. Kinsie, GWU MS student)*

theory about the suspect's access to the building must be revised. Capturing all the doors and windows on all sides of the building in your exterior overall photographs is good insurance against this possibility.

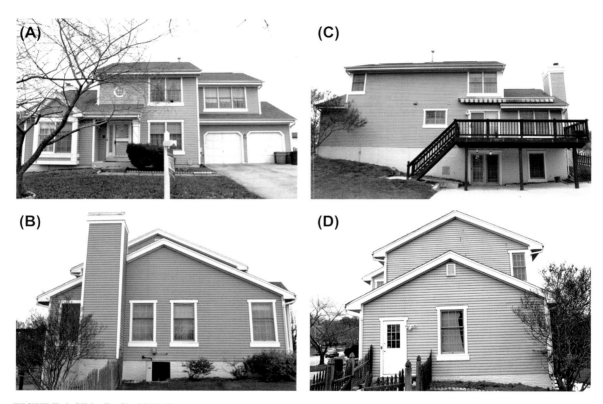

FIGURE 1-27A, B, C, AND D
Four sides of home *(courtesy of L. Etheridge, GWU MS student)*

When photographing the exterior of buildings, try to keep the back of the camera parallel to the building's façade. There are several good reasons for this recommendation:

■ If you take a diagonal view of a wall, the doors and windows closer to the camera will appear larger than doors and windows farther from the camera. Early in the investigation, it may not be known which of these doors and/or windows are important to the investigation. Why emphasize some, which may not ultimately be important, and deemphasize others, which may later become more important? If the film plane is parallel to the façade, all the door and windows share an equal emphasis.

- If you take a diagonal view of a wall, you create a situation in which important aspects of the scene are both near and far from the camera. If the entire façade is important, then its entire length should be in focus. Depending on the lighting, it may be increasingly more difficult to ensure that the entire façade is in focus if it is photographed from a diagonal view. The depth of field range—the distance from foreground to background that will ultimately be in focus—may not encompass the entire building's depth. On the other hand, if the façade is viewed and photographed with the film plane parallel to it, ensuring that the entire length of the façade is in focus is easier.
- If you take a diagonal view of a wall for which the lighting is dim and an electronic flash will have to be used to light the structure, then properly lighting the entire façade becomes problematic. Setting the flash to properly expose the near part of the building will cause the part further from the flash to be underexposed. Setting the flash to properly expose the far part of the building will cause the part nearer the flash to be overexposed. If the façade is viewed and photographed with the film plane parallel to it, on the other hand, properly exposing the façade with the flash is simpler.

Keeping the film plane parallel to the back of the camera has recurring benefits for other forms of crime scene photography. This concept will come up frequently; hence its designation as a cardinal rule.

Of course, there are some times when maintaining the film plane parallel to the façade of a building isn't possible. The most obvious is the situation in which the building façade is very close to another building façade and one simply cannot get far enough away from the façade to have the film plane parallel. In this case, only diagonal views will be possible. Reality will sometimes dictate what can and can't be done.

The other situation is when the façade has many windows, and when you are positioned across from the façade with the film plane parallel, your own reflection can be seen in the window opposite. You usually don't want to take photographs that include yourself, your equipment, or law enforcement personnel present at the scene. In this situation, the photographer must reposition him- or herself so you're not in view. Stand opposite a portion of the façade without a window directly opposite your own position. Doing so may require the camera to be positioned at a slight diagonal to the façade, but that is necessary to avoid photographing yourself within the crime scene image.

Besides documenting the approach to the crime scene, if the suspect's exit from the crime scene can be determined, that path should also be photographed. This task will sometimes lead to abandoned or dropped evidence or to evidence not otherwise available when the suspect's possible approach to the crime

FIGURE 1-28
Diagonal and film plane parallel views

scene is searched or the crime scene itself is checked for evidence. An obvious example might be when the approach to the scene is via pavement and sidewalks and the interior of the scene is all hard surfaces, but the path leading away from the crime scene reveals three-dimensional (3D) impressions in dirt or other soft surfaces. Following the path taken by the suspect when leaving the primary crime scene may lead to secondary scenes where evidence needs to be documented and collected.

Photographing the area around the immediate crime scene is frequently recommended, even when an obvious path to and from the crime scene cannot be determined. Most investigators have had an experience similar to this one. When

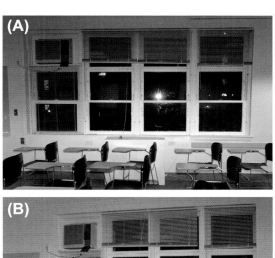

FIGURE 1-29A, B, AND C
Slight diagonal views to avoid photographing yourself *(courtesy of M. & M. Hashemi, GWU MF students)*

arriving at the crime scene, the suspect parks his or her vehicle nearby. For many reasons, it may not be prudent to return to this vehicle immediately after committing the crime. For instance, there might be people in the area of the vehicle who may be able to subsequently identify the suspect. So the suspect leaves on foot in another direction. Once at the crime scene, police photographers routinely photograph all the vehicles in the immediate area, check for which are registered to neighbors, and use the others as leads to possible suspects. More than one perpetrator has been caught because of this procedure.

Interior Overalls

Once the exterior overall photographs are completed, the crime scene photographer next documents the path or paths from doors and windows toward areas within the structure where items have been disturbed or other criminal activity is obvious. This area can include paths from one room to another or from a door, through a hall, to a room.

FIGURE 1-30A, B, AND C
Entry to scene *(courtesy of K. Kinsie, GWU MS student)*

Within a room where significant criminal activity has been located, it is customary to begin by photographing a complete 360-degree panorama of the room that includes every wall. These walls, as you should now anticipate, will be photographed with the film plane parallel to them whenever possible for the same reasons mentioned earlier for exterior overalls.

Many law enforcement agencies have policies dictating that interior overall photos should be taken from corner to corner, while also recommending that these shots be taken with wide-angle lenses. One reason for this is that frequently only four photos are required for the entire room this way, whereas—depending on the size of the room—having the film plane parallel to the walls normally requires six shots or more. Is there any appreciable difference? The use of wide-angle lenses usually results in the scene looking a bit larger because wide-angle lenses tend to elongate the distance between foreground and background. The deciding factor should be your agency's SOPs. Follow them.

FIGURE 1-31
Film plane parallel to walls

Even when there is no obvious evidence present on a particular wall, all walls are photographed. One reason is because the walls have the **fixed features** to which each item of evidence will eventually have to be related. These fixed features include doors and windows, corners, electrical outlets, and other

FIGURE 1-32
Corner-to-corner shots

features that won't move or change, should it ever be necessary to return to the original crime scene at a later date. And early in the investigation, all the evidence may not have been located, so it is undetermined which wall's fixed features will be required to properly document the location of all the evidence eventually found. Furniture cannot be regarded as a fixed feature because it can be moved or removed.

It is usually a requirement to use an electronic flash whenever doing interior overall photographs, but this will be discussed at length in Chapter 4.

When composing an overall photograph, ask yourself what is essential to be included in the composition, and what details can or should be eliminated. Just because these are overall photographs does not imply that we should be less careful about what is included in the background or at either the left or right side of the composition. The term "composition" suggests that a purposeful choice is made by the photographer. Include the primary subject; exclude what is irrelevant or unnecessary to the success of the image.

Midrange Photographs

Once the crime scene room has been photographed, it is time to photograph each item of evidence. The proper photography of each item of evidence always begins with what is termed a midrange photograph. A **midrange photograph** is an attempt to show an item of evidence in its spatial relation to a fixed feature of the crime scene. We want to show the accurate distance between the evidence and a fixed feature of the scene. This is easier said than done!

There are two types of distortion that must be avoided with taking midrange photographs.

- Lens distortion
- Perspective distortion

Many cameras used by crime scene photographers come with a zoom lens as the standard lens. Two examples of such standard zoom lenses are an 18—55mm lens and a 35—80mm lens. The first number for each lens represents the widest focal length of the lens, and the second number represents a short telephoto focal length. Somewhere in between is the "normal" focal length for the 35mm camera you are using. Complete details about lenses are covered in Chapter 3, but a brief description is appropriate for this discussion of midrange photographs.

Look through your viewfinder while you point the camera at a wall across from you. Now, while looking through the viewfinder, change focal lengths from the widest focal length to its short telephoto setting. Notice what happens to the wall. When set to the wide-angle focal length, the wall will appear farther away than it appears to your eyes when you look over the camera body. When set to the short telephoto focal length, the wall will appear closer than it appears to your eyes when you look over the camera body. In other words, the use of a wide-angle focal length or telephoto focal length can change the perceived distance between the photographer and any object. If the goal is to accurately depict the distance between the evidence and a fixed feature of the crime scene, then the only focal length you should use when taking midrange photographs is the "normal" focal length for your camera.

How do you determine the normal focal length for your camera? If you are using a film camera or a digital camera with a full-sized digital sensor (where the digital sensor is the same size as a film negative, 24mm × 36mm, or approximately 1 × 1.5 inches), the normal focal length is usually considered to be 50mm. If you are using a digital camera with a digital sensor smaller than a film negative, usually called an APS-C digital sensor, then the normal focal length of your camera will be around 33.3mm.

The bottom line: when taking midrange photographs, using anything besides the normal focal length lens for your camera will result in lens distortion, making the evidence look either closer to or farther from the fixed feature of the scene. This effect should always be avoided. Determine your normal focal length, and when taking midrange photographs, use that focal length only! Which of the following four images shows the scene as the

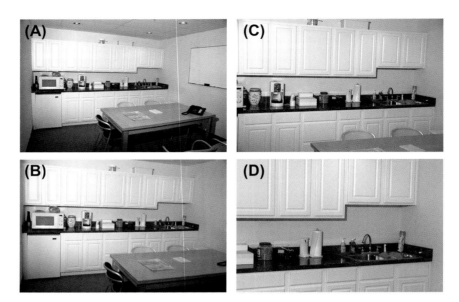

FIGURE 1-33A, B, C, AND D
Focal lengths of 28mm, 35mm, 50mm and 80mm

eye saw it? Figure 1-33C, or the 50mm focal length, shows the scene as the eye saw it.

Besides lens distortion, one must also avoid perspective distortion. This is a type of distortion that is created merely by assuming an improper viewpoint with relation to the evidence and the fixed feature. The easiest way to explain this is to show you a wagon wheel, viewed from two different directions.

When looking straight at the side of the wheel, all the spokes appear to be the same length. That is because they *are* all the same length. However, drop the wheel to the ground, and the round wheel now appears to be an ellipse, and the spokes appear to be different lengths. The horizontal spoke has been covered by a blue line. The green and red lines are the same length as the blue line and are now superimposed over a diagonal spoke and the vertical spoke. Which of these spokes depicts the accurate length of all the spokes? Only the horizontal/blue spoke. Why? Because viewing the wheel from a perspective view/oblique view makes the spokes appear to be different lengths even though we know they really are all the same length.

If the purpose of a midrange photograph is to show the correct distance between the evidence and a fixed feature of the crime scene, and it is, then when taking any midrange photograph, one *must* assume a viewpoint of the *two* for which they are the same distance away from the photographer: one should be

FIGURE 1-34A
Round wheel seen straight on

FIGURE 1-34B
Round wheel seen obliquely

on the right side of the composition, and one should be on the left side of the composition, so they appear to be the same distance from the photographer. Mentally connect the item of evidence and the fixed feature of the scene with an invisible line, and this line should be parallel to the back of the camera. The concept of film plane parallel is revisited.

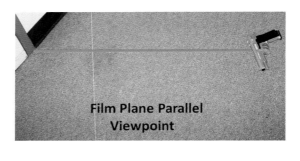

FIGURE 1-35A
Film plane parallel

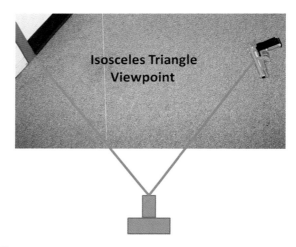

FIGURE 1-35B
Isosceles triangle

Another way to understand this is that for a midrange photograph, the photographer should be one point in an isosceles triangle, with the photographer at one point of the triangle and the evidence and the fixed feature each completing the two equal sides of the isosceles triangle. Create whichever is easiest for you to understand and practice: a film plane parallel point of view or an isosceles triangle point of view. Any other point of view will cause the evidence to appear as if it is closer to the fixed feature, which deceives the viewer about the real distance between the two. See Figure 1-36. Each example is supposed to be a midrange photograph showing the distance between a cartridge casing and an electrical outlet. The top three images are called linear viewpoints because the photographer, the casing, and the electrical outlet form a straight line. The difference between them is that the one on the left was taken from a natural perspective, the middle one has the photographer bent at the waist, and the right one has the photographer sitting. The image at the bottom shows the proper film plane parallel/isosceles triangle viewpoint, and it is the only one depicting the distance between the evidence and the fixed feature accurately.

FIGURE 1-36
Three linear and one proper viewpoint

When composing a midrange photograph, ask yourself what is essential to be included in the composition, and what details can, or should be, eliminated. Just because these are midrange photographs does not imply that we should be less careful about what is included in the background or at either side of the composition. The term "composition" suggests that a purposeful choice is made by the photographer. Include the primary subject (in this case, the evidence and a fixed feature of the crime scene) and exclude what is irrelevant or unnecessary to the success of the image. The invisible line between the evidence and the fixed feature can be moved up or down in the composition if it helps eliminate distracting details.

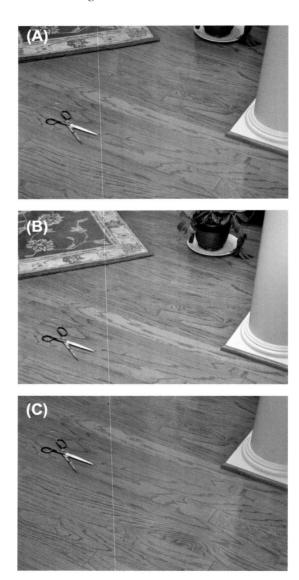

FIGURE 1-37A, B, AND C
Midrange composition variables *(courtesy of M. Blake, GWU MS student)*

Figure 1-37A seems like the proper midrange composition of a pair of scissors and a column base. But is it really? Remember the concept of being responsible for the clutter in the scene also? Figure 1-37B isn't any help at all, but Figure 1-37C shows the same item of evidence and the fixed feature in the proper alignment as well as the photographer's ability to control what is included and excluded from the scene. Because this one image has to show only the spatial relationship of the evidence and the fixed feature, Figure 1-37C is the best of the three.

It is frequently asked whether a midrange photograph is necessary for each piece of evidence. Usually, the answer is "yes." However, if there are several items of evidence very close together, one composition of the grouping of several items of evidence with one fixed feature can be sufficient, and it can be used as the midrange photograph for each individual item of evidence in the grouping.

FIGURE 1-38
Multi-item midrange *(courtesy of M. Blake, GWU MS student)*

Actually, completely photographing all items of the group, and then measuring one of them and packaging it, followed by a new midrange photograph of the remaining items of evidence, and then yet another with two of the original items removed, and so on, can be very confusing to viewers of these photographs. Avoid taking any photographs that tend to be confusing to the viewer. If pieces of evidence form a tightly knit grouping, the grouping can be considered one item of evidence as far as the midrange photograph is concerned. It is recommended that the items of evidence still be photographed into separate close-up photographs and then individually measured, however.

Close-Up Photographs
After the midrange photograph is taken of an item of evidence, we proceed by taking the close-up photos of that item of evidence. The purpose of a **close-up photograph** is to fill the frame with the evidence. Make it as large as you can.

If your regular zoom lens cannot fill the frame with the evidence, then some variation of macro equipment is called for. This can be a macro lens, an extension tube, or a set of close-up filters.

A **macro lens** excels at filling the frame with small evidence. Many allow the photographer to vary magnification power from 1:1 to 1:10. A 1:1 magnification ratio enables the lens to fill the frame with a single-digit fingerprint. In other words, with a 1:1 magnification ratio, a fingerprint will not have to be enlarged at all to be life size on the negative or as captured with a digital camera. A 1:2 magnification ratio would enable two adjacent fingerprints to fill the frame. When printed, without enlargement, each fingerprint would be half of its actual size. A 1:3 magnification ratio would fill the frame with three adjacent fingerprints, and when printed, without enlargement, each fingerprint would be one-third its actual size. Macro lenses are quite expensive, but they offer the highest-quality method of photographing small evidence.

FIGURE 1-39A
1:1 magnification ratio

FIGURE 1-39B
1:2 magnification ratio

FIGURE 1-39C
1:3 magnification ratio

An **extension tube** is a supplemental lens that fits between the camera body and the normal lens. Moving the lens elements farther from the sensor produces magnification, just as using a longer telephoto lens allows distant objects to be magnified.

Close-up filter sets usually come in three incremental strengths that can be used alone or in combination with one another to achieve different magnification possibilities. They are the least expensive method of producing magnification.

All three of these macro possibilities will be discussed further in Chapter 3.

Do not move around the crime scene taking midrange photographs of all the items of evidence before beginning any of the close-up photographs. When you begin dealing with Item #1, continue with it until it is completely photographed, measured, and packaged before dealing with Item #2 in any way (barring the exception of a tightly knit grouping of evidence as noted earlier).

For each piece of evidence, you should take at least two, and sometimes more, close-up photographs.

As Found, As Is, or In Situ

In each case, the first close-up photograph taken is one in which the evidence is photographed before any changes have been made to the scene, and the evidence is in the same position it was first noticed at. This is sometimes referred to as being an **as found** photograph. Nothing has been added to the area of the evidence, and nothing has been taken away. One might also say that the evidence is photographed "as is." It has also be said that the evidence is photographed "in situ," or in the situation as it was originally found.

If for any reason the evidence had been picked up prior to the arrival of the crime scene photographer (there are several valid reasons for doing so), do not let the evidence be replaced into the scene before you begin photographing it. Your photography should reflect the scene as it was when you arrived. The person who picked up the evidence must document his or her reasons for doing so in their report and must attempt to describe the location of the evidence when it was picked up.

If the person responsible is insistent that the evidence be photographed within the crime scene, offer him or her this option: once you have completely cleared the crime scene of all the evidence, the person originally removing the evidence from the scene prior to your arrival can then replace it within the scene, and then you can give the person your camera to take the photo of where he or she thinks it originally was when it was picked up. Before the person does so, fill out a new photo identifier and have him or her photograph it, indicating that a new photographer is taking the photo. After he or she takes the photo, fill out a new photo identifier indicating that you are resuming your own photography.

The "as is" close-up should fill the frame with the evidence. If the evidence isn't filling the frame, that just means you are photographing more of the area around the evidence and less of the evidence itself. Figures 1-40A and 1-40B make this point perfectly.

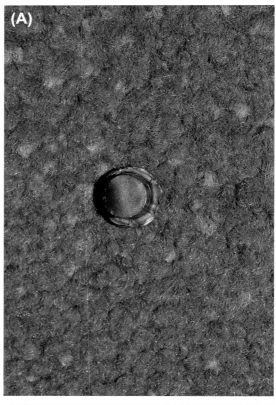

FIGURE 1-40A AND B
Close-up not filling the frame and properly filling the frame *(courtesy of K. Kinsie, GWU MS student)*

With a Fully Labeled Scale, on the Same Plane

After the first close-up photograph, a second close-up photograph is taken with a fully labeled scale, on the same plane, aligned next to the evidence. Again, this scale should be as high as the evidence is above the surface it is lying on or as low as the evidence is depressed into a softer substrate. Do not just set the scale next to the evidence, on the surface the evidence is on, unless the evidence is thin like a piece of paper, with no appreciable difference between the evidence and the surface it is on. The scale should contain the same information as the photo identifier:

- The case number
- The date and time
- The address/location
- Photographer: name/initials/badge number/ID number

The fully labeled scale can be a 6-inch ruler, with a label attached for the necessary information, or it can be a variety of preprinted forms that are available, some produced by the agency and some obtained from crime scene product distributors.

If the labeled scale is going to be raised to the same height as the evidence, props can be used as long as they are not visible in the composed image.

With Just a Portion of the Scale in View

When the item of evidence is larger than the fully labeled scale, filling the frame with the item of evidence and the fully labeled scale will have the evidence about the same size as the evidence composed in the as-is close-up, which does not have the fully labeled scale added next to the evidence. If, however, the evidence is smaller than the fully labeled scale, then to compose that image, it will be necessary to back away from the evidence to include the complete fully labeled scale. In this close-up photograph, the evidence is not filling the frame. Therefore, another close-up photograph will be necessary. In

FIGURE 1-41A
Props used to raise the labeled scale *(courtesy of K. Kinsie, GWU MS student)*

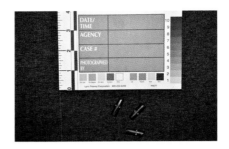

FIGURE 1-41B
Props not visible in the composed image *(courtesy of K. Kinsie, GWU MS student)*

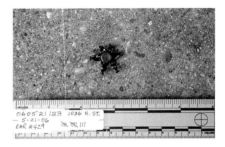

FIGURE 1-41C
Props not visible in the composed image

FIGURE 1-41D
Props not visible in the composed image

this case, the goal is to again fill the frame with the evidence, but now a portion of the scale showing inch/mm increments must also be in view on one long side of the composition. Of course, that partial scale must be on the same plane as the evidence.

FIGURE 1-42
Close-up with partial scale in view

An Altered Close-Up

At this point, the evidence can be measured to place it within the scene when a crime scene diagram is created, and it can then be picked up, with gloved hands, and examined. Sometimes, but not always, when examining the item of evidence on all sides, a new important aspect of the evidence is noticed and should be documented. This can be identifying evidence such as a serial number, any kind of trace evidence, or possibly a bloody fingerprint on the reverse side of a knife blade. When this is the case, and another close-up photograph is called for, we don't want this altered close-up to be confused with any of the other close-ups we have already taken.

 ### RULE OF THUMB 1-3

Altered close-up photographs should be taken in a way that makes it immediately obvious to the viewer that this photo is of evidence that has been moved. The photographer must be assured that no one viewing the altered photograph can confuse it with the as-found photographs.

The best way to photograph this newly discovered aspect of the evidence is to place the evidence on a clean surface, usually your own evidence packaging materials, with the new aspect face up. This approach serves two purposes. First, the evidence isn't just rolled over on the original crime scene surface, possibly contaminating it. And second, this new close-up photograph now has an obviously different background, so it cannot be confused with any of the previous close-up photographs.

FIGURE 1-43
Altered close-up

Examination-Quality Close-ups

The close-up photographs mentioned up to this point were taken to document the presence of the evidence within the crime scene. Some types of evidence, however, require another kind of close-up. When it can be anticipated that the close-up photograph of an item of evidence from the crime scene will eventually be used for comparison purposes, then **examination-quality close-ups** are taken. For example, the following possibilities:

- Shoe tread patterns
- Tire impressions
- Fingerprints
- Bite marks
- Evidence left behind with a broken edge

may later be able to be compared to:

- A recovered shoe
- The tires on recovered vehicles
- Known fingerprints of a suspect
- Known dentition of a suspect
- Evidence with a broken edge

This is probably the most demanding type of crime scene photography. These are the photographs that may be responsible for a person being sent to prison or sentenced to the death penalty. We rely here on the recommendations of SWGIT, SWGFAST, and SWGTREAD so that readers aren't presented with just the opinions of the authors. Their guidelines, however, will be paraphrased because they presume some experience in the field, certainly more than the reader to this introductory text may have. It is hoped this will make the SWG guidelines easier to understand. By all means, you should take the time to read the actual SWG guidelines at your convenience.

Examination-quality photography equipment recommended by SWGIT:

- This is a natural progression of close-up photography types. Other types of close-up do not have to meet these demanding requirements.
- A professional film or digital SLR camera system with a minimum of 8-megapixel (MP) resolution, interchangeable lenses, and manual override for both exposure and focusing. Of course, as digital cameras are becoming more affordable, the authors have noticed many crime scene photographers using 10- to 14MP digital cameras.
- A detachable electronic flash unit with a 6-foot extension cord or a flash with remote capabilities to allow for side lighting. Though many flash units come with a standard 3-foot remote flash cord, some of these allow two to be connected together to achieve the desired 6-foot distance between the flash and the evidence. The reason for the extra distance is that the light reaching the evidence from 6 feet away will be more uniform than light coming from just 3 feet away, making the analysis and comparison of the examination-quality photograph and the known item of evidence easier on the examiner. Because the whole purpose for this type of photography is to effect a comparison leading to a possible identification, making it easier for the examiner to do his or her job is critical.
- The use of a macro lens, or equivalent, capable of filling the frame with the evidence, when doing this type of photography.
- A remote shutter release cable. Whenever the camera is mounted on a tripod (to be discussed shortly), the shutter button should not be depressed with your finger in order to take the photo. One of the purposes for using a tripod is to reduce camera movement. Depressing the shutter button manually can cause some camera movement. Instead, use a remote shutter release cable to capture the image. Or use your camera's delayed shutter release capability, usually set to a ten-second delay. During the ten seconds, any vibration transferred to the camera by depressing the shutter button will have dampened.
- A sturdy tripod mount capable of various angles and positions. Impressions are located on various surfaces, and the tripod should have the capability to securely position the camera body so that the film plane is parallel to the impression regardless of the orientation of the impression.
- Level/angle finger. It is important to have the film plane parallel to the evidence, and this tool can help ensure that you have positioned the camera correctly.

- Suitable black-and-white and color negative film or digital storage media. This is not the time to skimp on the flash card used. Buy only high-quality name-brand flash cards.
- Flat rigid scales. Flexible tape measures have a place at crime scenes, but this isn't it! And, for this type of photography, avoid using the curved types of rigid scales.
- A tape measure for taking multiple overlapping images of long tire marks. In this case, the tape measure helps ensure that the overlaps are adequate. The tape measure is not used as the scale for the individual tire segment. A flat rigid scale does this job.
- A photographic log (what we have been calling the photo memo form).
- A reflector. When an electronic flash is used obliquely, it creates a hard shadow. It is counterproductive to have our own photography technique be the reason parts of the evidence cannot be seen and used for comparisons. When using a reflector on the opposite side of the evidence from where the flash is, light strikes the reflector and bounces back toward the impression. This is not enough light to overexpose any areas of the impression that received direct light from the flash. But it is enough light to increase the lighting of the impression in areas that had been in shadow. Now details in these areas can be seen. The shadows are not eliminated with this reflected light. The shadows are lightened to the point that details can be seen inside them (soft shadows).
- A device for blocking ambient lighting. Sometimes impressions need to be photographed during a sunny day. Examination-quality photographs are best lit by the oblique electronic flash. If the sun is shining on the impression, or there is other ambient lighting, this will affect the photography of the impression, so it is best to block the ambient lighting. One way is to have a yard or so of dark fabric you can wrap around the legs of the tripod to make a teepee around the evidence. Then the flash coming in through the "door" of the tepee will be the only lighting reaching the impression.

Additional SWGTREAD recommendations:

- Each image must fill the frame with the impression and scales. (This sounds familiar, doesn't it?)
- Manually focus on the bottom of the impression and close the aperture to maximize the depth of field (e.g., set the aperture to f/16 or f/22). Focusing techniques and managing the depth of field will be thoroughly discussed in Chapter 3.
- If using a digital camera, set the camera to the highest resolution available, and select an uncompressed or lossless compression file format like

RAW/NEF or TIFF. Do not set the camera to capture the image with a JPG or JPEG compression format. The job of the JPEG file format is to reduce the image's file size so that more images can be saved on the camera's flash card or the computer's hard drive. This is not the time for frugality! Capture the image with all the resolution the camera is capable of, and don't throw away any of this detail.

- Take multiple overlapping exposures, mapping the *entire* tire impression. This method revises previous recommendations to photograph just one complete tire rotation. If just one complete tire rotation is documented with photographs, areas with imperfect impressions will show fewer or no details. Photographing the entire length provides the opportunity to capture details in these areas in the second or third tire rotation. One cannot presume that all the detail required for a proper comparison will occur in just one tire rotation.
- For a long tire impression, a series of overlapping photographs of 12 inches each should be taken. A tape measure should be extended along the side of the entire length of the impression for orientation purposes.
- Multiple exposures using various settings (bracketing) may be required. A minimum of three images should be taken with oblique lighting in at least 100-degree increments around the entire impression. Rather than having to measure 100 degrees, it is easier to think of three photos, with the flash coming between each pair of the three tripod legs.
- If the impression is processed in any way with powders or chemicals, rephotograph the impression after each process. Processing 2D or 3D impressions is usually done to improve the visibility of the impression. However, it is best to photographically document each step, just in case the impression is degraded in any way.

Additional SWGFAST recommendations:

- Although SWGFAST also recommends that an 8MP digital camera is the minimum resolution required to capture examination-quality 1:1 images of fingerprints, they recommend one more camera variable. They also require that 1:1 images be captured at a minimum resolution of 1,000 pixels per inch (ppi) when the image is sized to 1:1.
- SWGFAST also indicates that images captured for comparison purposes shall be stored and transmitted without compression or with lossless compression. They recommend capturing these types of images in the RAW file format.

Lossy and lossless compressions and RAW, TIFF, and JPEG file formats are covered in Chapter 7.

But how does the recommendation of capturing examination-quality images at 1,000ppi affect our actual photographic process? Consider an example of photographing a single fingerprint. This image will fill the frame when captured with a 1:1 magnification ratio and the image is the same size as a full-sized digital sensor. The full-sized sensor is 24mm × 26mm, or approximately 1 × 1.5 inches. At 1,000ppi, this translates to 1,000ppi × 1,500ppi, or the equivalent of a 1.5-MP camera. Because an 8-MP camera is recommended, this is quite easy to do. Now, consider a situation in which two fingerprints are adjacent to each other and you want to capture them together in the same image. Because two fingerprints now fill the frame, each will be roughly half the size as a single fingerprint filling the frame. Therefore, the image will have to be enlarged to about 2 × 3 inches. At 1,000ppi, this results in 2,000ppi × 3000ppi, or the need for a 6MP camera. Again, this is easy if the camera you have has 8 MP.

What if you are now faced with the task of photographing three adjacent fingerprints, or a partial palm print of roughly the same size? Because these three fingerprints are now filling the 1 × 1.5-inch frame, it would be necessary to enlarge the image to roughly 3 × 4.5 inches in order to be used for comparison purposes. At 1,000ppi, this translates to 3,000ppi × 4500ppi, or a 13.5MP camera being necessary to take this shot at the required resolution. If you are using an 8MP camera, the solution is to capture overlaps. Take one image of the left and middle fingerprint and another image of the middle and right fingerprint. This is the only way to capture all three fingerprints at the resolution recommended by SWGFAST when using the 8MP camera, which is the minimum resolution required.

Is the solution to this problem to go out and buy a 13.5MP camera? That will solve the problem of capturing three adjacent fingerprints or a partial palm print of the same size. But Murphy's Law dictates that as soon as you buy the 13.5MP camera, the first scene you take your shiny new camera to will feature four adjacent fingerprints or a partial palm print of the same size. In order to capture this 4 × 6-inch area, you'll need 4,000ppi × 6,000ppi, or a 24MP camera! Although digital cameras with this resolution do exist, they are not likely to be found in the hands of crime scene photographers because of their cost. What to do? Determine the largest area your particular camera can place 1,000ppi, and when the area to be photographed is larger than this, begin doing overlaps.

The Photographic Documentation of Bodies and Wounds

When deceased bodies are encountered at crime scenes, they must be completely documented with photography. These crime scene photographs will eventually be supplemented with additional photographs taken at the medical examiner's office when the autopsy is done. Many crime scene photographs of the body have similar aspects to the photos of any kind of

FIGURE 1-44
Midrange of body *(courtesy of S. Dickson, GWU MFS student)*

evidence. One of these is that before taking close-up photos of the body, we must first begin by taking a midrange photograph of the body. Because a series of close-up photographs will follow this midrange photo, it is not necessary to include the complete body in the midrange image.

FIGURE 1-45A
Head to toe *(courtesy of S. Dickson, GWU MFS student)*

FIGURE 1-45B
Toe to head *(courtesy of S. Dickson, GWU MFS student)*

The Full Body Panorama

No matter how the body is originally positioned, face up, face down or on its side, the body is photographed from all four sides.

When photographing the body from the head to the feet, or from the feet to the head, because the body stretches out away from the photographer, it is best to orient the camera vertically in order to better fill the frame with it. If the camera is kept at the horizontal position, there will usually be large areas to the left and right of the body, and the body will be smaller in the field of view than necessary. Remember to fill the frame with your primary subject.

When photographing both sides of the body, the more common horizontal camera position can be used.

There is an issue of composition that relates to these side photographs. Whether the body is positioned high in the field of view, centered in the field of view, or low in the field of view, the body is the same size in each composition. Each of these three compositions succeeds in filling the frame with the body. So what would prompt us to select one of these variable compositions over the other? Remember that the suggestion to fill the frame with the evidence has two parts: one is to make the evidence as large as it can be in the field of view. In these three compositions, we have succeeded in doing this. However, the instruction to fill the frame also includes eliminating as much as possible that is not the

FIGURE 1-46A
Right side *(courtesy of S. Dickson, GWU MFS student)*

FIGURE 1-46B
Left side *(courtesy of S. Dickson, GWU MFS student)*

FIGURE 1-47A
Body low in the field of view *(courtesy of S. Dickson, GWU MFS student)*

FIGURE 1-47B
Body positioned in the middle *(courtesy of S. Dickson, GWU MFS student)*

FIGURE 1-47C
Body high in the field of view *(courtesy of S. Dickson, GWU MFS student)*

primary subject. Depending on the amount of irrelevant, distracting clutter on either side of the body, we may be able to successfully remove it from the composition simply by raising or lowering the camera a bit. The body remains the same size, but the amount of clutter around the body may be controlled by a careful composition of the body. In this case, Figure 1-47C includes the body and the least amount of clutter in view.

The fifth photograph taken of the body is usually of the full face. Sometimes the face is not able to be seen with the body in many different positions. But eventually, the body will be rolled over to enable photography of the other side of the body. During the time both sides of the body are being photographed from four directions, there will be a time to photograph the full face.

Filling the frame with the full face while using your normal focal length lens is, however, not recommended. In this case, crime scene photographers borrow a trick used by professional portraiture photographers.

 ## RULE OF THUMB 1-4

To fill the frame with a face, while remaining back a distance so as to not enlarge the nose, a lens in the 100—120mm length is necessary; it's the perfect portraiture lens focal length range.

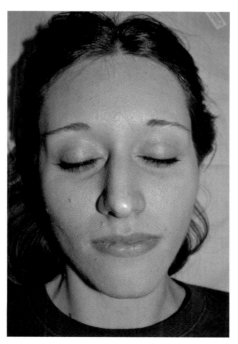

FIGURE 1-48A
Focal length of 50mm *(courtesy of Min Hur, GWU MFS student)*

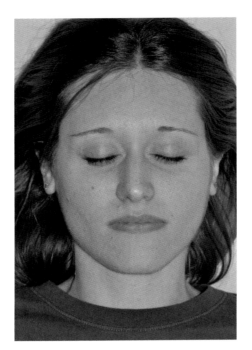

FIGURE 1-48B
Focal length of 100mm *(courtesy of Min Hur, GWU MFS student)*

The optimal focal lengths to use when filling the frame with faces are the 100–120mm focal lengths. If you get too close to the face, when using your normal lens, the relative distance between the nose and the ears seems to increase, resulting in a larger than normal nose and smaller ears. This effect is not only unflattering but may also distort the face to the point that the subject may be unrecognizable when the photo is shown to people who might otherwise be able to recognize the subject.

Another issue related to faces is that sometimes the sun can light them from angles that cast unattractive shadows, to the point where it may make the person difficult to recognize. Because the purpose of this photo is to enable it to be shown to people who may be able to recognize the victim, the sun's shadows can make this more difficult. The solution is easy: block the sun so that the face in completely in shadow, and then expose for the shade, and the face will be properly exposed.

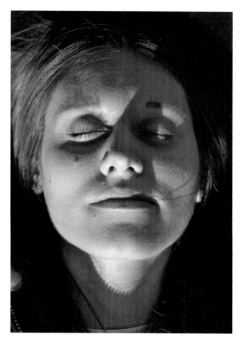

FIGURE 1-49A
Sun shadow *(courtesy of M. Hur and J. Buffington, GWU MS students)*

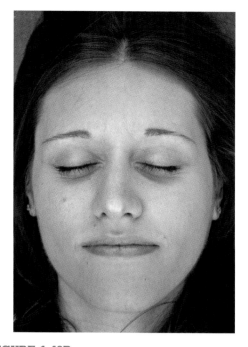

FIGURE 1-49B
Sun blocked, exposed for the shade *(courtesy of M. Hur and J. Buffington, GWU MS students)*

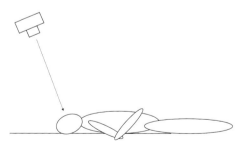

FIGURE 1-50
Camera with the film plane parallel to the face

Finally, when capturing an image of the face of a victim, do not just stand over the body and position the camera directly over the face of the victim. Often, the victim's face will be tilted a bit, with the chin higher than the forehead. Aiming the camera straight down in this case would show more chin and neck, and the digital camera would not be parallel to the face even if it is parallel to the surface the body is lying upon. Figure 1-50 shows the proper angle for positioning the camera when the head is tilted back.

FIGURE 1-51
Tripod handle position reversed

The next photograph in the full body panorama series is a full body shot from overhead. This shot is created by mounting the camera on a tripod, extending all the tripod legs and the center stem, and raising the camera above the body, with the lens positioned perpendicular to the body. If this shot is done indoors, there is one additional modification to the usual mounting of the camera on the tripod. Normally, the tripod handle for adjusting the camera's vertical tilt extends behind the camera, as is seen in the left of Figure 1-51. Because the camera will frequently be positioned near the ceiling, with the back of the camera actually touching the ceiling to help steady the camera, the camera can be mounted on the tripod backward so the handle is reversed, as in the right of Figure 1-51.

Then raise the camera over the body so it is positioned over the middle of the body and take the picture. It is not quite that easy, however. From the camera's position above the body, you must determine the following:

- The proper focal length to use to prevent cutting off either the head, or the feet or both.
- The proper exposure.
- The proper focusing technique.
- Positioning the camera not only so that it is midway between the head and the feet but also so that it isn't aimed more to the right or left side of the body. From the photographer's position, at the side of the body, this position is not always easy to determine.
- With the camera positioned as described, it is not being held as steadily as it is when we take our normal photographs. You must use a technique to ensure that the resulting image is not blurred from camera shake.
- How to take the picture when your finger is not near the shutter button.

Before taking this picture, do a dry run. First, position the camera above the body on the tripod, just to determine how high above the body the camera will eventually be positioned. Indoors, this may be the ceiling height unless the ceiling is very high. Then, stand this distance (the height of the camera above the body) away from the side of the body.

- In this position, vary your lens's focal lengths to determine which focal length does not cut off any parts of the body. Give yourself a little more room than you would if composing the camera normally. For a normal adult body, this usually results in a 35mm focal length. If using a digital camera with an APS-C-sized sensor, this position usually requires a 24mm focal length.
- From the same position away from the body, take a meter reading and set the camera for that exposure if the body is well lit outside. When this is done outside, and flash is not being used, set the shutter speed to 1/125 second. This speed will help freeze the motion from the camera held above the body, as is explained in more depth in Chapter 2. If you're working inside or under darker lighting conditions, you will need to affix your flash, set to the manual flash mode, to the camera's hot-shoe, and calculate the exposure based on your electronic flash's distance to the body.
- From the same position, focus the camera on the subject. However, when this shot is taken, the camera will be aimed straight down. Many lenses have a tendency to extend a bit and lengthen when aimed straight down, and this may change your focal length. If you know your camera has this propensity, after selecting the focal length and focus you may want to tape the lens so that it does not change focal length or focus.
- To deal with whether the camera is being properly aimed straight down over the body, this is best resolved by having another person

stand down the body's long axis. They are in the best position to see whether the lens is directly over the body or if it is aimed to the left or right of the body. See Figure 1-52C.

■ To take this photograph, set the camera for a ten-second delayed shutter release. Once you depress the shutter button, you'll have ten seconds to get the camera positioned properly. This method will take a few practice tries but is easily learned.

One final issue related to this technique: with the flash mounted on the camera's hot-shoe and the camera held diagonally above the body, many feel like just holding the tripod securely is precarious. Two suggestions will help reduce this concern.

First, rather than holding the camera diagonally over the body for ten seconds, try this. During one of your dry runs, in order to determine just how high the camera will eventually be positioned, mark that area in space visually that you have to return to the best way you can. If inside a building, note what area of the ceiling you end up at. Then, when actually taking the photo, push the shutter button, wait a few seconds, and then put the camera into the correct location. You do not have to hold the camera diagonally for ten seconds.

FIGURE 1-52A
Tripod held with hands alone *(courtesy of M. Hur, GWU MS student)*

FIGURE 1-52B
Right forearm on the tripod *(courtesy of M. Hur, GWU MS student)*

FIGURE 1-52C
Camera held above the body *(courtesy of M. Hur, GWU MS student)*

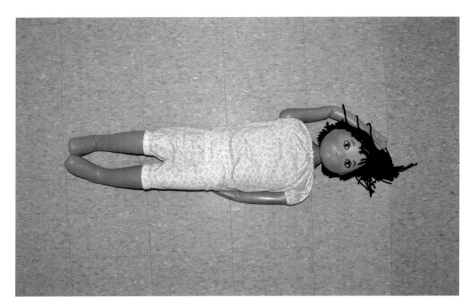

FIGURE 1-52D
An overhead image *(courtesy of M. Hur, GWU MS student)*

Second, rather than just holding the camera with your hands, which makes you rely a lot on finger strength, slide up your lower hand several inches, and now position your lower forearm until it rests on the tripod legs, as in Figure 1-52B. Rather than finger strength controlling the tripod, it is now bones supporting the tripod. Your lower forearm on the tripod supports the lower end of the tripod. Your upper forearm, positioned almost vertically while holding the tripod, supports the tripod held by your higher hand. This approach should make you more confident about using this technique. Figures 1.52A through 1.52D show this sequence.

Wounds

When photographically documenting individual wounds, bruises, or injuries on a subject, whether alive or dead, the first step is to take a midrange photograph. However, rather than documenting the wound/bruise/injury in its spatial relationship to a fixed feature of the crime scene, we now want to document its relationship to a fixed feature of the body. These fixed features are usually joints or other easily recognized sites. Once we begin the close-up

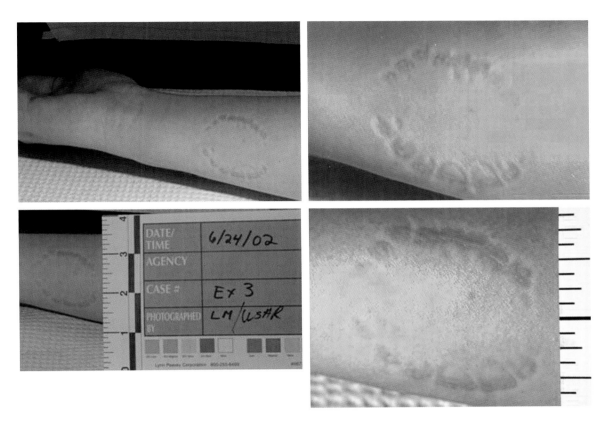

FIGURE 1-53
Injury midrange and close-ups

photographs, filling the frame with just the wound/bruise/injury, it may not be obvious where on the body these sites are. The midrange photograph orients the viewer of the close-up photographs to the location on the body where the injuries are.

As with other close-up photographs, the first to be taken is an as-is close-up, followed by a close-up with a fully labeled scale and then a close-up with just a portion of the scale when the injury is small.

Identification
If the identification of a deceased subject has not yet been determined, possibly because decomposition makes a visual identification of the subject impossible,

any aspects that may assist in the ultimate identification should be photographically documented. These include, but are not limited to:

- Fingerprints and palm prints
- Dental artifacts that can be seen: dentures, gross tooth misalignment or missing teeth, etc.
- Scars, marks, tattoos, birthmarks, warts, moles
- Jewelry
- Glasses, contacts, hearing aids
- Personal effects in pockets and wallets
- Hair length, color, style
- Signs of medical procedures: pacemakers, prostheses, medicines
- Clothing size, style, brand name

Post-Mortem Interval (PMI)

Finally, obvious signs that can be used to determine how long the body has been dead should be photographically documented. These signs may include:

- Scene markers: scene conditions such as mail, newspapers and other dated material; signs of food preparation; is the clothing worn appropriate for the time, for example, is the body found at 3:00 p.m. still wearing pajamas?
- Rigor mortis: is it present and consistent with the body's current position?
- Livor mortis: is it present and consistent with the body's current position?
- Decomposition changes.
- Stage of insect infestation.

 ## CARDINAL RULE III: MAXIMIZE THE DEPTH OF FIELD (DOF)

If it has been included in your composition, it should be in focus.

Depth of field (DOF) is the variable range, from foreground to background, of what appears to be in sharp focus. It is very easy to ensure that any individual object at just one distance from the camera is in focus. Just turn the focusing ring on the lens until that object comes into focus. However, the crime scene photographer must often photograph areas, not just one object. This area will have its foreground closer to the camera, and its background will be farther from the camera. How does the photographer ensure that the entire area of concern is in focus at the same time? Different focusing techniques must be

FIGURE 1-54A
Wide aperture, focused on #1

FIGURE 1-54B
Wide aperture, focused on #15

FIGURE 1-54C
Small aperture, zone focused; everything in focus

employed to maximize the DOF. An entire chapter in this book (Chapter 3) is devoted to focus topics.

When one composes shots of different areas of the crime scene, the foregrounds and backgrounds are constantly changing. The photographer must think about ensuring that each of these different scenes is in focus when the image is captured. This result does not happen by accident. It happens because the crime scene photographer carefully manipulates the variables that affect the depth of field. The DOF variables are mentioned here because they are extremely important! In Chapter 3, they are fully explained. For now, know that DOF variables include the following:

- F/stop selection: the f/stops will typically range from f/2 through f/22. The f/stops with the smallest apertures, such as f/8, f/11, f/16 and f/22, provide the best DOF ranges.
- Lens (focal length) selection: a wide-angle lens has a better DOF than a normal lens; a normal lens has a better DOF than a telephoto lens.
- Camera to subject distance: when the camera is further from the subject, the DOF is longer; as the camera comes closer to the subject, the DOF range becomes smaller.

CHAPTER SUMMARY

Chapter 1 has introduced you to the multiple concepts related to composition and related the concepts to the typical types of photographs captured by crime scene photographers. If Chapter 1 is clear, you can now go out and begin applying these concepts. Set your camera to autoexposure and autofocus, because exposure and focusing concepts have not yet been covered. The reader can even use a point-and-shoot digital camera; an SLR camera is not required for these first exercises. Because the proper use of an electronic flash has not been covered, the following exercises are designed to be done outside on a sunny day. If your camera has a flash, turn it off. The images you will be capturing involve only the proper composition of various types of photos and applying what you have learned about overall, midrange, and close-up photographs.

With each new chapter, you will become increasingly responsible for the settings on the camera. Eventually, you will be required to take all the images in the exercises by (1) intentionally choosing the composition, (2) manually setting the exposure controls, (3) manually setting the focusing and DOF controls, (3) selecting the proper focal length of the lens for each photographic situation, (4) using various electronic flash techniques—all the while (5) ensuring that the images will eventually be acceptable in court as evidence.

Crime scene photography is very different from the photographs you have previously taken. But it is nice to know that having learned crime scene photography, your other kinds of photography will also vastly improve.

Enjoy the ride!

Discussion Questions

1. Briefly explain why photography can be considered to be both a scientific enterprise and an artistic expression of the photographer.
2. Can a properly exposed crime scene photograph still be unsuccessful? Why?
3. How can the photographer's viewpoint affect whether an image correctly depicts the spatial relationship between two objects?
4. How can both ambient and flash shadows be controlled?
5. Briefly explain the written documentation that should accompany each photograph.
6. When scales are used, explain why they should also be labeled.
7. Briefly explain the types of exterior overall photographs. Explain the issues related to the different lenses that can be used and the perspective that is suggested.

8. Briefly explain interior overall photographs. Explain the issues related to the different lenses that can be used and the perspective that is suggested.
9. Midrange photographs have a specific purpose: explain it. Explain also their lens and perspective aspects.
10. Explain the four different types of close-up photographs that can be taken of evidence.
11. Explain the full body panorama series of photographs.

Practical Exercises

The following are composition exercises only. As such, issues of exposure, focus, depth of field, and flash techniques are not considered. You may use an SLR set to program exposure mode and set the camera to autofocus. Or you may use a point-and-shoot film or digital camera. Composition is the only issue in these exercises.

Construct an exterior mock crime scene with several items of evidence included in it:

1. Fill the frame with a photo identifier and photograph it at midday on a sunny day.
2. Take an exterior overall image that shows the crime scene in its relationship to the surrounding neighborhood. Attempt to locate a single easily recognizable feature of the surroundings, and include this feature with the crime scene. It may be a particular business, a house, intersection street signs, or a natural feature of the scene.
3. Take one exterior overall photograph, encompassing an entire outdoor crime scene, while attempting to eliminate everything not within the crime scene.
4. Take a series of images, capturing two sides of any building. Some larger buildings will require overlapping images if a single image does not capture the entire façade.
5. Select one of the items of evidence that is outside, and take a midrange photograph of it with a fixed feature of the scene.
6. Take one close-up, as is, of that item of evidence, filling the frame with it.
7. Take a close-up with a fully labeled scale in view.
8. Take an altered close-up of the evidence.
9. With a body outside, take a midrange photograph and a complete body panorama of it.
10. On this body, draw a 1-inch wound on it, and take a midrange photograph and a series of close-ups of it.

Suggested Readings

Adams, Ansel. 1985. *The Camera*. Boston: Little, Brown, and Company. Chapter 1: Visualization.

Barbara London Upton with John Upton. 1989. *Photography*, Fourth Edition. Glenview, IL: Scott, Foreman and Company, Chapter 14: Seeing Photographs.

Davis, Phil. 1995. *Photography*, Seventh Edition. Boston: McGraw-Hill. Chapter 2: Qualities of a Good Photograph.

Doeffinger, Derek. 1984. *The Art of Seeing*. Rochester, NY: Eastman Kodak Company.

Editors of Eastman Kodak Company. 1976. *Using Photography to Preserve Evidence*. Rochester, NY: Eastman Kodak Company.

Lester, Doug. 1995. *Crime Photographer's Handbook*. Boulder, CO: Paladin Press.

McDonald, James A. 1992. *Close-Up & Macro Photography for Evidence Technicians*. Arlington Heights, IL: Photo Text Books.

McDonald, James A. 1992. *The Police Photographer's Guide*. Arlington Heights, IL: Photo Text Books.

Miller, Larry S. and Richard McEvoy, Jr. 2010. *Police Photography*, Sixth Edition. Cincinnati: Anderson Publishing Company.

O'Brien, Michael F. and Norman Sibley. 1995. *The Photographic Eye: Learning to See with a Camera*, Revised Edition. Worcester: Davis Publications Publisher. Part 2: Elements of Composition.

Redsicker, David R. 1994. *The Practical Methodology of Forensic Photography*. Boca Raton: CRC Press.

Siljander, Raymond P., and Darin D. Fredrickson. 1997. *Applied Police and Fire Photography*, Second Edition. Springfield: Charles C. Thomas.

Staggs, Steven. 1997. *Crime Scene and Evidence Photographer's Guide*. Temecula, CA: Staggs Publishing.

Exposure

KEY TERMS

Aperture
Aperture Priority exposure
    mode (Av)
Bracketing
Burning and dodging
Diaphragm
Digital noise/dark noise
Dirty snow
Exposure compensation
Exposure latitude

Exposure stops
Fill-in flash
F/stop
F/16 Sunny Day Rule
Graininess
18% gray card
Manual exposure mode (M)
Neutral density filter
Polarizer filter
Polarizer filter

Program exposure mode (P)
Reflective light meter
Shutter
Shutter Priority exposure
    mode (Tv)
Theory of reciprocity
UV filter
White balance

LEARNING OBJECTIVES

Upon completion of this section, you will be able to:

- Explain the four exposure variables and their interrelationships
- Explain that shutter speeds are not only exposure controls but also motion controls
- Explain the concept of the Theory of Reciprocity
- Explain how a reflective light meter works
- Explain what "tools" are available to help determine the proper exposure for a tricky scene
- Explain the typically encountered "non-normal" scenes that require exposure adjustments
- Explain the various exposure modes available with different cameras
- Explain how to bracket in manual and automatic exposure modes
- Explain the F/16 Sunny Day Rule
- Explain the basic uses of filters as lens protection, reflection removers, and "sunglasses"

79

Introduction to Crime Scene Photography.

THE PROPER EXPOSURE TRIANGLE

Images can be considered properly exposed, overexposed, or underexposed. For the most part, it should be a goal to have most images properly exposed. Why just "most" of our images? There will be times when we intentionally "bracket" a particular image.

To **bracket** an image means that after taking what we consider to be a properly exposed image of a particular subject, we immediately take two or more additional shots of the same subject from the same point of view; these additional shots are intentionally overexposed and underexposed. Usually, there are two good reasons for following one photo with a series of brackets, as are shown in Figures 2-1, 2-2, and 2-3.

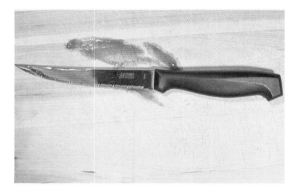

FIGURE 2-1
A +1 bracket

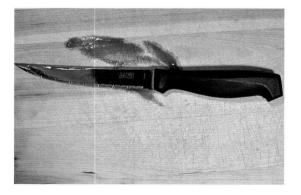

FIGURE 2-2
Properly exposed

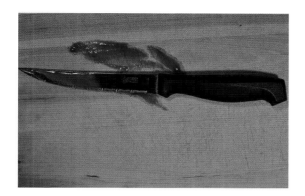

FIGURE 2-3
A —1 bracket

One is that the lighting at the scene might be particularly problematic for any number of reasons, and we are actually unsure if our exposure setting on the camera will truly produce a "proper exposure." In this case, it is just being smart to take additional exposures, in the hopes that at least one of them may truly be "properly exposed." Think of it as taking "insurance shots." We won't get the opportunity to capture this image of the subject ever again, and we want to be assured that at least one of this series of bracketed shots has a properly exposed image among them.

Another good time to take a series of bracketed shots of the same subject is when that subject is a candidate for examination-quality images. As discussed in the previous chapter, these are extremely important images that will be either analyzed or examined in a forensic laboratory by an expert who will be comparing the image to something else to try to establish identity. For example, an image of a fingerprint from the crime scene will be compared to known fingerprints from a suspect. Or an image of a shoe print from the crime scene will be compared to a suspect's shoe. Or an image of a bite mark on a victim will be compared to the known dentition of a suspect. In these situations, it is extremely important that the examiner be able to distinguish all the details in the image. Even if the image is "properly exposed," some of the details necessary to make the identification may be in an area that is a bit more brightly lit than the rest of the image. Additionally, some of the details necessary to make the identification may be in an area that is a bit less brightly lit than the rest of the image. In these situations, in order to provide the best opportunity for the examiner to clearly distinguish all the markings within the image that are there, having additional brackets of the "properly exposed" image might help ensure that the examiner can see all that is present in the series of images necessary to make the determination of either an identification or an exclusion.

Exactly how to change the exposure settings to capture a series of brackets of an important item of evidence will be explained immediately after the exposure variables themselves have been explained.

There are four variables that affect an image's exposure:

- The f/stops
- The shutter speed
- The ISO setting
- The lighting at the scene that affects the subject of our image: the ambient lighting at the scene or the lighting we choose to supplement the ambient lighting with, be that an electronic flash, a flashlight, an alternate light source (ALS), or any other lighting to supplement the ambient lighting

If any of these four variables changes, the exposure of the image is changed. To help us remember the four variables that affect an image's exposure, we group them into what is referred to as the **proper exposure triangle.** Although a triangle has just three sides, adding the "inside" of the triangle as an element of proper exposure practices allows us to group these four variables together. A typical proper exposure triangle looks like this:

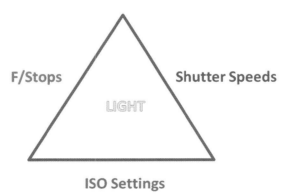

FIGURE 2-4
The proper exposure triangle

EXPOSURE STOPS

Before discussing the individual exposure variables, it is best to understand gross exposure changes first. An image may be described as being properly exposed, overexposed, or underexposed. Of course, any one of the three can happen accidentally, or they can happen because the camera's exposure variables were carefully chosen to create that effect.

When intentionally choosing to alter the camera's exposure, it is possible to increase or decrease the exposure by precise amounts. When we discuss exact exposure amounts, the first concept to understand is the idea of an **exposure stop**. It is possible to take any properly exposed image and to increase its exposure by precisely one stop or decrease its exposure by precisely one stop. A +1 exposure stop means that you're *doubling* the lighting of the original image. A −1 exposure stop means that you're *halving* the lighting of the original image. You may hear a photographer talk about "opening up one stop," or "increasing the exposure by +1." Conversely, you may hear that they intend to "close down one stop," or "decrease the exposure by −1."

Many years ago, cameras offered the photographer controls that altered exposures only by a full stop. Today's cameras, both film and digital, usually allow a photographer to vary exposures by different incremental amounts. Most cameras today include menu selections to change exposures by full stops, 1/2 of a stop or 1/3 of a stop. This point is very important to remember, because depending on how the camera's menu has been set, changing a camera's exposure by pushing a button or rotating a dial may result in either a full stop alteration with just one push of a button or one click when rotating a dial—or pushing the same button once or rotating the dial to the next click may only be a 1/3 stop or a 1/2 stop adjustment. You might be trying to increase or decrease exposure by +1 or −1, but if your camera has been set previously to provide 1/2-stop increments or 1/3-stop increments, one push of a button or one rotation click of a dial may not provide you with a full stop change. The solution is to check your camera's menu selections, especially if the camera you are using has been used by another photographer who prefers different increments of bracketing.

EXPOSURE VARIABLES

Now that you understand how an exposure can be altered in precise amounts with both overexposures and underexposures, it is now time to learn how this information applies to each of the exposure variables.

Shutter Speeds as an Exposure Variable

The shutter of a **single-lens reflex (SLR)** camera lies just in front of the film or digital sensor. For this reason, the shutter of an SLR camera is called a **focal plane shutter**. In other camera systems, the shutter might be located in the lens instead of the camera body.

The shutter covers the sensor until the shutter button is depressed, when it will open and allow light coming in through the lens to strike the sensor for a predetermined amount of time. The times the shutter is open can typically vary from several seconds to just fractions of a second. A typical range of shutter speeds on most current cameras includes: 30, 15, 8, 4, 2, 1, 1/2, 1/4, 1/8, 1/15, 1/30, 1/60, 1/125, 1/250, 1/500, 1/1000, 1/2000, and 1/4000.

As mentioned earlier, these shutter speeds appear to follow the exposure stop concept of halves and doubles. Selecting any of the listed shutter speeds will have its neighboring shutter speed either doubling or halving the light from the shutter speed originally selected. For instance, if one begins with a 1/60-second shutter speed, a 1/125-second shutter speed would close the shutter sooner, allowing just half of the light as 1/60 let through. A 1/30-second shutter speed remains open longer, allowing twice the amount of light through. Each of these two changes would be regarded as a −1 or +1 exposure stop, respectively. See Figures 2-5 through 2-7.

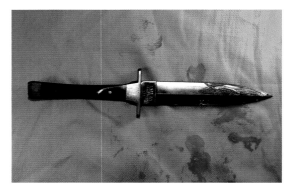

FIGURE 2-5
A −1 exposure with 1/125

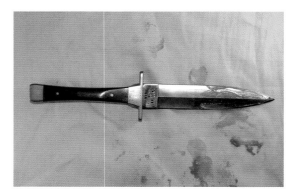

FIGURE 2-6
A proper exposure with 1/60

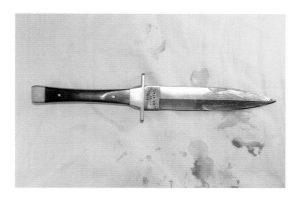

FIGURE 2-7
A +1 exposure with 1/30

Any particular camera may also have offerings in addition to these numbers, allowing for a shutter-speed exposure change in 1/2 of a stop or 1/3 of a stop. Be aware of this, because changing the shutter speed by one click of the dial or one push of a button may be a full-stop change, a 1/2-stop change, or a 1/3-stop change. For instance, at 1/2-stop increments, changing from 1/60 to the next longer shutter speed would be 1/45. At 1/3-stop increments, changing from 1/60 to the next longer shutter speed would be 1/50. Changing from 1/60 to 1/30 would be a full stop change.

In addition to these shutter speed numbers, most cameras also have the option of a Bulb (B) setting. See Figure 2-8. This setting is used when there is a need to have a longer shutter speed than the 30 seconds that is normally the longest option on most cameras. Depress the shutter button, and keep it depressed, and the shutter will remain open for as long as the shutter button is depressed. To alleviate the need to keep your finger on the shutter button, an electronic shutter release cable is available that can open and then lock the shutter open for any desired time (Figure 2-9). Keeping your finger on the shutter button for prolonged times, even if the camera is mounted on a tripod, can transfer some vibration to the camera, resulting in blur.

Shutter Speeds as a Motion Control
Although shutter speeds are certainly an exposure control, they are also a means of controlling motion that is just as important as determining the proper exposure. There are several types of motion that can be controlled by the proper selection of the shutter speed:

- Photographer motion
- Camera motion
- Subject motion

Motion Control with Fast Shutter Speeds

Just by holding a camera in your hands, you transfer enough vibration to the camera to result in a blurred image. The solution is to use a shutter speed that is fast enough to eliminate this tendency to blur. Or you can mount the camera on a tripod so that your heartbeat does not influence the camera. But because using a tripod to capture most of your images would be very awkward, most photographers just learn the appropriate shutter speed to get the job done.

The standard recommendation for eliminating blur from hand-holding the camera is to notice the current focal length of the lens you have selected, turn that focal length into a fraction, and use the closest shutter speed to this fraction or the next faster shutter speed. For example, if you are currently using a 50mm lens, or have your 35—105mm zoom lens set to 50mm, that would convert to 1/50, and if your camera has a 1/50 of a second shutter speed, then use it. If not, the next faster shutter speed would be 1/60 of a second. If you cannot use 1/50, then use 1/60.

If you take your 35—105mm zoom lens and select the 105mm setting for a particular shot, then use a shutter speed of 1/105, or the next faster shutter speed available, which might be 1/125.

This recommendation works for all longer focal lengths. However, it is *not* recommended for focal lengths wider than 50mm. For instance, should you select the 35mm setting of your 35—105mm zoom lens, it is not recommended that you also select a shutter speed of 1/35. Although some professional photographers brag about their ability to use shutter speeds slower than 1/50, this method is not recommended for the general photographer. Do not risk a blurred image because you want to test your ability to hand-hold a camera. Crime scene photography is too important to take such risks.

Camera motion and subject motion share the same shutter speed recommendations. If you arrive at a multicar accident as bodies are still being pulled from the wreckage and carried to ambulances, you might want to photograph some of these victims before they get to the hospital. But you cannot stop the gurney with a victim on it just so you can take some pictures. Your shutter speed selection must be adequate to stop the motion of the moving gurney and your own body as you move alongside the gurney as it nears the ambulance.

Or perhaps you are doing surveillance on a subject expected to move from the front door of an apartment to a car parked on the curb. Your shutter speed must be adequate to freeze the subject moving on the sidewalk, at least enough so that you can recognize the face.

There are well-known shutter speeds that will stop some commonly encountered types of movement:

- 1/60 will freeze the motion of the photographer when hand-holding the camera, with a 50mm lens, aimed at a unmoving item of evidence.

- 1/125 will stop/freeze a walker.
- 1/250 will stop/freeze a jogger, a slow bicyclist, or someone who is jumping.
- 1/500 will stop/freeze a car moving at about 30 miles per hour (mph), enough to recognize an occupant.
- 1/1000 will stop/freeze a vehicle moving about 60 mph.
- 1/2000 will stop/freeze WWII propeller planes at air shows; even the propellers will appear frozen. (However, today's propellers rotate faster.)

FIGURE 2-8
Bulb exposure mode: B.

FIGURE 2-9
Electronic shutter release cable

FIGURE 2-10
1/125 freezing a walker

When using these fast shutter speeds, you must constantly remember that these shutter speeds also effect the exposure of the image, so some kind of exposure compensation will have to be made to avoid underexposing the image. One or more of the other three exposure variables must be manipulated to allow faster shutter speeds while also providing proper exposure.

Motion Control with Slow Shutter Speeds

Is there ever a benefit for a crime scene photographer from using slow shutter speeds? Yes.

Consider an outdoor crime scene at which it is currently raining or snowing. Because we never want to deceive the viewers of our images, we certainly do want to document the fact that it was raining or snowing when we arrived to begin our photography. However, after the fact that it was raining or snowing has been documented, from then on the rain or snow can be considered to be a visual contaminant, obstructing our view of both the crime scene and the evidence within the scene.

FIGURE 2-11
1/250 freezing a jumper

FIGURE 2-12
1/500 freezing a car moving at 30 mph

If you approach a crime scene room that has a screen door, you must document the fact that there was a screen door present, because that might affect a witness's view into the scene through the screen door. After this is done, however, capturing images of the inside of the room and the evidence within the room through the screen door makes no sense. The screen prevents a good view of the room and the evidence.

The same goes for rain and snow. Once their existence has been documented, they are only obstacles. With the proper shutter speed, rain and snow do not have to appear in any remaining images. The answer is not to wait for the rain or snow to stop. The answer is not to put up a tent around the crime scene (although, if the crime scene is small enough, this is an option to consider). The answer is to use a shutter speed that will make the rain or snow disappear!

Trial and error teaches us that if we use a shutter speed of 2 to 3 seconds, then the rain and snow vanish from our images. If we carefully expose for a crime scene using a shutter speed of 2 to 3 seconds, then only objects in the field of view for 2 to 3 seconds will appear in the image. None of the rain drops or snowflakes were in the field of view that long, so they disappear.

FIGURE 2-13
Snow shown coming down

FIGURE 2-14
Snow eliminated with the proper shutter speed

However, a 2- to 3-second shutter speed does let in a tremendous amount of light. The exposure will have to compensate for this light to ensure that a proper exposure is still maintained. The required compensation frequently involves using low ISO settings, the smallest aperture on the lens, and using neutral-density filters or polarizer filters over the lens to help block out some of the light. (All of these exposure variables are discussed later in this chapter.)

On the more modern film and digital cameras, shutter speeds are usually selected by using a rotating dial on the camera body.

Shutter Speed Rule of Thumb

If you are an experienced photographer, you already know what shutter speeds you tend to use most frequently. If you are a novice to SLR photography and you have to make a decision about each exposure variable (presuming that you are using the manual exposure mode) then a little guidance would probably be appreciated at this point. With all those shutter speeds to choose from, are there a few most frequently used? Or is there one most frequently used? Or can it be true that all 18 different shutter speeds mentioned thus far are equally likely to end up being selected for any particular shot?

A general suggestion can be offered here. Because ultimately we may want any particular image to be admissible in court as evidence, one of our constant goals should be to make the image a "fair and accurate representation of the scene." Although this goal will be explained more later, the focal length of the lens that does this job the best is an SLR camera's "normal" lens. This is a 50mm lens for cameras with a film camera or a digital camera with a sensor the same size as a film negative. Therefore, because we will be using a 50mm lens for much of our photography and we will be hand-holding the camera to capture most of our images, we will need a shutter speed that is the reciprocal of 50, that is, 1/50. Many cameras do not have a 1/50-second shutter speed as an option. In that case, 1/60 is the best shutter speed to use when hand-holding a 50mm lens.

 ### RULE OF THUMB 2-1

The optimal shutter speed for most images is 1/60 of a second.

Use a slower or longer shutter speed such as 1/30 or 1/15 and you risk capturing a blurred image. Use a shutter speed that is faster than necessary to eliminate the blur from hand-holding an SLR camera, such as 1/125 or 1/250, and it is more difficult to arrive at an exposure combination with the smaller f/stops that maximize the depth of field. This concept is further explained later in this chapter, when the Theory of Reciprocity is explained.

What ideas govern our choice of a shutter speed?

1. We need a shutter speed that will help provide a proper exposure.
2. We need a shutter speed which will eliminate the blur that can come from motion:
   - The blur that can result from hand-holding different lenses with different focal lengths
   - The blur that can result from a subject's motion
3. We need a shutter speed that is the *slowest* considering the previous two points, because if a *faster* shutter speed is selected, this speed may necessitate a wider aperture that will in turn provide a smaller depth of field.

F/Stops

The terms "f/stops" and "apertures" are frequently confused and sometimes used to mean the same thing. In the lens, there are diaphragm blades that create a variable-sized opening through which light travels on the way to the sensor. This opening, or aperture, can be larger or smaller, to allow more or less light to reach the sensor. The changeable size of the aperture is therefore an exposure control.

The term **f/stop** relates the aperture opening to the focal length of the lens being used. Consider the setting "f/8." First, notice that this term is properly expressed as a fraction. One can sometimes find this improperly expressed as "f-8." If "8" is properly the denominator of a fraction, what does the numerator, or "f," signify? The "f" of "f/stops" refers to the *focal* length of the lens currently being used. This relationship is expressed in the following equations:

$$FLL/f/stop\ number\ =\ DOD$$

$$FLL/DOD =\ f/stop\ number$$

where:

FLL = focal length of the lens
f/stop number = the f/stop selection
DOD = diameter of the diaphragm

For instance, if the lens currently being used is 50mm, and the f/stop currently selected is f/8, then the size of the aperture, the diameter of the opening made by the diaphragm blades (the DOD) is 50/8, or 6.25mm. Or, if a camera with a 50mm lens currently has a diameter opening of 6.25mm, then the f/stop selected is f/8.

What are the f/stop numbers? Although different lenses have different f/stops available, here is the entire continuum of whole f/stop numbers most likely found on most lenses: 1.4, 2, 2.8, 4, 5.6, 8, 11, 16, 22, 32.

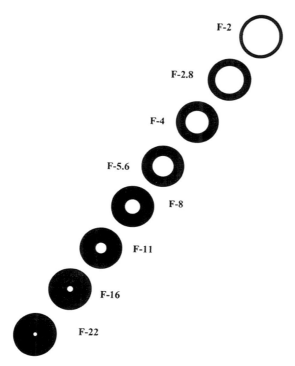

FIGURE 2-15
The relative sizes of the f/stops and the apertures they produce

Certainly, the f/stop numbers seem a bit strange, and they definitely do not look as logically sequential as the shutter speeds did. They do not seem to be halves and doubles of their neighbors, like the shutter speeds. The derivation of these numbers will eventually be explained. And it will eventually be proven that although the f/stop numbers are not numerically halves or doubles of their neighbors, they do represent a halving or doubling of the light being transmitted through the apertures they control. This explanation can be found in Chapter 4.

As with the shutter speeds, although the listed numbers are the whole f/stop numbers, your camera may allow incremental f/stop changes between whole f/stop numbers. For instance, a change from an f/8 to an f/11 is a −1 stop exposure change. If your camera allows for 1/2-stop changes, then rotating the dial or pushing the button that changes the f/stops may result in changing from f/8 to f/9.3 to f/11. If your camera allows for 1/3-stop changes, then rotating the dial or pushing the button that changes the f/stops may result in changing from f/8 to f/9 to f/10 to f/11.

FIGURE 2-16
A −1 with an f/16

FIGURE 2-17
A proper exposure with an f/11

FIGURE 2-18
A +1 with an f/8

Because these f/stop numbers are the denominator of a fraction, it also explains why the f/2 and f/22 setting are frequently misunderstood. Usually, we think of 22 being a larger number than 2. So, if the f/stop numbers cause the apertures to be different sizes, one's first inclination may be to think that an f/22 would produce a larger aperture than an f/2. But, in fact, the opposite is the truth. Considering the f/2 as 1/2 of the focal length and f/22 as 1/22 of the focal length, one quickly learns why the f/22 produces the smaller aperture. Considered with a 50 mm lens:

50/2 = an aperture of 25mm

50/22 = an aperture of 2.27mm

That is, 1/2 of anything will always be more than 1/22 of it. Therefore, an f/2 aperture will be larger than an f/22 aperture. See Figures 2-19 and 2-20.

FIGURE 2-19
An f/2 produces a wide aperture

Just as shutter speeds are both exposure controls and motion controls, f/stops are more than exposure controls. They also partially determine the **depth of field range**. As this is a very complicated subject, it will be covered in the next chapter. But a brief explanation will be provided here. With wide apertures, like f/2, the depth of field range will be very small. With small apertures, like f/22, the depth of field range can include wider ranges. See Figures 2-21 through 2-23.

FIGURE 2-20
An f/22 produces a small aperture

FIGURE 2-21
An f/2 with focusing on the front number has a very small area in focus

FIGURE 2-22
An f/2 while focused on the rear number has a very small area in focus

FIGURE 2-23
An f/22 results in a deep depth of field, covering all the numbers

On the more modern film and digital cameras, f/stops are usually selected by rotating a dial on the camera body.

F/Stop Selection Rule of Thumb

As was done with shutter speeds, it is important at this stage of the text to provide some guidance as to how f/stops are most likely to be used when taking crime scene images. Although ten f/stops are mentioned in the f/stop continuum in the previous section, there are just four that are used most frequently. A fuller explanation will be provided later in this book, in Chapter 3. But a brief explanation is appropriate here.

Besides having an image properly exposed and besides having the image avoid blur from motion it is just as important to have the image in focus. And, to the extent possible, most of the image should be in focus. This range, or area, that is in focus is normally referred to as the **depth of field (DOF)**. The depth of field is the variable area, from front to back, of what appears to be in sharp focus. The f/stop selection is one of the settings or camera variables that controls depth of field. Because the f/stops that produce larger depth of field ranges are the f/stops that produce the smallest apertures, these are the f/stops most frequently recommended.

 RULE OF THUMB 2-2

The optimal f/stops to produce the largest depth of field ranges are f/8, f/11, f/16, and f/22.

If the camera body exposure meter ever recommends using any wider apertures, such as f/4 or f/5.6, bells and whistles should go off in your head because these apertures will result in a much poorer depth of field range. Instead, you should immediately ask yourself what has to be done to use one of the four recommended f/stops. The options usually are:

1. Use a slower shutter speed so that you can use a smaller aperture. However, if the shutter speed is slower than 1/60 second, you will have to put the camera on a tripod to avoid blur.
2. Use a higher ISO setting so that you can use a smaller aperture. This setting is reasonable up to ISO 400 or ISO 800. After that, a higher ISO selection may result in increased digital noise (see the following section).
3. Add light in the form of an electronic flash. By making the scene brighter with a flash, a smaller aperture can be used for a proper exposure, and the smaller aperture will also result in a better depth of field.

What ideas should govern our choice of an f/stop?

1. We need an f/stop that will help provide a proper exposure.
2. We need an f/stop to maximize the depth of field.

When possible, we should use an f/stop that produces a proper exposure and at the same time also maximizes the depth of field. These goals can both be achieved by using the f/stops f/8, f/11, f/16, and f/22 as much as possible. If a meter reading suggests a different f/stop, manipulate the other exposure variables so that these smaller apertures can be used.

ISO Speeds

ISO stands for International Standards Organization. At one time, films made and used in the United States were rated by the American Standards Association (ASA), but eventually we joined the rest of the world and began using international standards.

Several camera manufacturers seem to be battling for the title of offering the fastest ISO setting on their cameras. However, the standard range of available ISO speeds on the majority of cameras at this time are: 50, 100, 200, 400, 800, 1600, 3200 and 6400. The battleground for faster and faster ISOs has produced some cameras that now offer these additional ISO speeds: 12,800, 25,600, 51,200, and even 102,400! As can be seen, both of these digital ISO speed continuums nicely follow the halves/doubles concept as illustrated with the shutter speeds.

Previously, with film, the ISO number indicated the relative sensitivity of the film to light. When the lighting was strong, as on a sunny day, a low-numbered ISO film such as ISO 100 could be used. As the lighting became weaker, film that was more and more sensitive to light had to be used, like ISO 400 or ISO 800. At night, the highest film sensitivities were needed: ISO 1600 and ISO 3200. However, as the film ISOs became faster and faster, there was a penalty to be paid for this increased sensitivity to light. With the ISOs of 1600 and 3200, you could detect a decrease in contrast and an increase in the graininess of the image. You would begin to see that the image was losing its midtones, making the image more a recording of the extremes of the white-to-black continuum. There were less diverse gray tones, and these gray tones are what gives an image much of its depth and detail. The image would also begin to appear spotty or grainy, with less resolution.

Digital ISO equivalents follow a similar sequencing, although the digital sensor is not actually changing its sensitivity to light. Instead, the signal from the digital sensor being transmitted to the digital memory card in the camera is being electronically boosted. To the digital photographer, though, the similarity remains. When there is bright ambient light available, the low digital ISO

FIGURE 2-24
Normal contrast on the left, loss of contrast in the middle, and digital noise resulting in a spotty/grainy appearance

equivalents are normally selected; as the ambient lighting becomes weaker, we tend to use higher ISO numbers. Again, with faster digital ISOs, there is a price to pay. Normally, once you get beyond ISO 800, you begin to notice **digital noise** or **dark noise** more and more, because it is when the scene becomes darker that we tend to boost the digital ISOs up to the higher ISO numbers.

The main difference between film ISOs and digital ISOs is that with film, once the camera was loaded with a particular film, it no longer became a usable exposure variable. We had to use the entire roll of film until we could put in a more appropriate ISO. For instance, if we first began photographing in outdoor sunny conditions with a roll of 24-exposure ISO 100 film and finished photographing a few items of evidence that were outside at exposure #14, when we went inside a crime scene building to continue documenting all the evidence, we were stuck using the ISO 100 film until that roll was done. Then we could reload the camera with a more appropriate ISO 400 film.

With digital ISO equivalents, we now have the option of changing the ISO setting for every shot! Having more options is always a good thing. Now, when determining the particular exposure for any shot, the option to change the ISO setting is always in play. This option is sometimes difficult to remember for many of us who have a long history of using film on the job. The author frequently has to remind himself that altering the ISO is now an option for every shot.

ISOs are usually selected by buttons or dials on the camera body and can be seen in either the digital LED screen or in one of the Menu selections.

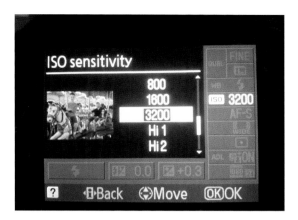

FIGURE 2-25
ISO 3200 selected *(courtesy of M. Hashimi, GWU MS student)*

FIGURE 2-26
ISO 6400 selected

ISO Selection Rules of Thumb

If you have a camera with 8 ISO selections to choose from, are there a few that are most frequently used?

 RULE OF THUMB 2-3

Outside on a sunny day (generally, daytime is considered to be between 10:00 a.m. and 3:00 p.m.) with the scene of interest lit by the sun, the normal recommendation is ISO 100.

Some digital cameras may not have an ISO 100 option. These may have ISO 200 as their lowest ISO option. If so, use the ISO 200 on sunny days.

RULE OF THUMB 2-4

For all other times and conditions: earlier in the morning, later in the afternoon, at night, and anytime you are inside a house or building, it is recommended to select ISO 400 as your starting selection. You may need to change this particular ISO selection, but it is a great place to begin.

These two ISO selections are great initial settings. They can always be changed if necessary.

What ideas govern our choice of an ISO selection?

1. We need an ISO selection that will help provide a proper exposure while maintaining a good resolution and minimizing digital noise.
2. We need an ISO selection that can help maximize the depth of field.

Light as an Exposure Variable
The Amount of Ambient/Existing Light

The amount of ambient light currently present at a crime scene is obviously going to affect exposure determinations. When the lighting is bright, it will be relatively easy to ensure the desired results:

1. A proper exposure
2. The elimination of blur from motion, also controlled by the shutter speed selection
3. A great depth of field (or the elimination of blur resulting from a critical area of the photo being out of focus); also primarily controlled by the f/stop selection

As the ambient lighting begins to dim, we can manipulate the exposure variables to a certain extent to maintain these three results, but if the lighting becomes too dim, at some point we will be forced to add supplemental lighting, usually in the form of electronic flash. At other times, a flashlight may be all that is required. And an ALS can even be introduced to light certain types of evidence; to induce fluorescence; or to achieve other lighting effects.

Shadow Control

At times, it may be prudent to consider the elimination of some of the ambient lighting. Sunny days result in areas that are both brightly lit and areas that are in shadows. There will be times when the evidence is affected by these shadows. It would be nice if all evidence located outside on a sunny day were completely sunlit. It would also be convenient if the evidence were located completely in the shade. In that case, all that would be necessary would be to take a meter reading of the evidence in the shade and set the camera for that lighting, and the resulting image would be properly exposed. But frequently there are partial shadows over the evidence that might be distracting because of their pattern. If there is a shadow of tree branches, power lines, fence designs, or any other items over the evidence, it may make it difficult to see the evidence. The solution is often an easy one: block the sun with your body (or the body of anyone else who may be nearby) so that the evidence is completely in the shade. Then just meter the evidence in the shade and take the photo. The evidence will be properly exposed without any distracting shadows present.

FIGURE 2-27
Lighting with shadows *(courtesy of M. Hashimi, GWU MS student)*

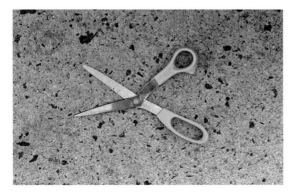

FIGURE 2-28
Sun blocked and the exposure determined with the scissors in the shade *(courtesy of M. Hashimi, GWU MS student)*

A variation on this theme is when the sun is low in the horizon, either early in the morning or late in the afternoon. The sun itself may cause the evidence to have distracting shadows around it. If you consider these shadows to be a distraction, just eliminate them by blocking the sun so that the entire area is in the shade. One obvious example is dealing with a body outside in the early morning or late afternoon. If the sun is low and positioned at the victim's feet, the face of the victim will have the look of a person holding a flashlight below their chin aimed upwards. These shadows may be so distracting that showing the photo to individuals who may be able to recognize the victim may make an identification more difficult or impossible.

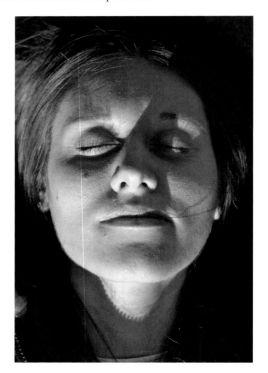

FIGURE 2-29
Distracting shadows over a face *(courtesy of M. Hur and J. Buffington, GWU MS students)*

When there are shadows over larger areas, this technique will not work. But for most close-up photography, it can be the solution to the problem of distracting shadows.

Lens Flare

Many outdoor photographs must be taken when the sun is in front of the photographer. When taking exterior overalls of buildings, one or two sides of

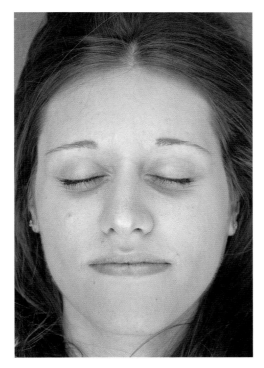

FIGURE 2-30
Shadows blocked and an exposure set for the shade *(courtesy of M. Hur and J. Buffington, GWU MS students)*

a building are often sunlit and the other sides are in shadow. Photographing accident scenes will also often mean that some of the sides of the vehicles are in shadow. Whenever the photographer has the sun in front of the camera when an image is captured, the possibility of lens flare occurring exists. Lens flare is created by the light of the sun coming directly into the lens, resulting in multicolored geometric shapes across the image. Sometimes lens flare resembles a misty cloud over the scene or streaks of light. All forms of lens flare compromise the intent of the image: to show clearly a part of the scene.

There are generally two solutions to the problem of lens flare. Many lens manufacturers provide a lens hood with each lens they sell. The lens hood projects from the end of the lens and hopefully blocks the sun from shining directly into the lens. If you don't have a lens hood handy, you can also use a clipboard or even your own hand to block the sun so that it cannot shine into the lens directly.

FIGURE 2-31
Lens flare

FIGURE 2-32
Lens hood on the lens *(courtesy of M. Simms, GWU MS student)*

At times, the photographer can actually see the lens flare in the viewfinder before the image is captured. Many times, however, the result won't be noticed until the image is captured, and then it is too late. The simple solution is to be aware of the possibility and to take the precautions mentioned here.

The Color of Light

In addition to considering the amount of ambient light that might be present to affect an exposure, the photographer must also be aware of the various colors of different lights. The colors of many lights may not always be apparent to a photographer, but they can be picked up by the camera in the form of tints or color changes to the scene.

FIGURE 2-33
Blocking the sun with your hand

Shade

On a sunny day with a blue sky, if the item of evidence is not directly lit by the sun, the blue sky may be the light that most affects the evidence. In this case, there can be a blue tint to the scene or over the evidence. The solution is to provide the proper light to prevent objectionable tints from occurring: electronic flash.

FIGURE 2-34
A blue tint from being in the shade *(courtesy of M. Hashemi, GWU MS student)*

FIGURE 2-35
Tint removed with the use of electronic flash *(courtesy of M. Hashemi, GWU MS student)*

Sunrise, Sunset

Early in the morning or late in the afternoon, the sun can take on an obvious orange or red tint. This tint can affect everything lit by the sun. The scene or the evidence will look like it has these tints over them.

FIGURE 2-36
Late afternoon sun producing an orange tint

FIGURE 2-37
The true color of the car

Tungsten

Normal indoor household light bulbs have tungsten filaments. Tungsten light can cause the area lit by it to have a yellowish tint. Again, to avoid this tint, use an electronic flash whenever capturing images indoors.

FIGURE 2-38
A yellowish tint produced by indoor tungsten light bulbs *(courtesy of M. Hashemi, GWU MS student)*

FIGURE 2-39
The yellow tint removed by using an electronic flash *(courtesy of M. Hashemi, GWU MS student)*

Fluorescent

Many homes are now lit by energy efficient mini fluorescent lightbulbs designed to replace the regular household tungsten lightbulbs. These can produce either yellowish or green tints. The long tubular fluorescent lightbulbs used in many offices and businesses are also well known to produce greenish tints.

FIGURE 2-40
A green tint from indoor fluorescent lighting *(courtesy of M. Hashemi, GWU MS student)*

Solutions to Color Tints

With all these tints resulting from different lighting, how is the crime scene photographer able to go into court and swear that the image being offered to the court as evidence is a "fair and accurate representation of the scene?"

FIGURE 2-41
The green tint removed by using an electronic flash *(courtesy of M. Hashemi, GWU MS student)*

The best way to avoid a challenge to the accuracy of the color of an image intended to be offered to the court as evidence is to first be aware that the problem does exist. After that, you should take the following precautions so that these color tints do not affect your images.

Capture the Image with the Right Light. If the original image is captured with the right light, then the colors within the images will be correct. What is the right light? Both of the following light sources will produce images with accurate colors:

- Midday sun
- Electronic flash

 RULE OF THUMB 2-5

When accurate colors must be recorded, it is recommended to use only midday sunlight or an electronic flash.

Ensure that the Properly Captured Colors Are Properly Printed. Once the image has been captured correctly, it is still possible that the image has been printed incorrectly, resulting in colors in the photograph not accurately representing the true colors of items that were photographed. How is this mistake avoided?

Whenever the proper color of anything can be anticipated as a possible issue in the future, one of the best ways to ensure that the image going to court has the same colors as the original items at the crime scene is to insert some sort of color scale into the image before the image is photographed. Then, this color scale will be submitted with the images and accompany all the images when they go to court. If the image was captured with the correct light, as mentioned earlier, and printed accurately, then the color scale in the photograph will appear to have the same colors as the real color scale going to court with the photographs. It will be easy for anyone looking at the images to determine that the colors of the color scale in the photo and in real life are the same. If so, then all the other colors in the photography are also accurate.

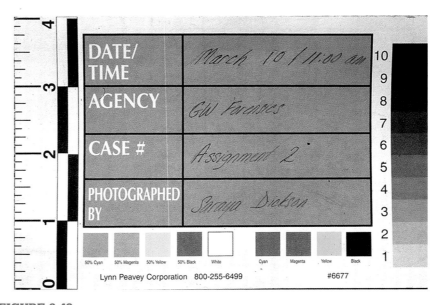

FIGURE 2-42
A color scale *(courtesy of S. Dickson and B. Pridgen, GWU MFS students)*

If the image of the scene with a color scale alongside the evidence was present but there was a green tint over the entire resulting image because the image was captured with office fluorescent tube lighting, with no flash, then the digital darkroom technician can use digital software such as Adobe Photoshop® to remove the green tint. After this is done, the color scale in the image should look like the color scale turned in with all the images taken at the crime scene.

Use the Proper Digital White Balance Setting. Today's digital cameras also have a **digital white balance** setting in the camera's menus. This feature allows the crime scene photographer to feel confident that improper tinting isn't being captured when the image is captured. Select the white balance

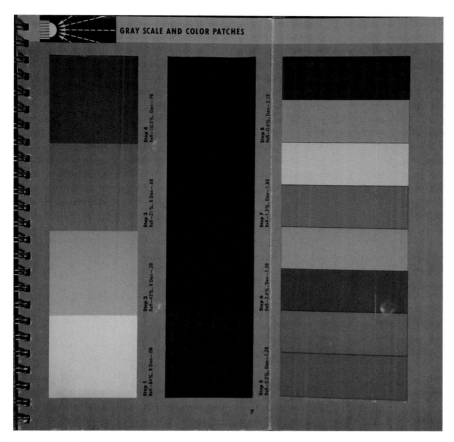

FIGURE 2-43
A color scale

setting that corresponds to the lighting at the scene. The digital camera's software will then adjust the colors so that they are correct.

There is also an **automatic white balance (AWB)** setting. This name is a bit deceiving. It suggests that the setting will automatically correct for any of the various lighting conditions that may be present. Actually, it does its job fairly well, as long as there is some white object within the composition. This element is required for the AWB setting to be truly effective.

However, rather than rely on the camera's software to correct this critical issue, it is better to be able to testify that you used the correct lighting and that you added a color scale to the scene, anticipating the accurate color of a particular image to later become an issue.

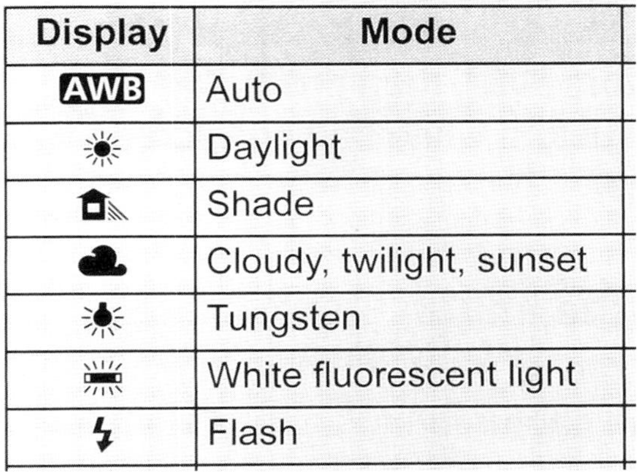

Display	Mode
AWB	Auto
☀	Daylight
⌂	Shade
☁	Cloudy, twilight, sunset
☀	Tungsten
▦	White fluorescent light
⚡	Flash

FIGURE 2-44
A typical white balance set of options

Electronic Flash

When the ambient lighting is insufficient to produce both a proper exposure and a good depth of field, supplemental lighting in the form of electronic flash can be utilized to provide the smaller apertures necessary to have a good depth of field. For example, as previously mentioned, if the current exposure recommendation is ISO 100, 1/60, and f/5.6, then adding extra light in the form of electronic flash may enable the use of smaller apertures such as f/22, f/16, and f/11.

Chapter 4 is an entire chapter on electronic flash, so you'll have a good command of the various flash techniques necessary to adequately photograph any crime scene after reading it.

Exposure Latitude and Dynamic Range

It is very important for photographers to understand these two terms. **Exposure latitude** (originally related to film photography), and its counterpart, **dynamic range** (a digital photography term with the equivalent meaning) are important to understand when considering the proper exposure of any scene. Many crime scenes are uniformly lit, making it easy to determine the proper exposure of that scene. However, there are just as many crime scenes that have substantial lighting differences within the area one wants to include in any one image. If it were possible to compose part of the scene that is brightly lit and take that photo, and then recompose on the other part of the scene that is more dimly lit and take that photo, there would be no problem. At times, however, the composition of an area of importance includes both brightly lit details and other details that are more dimly lit. When both areas are important and are juxtaposed in a way that requires both to be in the same image, then an exposure dilemma presents itself to the photographer.

Sensors Cannot Capture Details in Extreme Lighting Conditions

Both film and digital sensors lack the ability to capture all the details of the scene when there is a wide range of exposures in that scene. Sensors are limited in what they can properly expose when there are extreme ranges of lighting present. This concept is initially difficult to understand, because at such scenes, the human eye can effectively make out details in both extremes of lighting. We can focus with our eyes on an area brightly lit and see detail in that area because the eye will adjust for that lighting. We can then refocus on an area that is dimly lit; the eye will adjust for the dim area, and we can make out details there also. We sometimes forget that the camera cannot do the same thing and expect it to correctly capture details in both areas. Cameras cannot do that—at least not without help.

We can set the camera to properly expose the details in the brightly lit areas, and those areas will be properly exposed. Details in the darker parts of the scene will be obviously underexposed—sometimes vastly under-exposed. We can set the camera to properly expose the details in the dimly lit areas, and those areas will be properly exposed. Details in the brighter parts of the scene will then be obviously overexposed—sometimes vastly overexposed.

Is the solution to this problem to determine the exposure for both ranges, and then set an exposure midway in between the extremes? No. In this case, details in neither extreme will be properly exposed.

Consider this example. When the scene is brightly lit by the midday sun, a typical exposure determined by the camera's exposure meter (discussed later in this chapter) might be ISO 100, 1/60, f/22. Meter an area that is in deep shade, and the lighting might be at least five stops dimmer, resulting in an exposure recommendation of ISO 100, 1/60, f/5.6. Because the f/stop range is 22, 16, 11, 8, 5.6, 4, and so on, the f/stop midway between f/22 and f/5.6 is f/11. Is the solution to capture the image with an f/11? With that setting, you'll overexpose the area that is sunlit by two stops, because it requires an f/22 for a proper exposure. And you'll underexpose the area that is shady by two stops, because it requires an f/5.6 for a proper exposure. The middle ground is not the solution!

Because neither film nor digital sensors are sensitive enough to expose both areas properly at the same time, the solution is to light the dimly lit area with a supplemental electronic flash burst, bringing the dimly lit area into the range of lighting that either film or a digital sensor can properly expose. This flash technique is called *fill-in flash,* and it is covered fully in Chapter 4.

Exposure Corrections in the Digital Darkroom

It may be comforting to know that there are other solutions to incorrect exposures. It is also possible to correct exposure problems by processing the image with digital software. However, it is always preferable to have correctly captured an image initially than it is to be able to correct exposure problems after the fact. It is better to be a good photographer than it is to be good at fixing initial mistakes.

Globally Increasing or Decreasing Exposures

When the entire image is overexposed or underexposed, it is very easy to correct most exposure errors with software such as Adobe Photoshop. There is a limit to this correction ability, but if the image is just one or two stops over- or underexposed, then the correction is relatively easy. This approach is referred to as a **global correction** because the entire image will be uniformly lightened or darkened as needed.

Burning and Dodging Selected Areas of an Image

When processing film, photographic paper was white until subjected to light in the wet-chemistry darkroom. Adding light to the photographic paper darkened it; withholding light from the photographic paper kept it a lighter tone. When the majority of the image was properly exposed and isolated areas showed a marked overexposure or underexposure, it was possible to make corrections in just selected areas of the image.

Selected areas that were originally overexposed can be darkened to various degrees until they seem to blend with other properly exposed areas. This technique is called **burning** the area that was previously overexposed. After the "normal" exposure of the film print, selected areas previously overexposed can be subjected to additional light while the rest of the image is masked so that it does not receive any additional light. The effect is that previously overexposed areas (lighter areas) of the image now look properly exposed (darker). With Photoshop, the effect is the same. Selected areas that are overexposed can be darkened to various degrees until they blend with the properly exposed areas.

Areas that were originally underexposed can be lightened to various degrees until they seem to blend with other properly exposed areas. This technique is called **dodging** the area previously underexposed. With film, this effect was achieved by inserting an opaque form over the light-sensitive photographic paper in the areas that were underexposed, withholding light from specific areas of the photographic paper, thereby lightening those areas. With Photoshop, the effect is the same. Selected areas that are underexposed can be lightened to various degrees until they blend with the properly exposed areas.

RECIPROCAL EXPOSURES

Determining proper exposure is one of the fundamental duties of a crime scene photographer. However, there is not just one combination of exposure variables that results in a proper exposure. There are many available exposure variables that result in a proper exposure. Because the exposure variables are each available in increments of halves and doubles, it is possible to vary any exposure combination by changing one of the variables by +1 while at the same time varying another of the exposure variables by −1. The result will be a proper exposure with two different exposure variables. This concept is the basis for the term **reciprocal Exposures**.

Figure 2-45 is provided to make this concept easier to understand. On the left side are sequential shutter speeds and on the right side is a sequence of f/stop numbers. Each shutter speed is currently aligned with a particular f/stop number by a series of dashes. For example, 1/60 is currently aligned with f/5.6. If your camera's meter currently indicated that 1/60 and f/5.6 was a good exposure for the lighting of a particular crime scene, then every other pairing would also be exposure variables that result in a proper exposure. Notice that changing from 1/60 to 1/30 would be the equivalent of a +1 shutter speed change. And changing from an f/5.6 to f/8 would be a −1 exposure change. Therefore, the exposure variables of 1/30 and f/8 result in the *same* exposure as 1/60 and f/5.6—all the shutter speed and f/stop pairings in Figure 2-45 result in the *same* exposure!

There are always multiple exposure combinations that will result in the same exposure. How do we use this concept of reciprocity at crime scenes? When we take a meter reading at crime scenes, the initial combination of f/stop and shutter speed may not be the optimal combination of f/stop and shutter speed. The meter can recommend only one f/stop and shutter speed combination at a time. We have to constantly remember there are always multiple other combinations available. How do we decide which of the multiple combinations is optimal? The answer usually comes down to asking ourselves one of two questions:

1. Which of the available proper exposure combinations allows me to freeze motion best when there is movement in the scene?
2. Which of the available proper exposure combinations allows me to maximize the depth of field when that is the priority?

If question #1 applies, then gravitate towards to the shutter speed and f/stop combinations with faster shutter speeds. If question #2 applies, then gravitate towards the shutter speed and f/stop combinations with smaller apertures. Because most crime scenes are static and the evidence is unmoving, question #2 is the one most frequently applicable.

Notice in Figure 2-45 that the 1/60 shutter speed is red and the f/stops of 22, 16, 11, and 8 are blue. This color coding reiterates the previous recommendations for shutter speeds and f/stops.

 ### RULE OF THUMB 2-6

To the extent possible, it is desirable to capture as many images as possible with that shutter speed (1/60) and those f/stops (f/22,/f/16, f/11, and f/8). 1/60 allows the hand-holding of a 50mm lens without blur, and those four f/stops result in the best depth of field.

Should the camera's meter ever recommend a different shutter speed and f/stop combination, it is worth repeating the recommendations provided earlier:

- Use a slower shutter speed so that you can then use a smaller aperture. However, if the slower shutter speed is slower than 1/60 second, then you will have to put the camera on a tripod to avoid blur.
- Use a higher ISO setting so that you can then use a smaller aperture. This approach is reasonable up to ISO 400 or ISO 800. After that, a higher ISO selection may result in increased digital noise.
- Add light in the form of an electronic flash. By making the scene brighter with a flash, a smaller aperture can be used for a proper exposure with a better depth of field.

Make a copy of Figure 2-45 and then cut it vertically through the middle hash marks. In this way, you can align different shutter speeds and different f/stops. Ask yourself if any particular shutter speed and f/stop combination should be used for a scene with any particular lighting. Remember, the "correct" answer will usually be the combination that aligns the 1/60 shutter speed with one of the four designated f/stops.

THE REFLECTIVE LIGHT METER

The reflective light meter is located in the camera body. Its job is to recommend an exposure combination that will result in a proper exposure. To do this, it

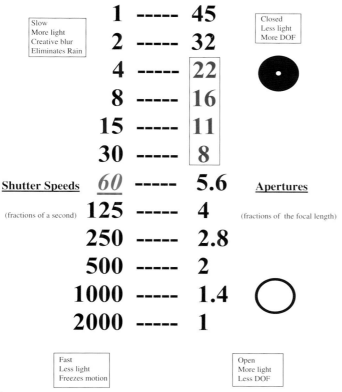

FIGURE 2-45
Reciprocal exposure

tries to balance the four exposure variables. The exposure variables are prioritized as follows:

1. Usually, the digital ISO equivalent is determined first. When film cameras were the norm, they first thing done was to load the camera with film. Recommendations have previously been made for this choice. On a bright sunny day, set the ISO to 100; otherwise, under all other lighting situations, set the ISO to 400. These are good beginning points and they may be altered later if necessary.
2. Set the shutter speed to avoid blur when hand-holding the camera with a particular focal length lens. Because the "normal" focal length selection will usually be a 50mm lens, 1/60 second is normally selected.
3. Compose the scene by looking through the viewfinder and take a meter reading of the reflected light coming into the lens from the composed crime scene. This is usually done by depressing the shutter button half way down.

When you are looking through the viewfinder to compose the scene and depress the shutter button halfway, in the viewfinder there is usually some form of a continuum from −2 to +2, frequently similar to the −2 to +2 continuum in Figure 2-46. When the meter is activated, there will be a hash mark or other form of indication that lets you know what exposure would result if you depressed the shutter button the entire way.

FIGURE 2-46
The exposure meter continuum: −2 to +2

4. F/stop selection for a proper exposure. If this hash mark is not aligned under the "0" or, in this case, the symbol that looks a bit like a baseball home plate, then the photographer needs to make f/stop changes until the hash mark is aligned in the middle of the continuum.

How does the light meter do this job? One can get the feeling that the meter is doing some kind of math to determine the proper exposure for a scene. It is. What is the standard by which the light meter determines whether a particular scene will be properly exposed, overexposed, or underexposed?

The Light Standard: The 18 Percent Gray Card

Figure 2-47 shows an 18 percent gray card. This shade of gray reflects 18 percent of the light that strikes it. Why is this shade of gray regarded as the standard around which camera exposure systems are designed? After exhaustive research, camera manufacturers have determined that when most people take photos, they aim their cameras towards subject matter that reflects 18 percent of the light back towards the camera. These camera manufacturers know that if their cameras produce unacceptable results in the majority of picture-taking situations, then customers will buy different cameras from other manufacturers.

FIGURE 2-47
The 18 percent gray card

What is this hypothetical 18 percent gray scene? It is one that is composed of multiple colors, various tones of these colors, light subject matter and dark subject matter. All together, the total scene reflects 18 percent of the light striking it towards the camera.

How can a photographer use the 18 percent gray card? If the reflectivity of any particular scene is in doubt, or the photographer has any doubt about whether the light meter in the camera will be making a correct exposure suggestion in any situation, the photographer can take a meter reading of the 18 percent gray card, lit the same way the scene in question is lit, and the resulting exposure recommendation will invariably be correct.

Light Meters

To make life interesting, there are different light metering systems available with different cameras, each doing its job just a bit differently.

Averaging/Center-Weighted Meters

Less expensive cameras once offered just one metering system. This was the **averaging** or **center-weighted meter**. It is easiest to envision as an oval in the viewfinder, with the meter concerned with just the light within that oval. Seldom did a photographer compose the most important element of the photograph in the corner of the viewfinder. Usually, a photographer composes with the most important elements toward the center of the viewfinder. At one time, this metering system was quite prevalent, and other options were not available. Today, two other metering systems are primarily used.

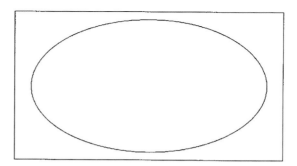

FIGURE 2-48A
Graphic of a center-weighted metering system

Spot Meters

There are times when the primary subject matter of the photograph is relatively small in comparison to the entire scene. For example, if one goes to a child's school play, and it is imperative to make sure that one child on the stage is optimally exposed, then all the surrounding elements on the stage, under various lighting conditions, are irrelevant.

If you are doing surveillance on a subject and the lighting conditions around the subject are variable, then it would be best to use a **spot meter** and put the spot on the subject so that he or she is properly exposed.

Various cameras have different-sized center spots in the center of the viewfinder. In these cases, only the light reflected by the area that this spot covers will determine the exposure for the entire image. The child, or the suspect under surveillance, will be properly exposed, and the surrounding areas will have no impact on the exposure determination.

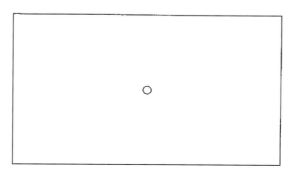

FIGURE 2-48B
Spot metering system

Matrix Meters

The most refined camera metering system on the most expensive film and digital cameras is the **matrix metering system**, a metering system featuring a variety of geometric segments covering the image in the viewfinder. Each segment will read the light in its own segment, and then the camera's computer chip will evaluate the light and dark areas in the image and determine the optimal exposure for that scene. For example, if the following image was being composed (Figure 2-50), then the computer chip in the camera would interpret it as an underexposed person being backlit by the sun, and the exposure recommendation would attempt to properly expose for the person. Some cameras may have a "backlight button" that tries to achieve the same effect. It usually works by forcing the meter to recommend an exposure that exposes the scene with a +1.5 stops to lighten the otherwise dark parts of the scene. A third way to solve the exposure problems encountered by backlit scenes is to use fill-in flash (see Chapter 4).

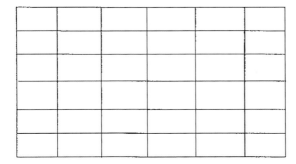

FIGURE 2-49
Matrix metering system

As matrix metering systems tend to do their job well, it is recommended they be used as your primary metering mode.

NORMAL VERSUS NON-NORMAL SCENES

The camera's internal light meter is supposed to assist the photographer in determining a proper exposure. But, just what does the camera meter use as a guide to determine one scene is either "properly" exposed, "overexposed," or "underexposed"? It must have some standard or some guide to determine whether the light currently coming through the lens is "enough," "too much," or "too little."

FIGURE 2-50
Backlit subject metered with an averaging metering system

FIGURE 2-51
Backlit subject lit with fill-in flash

The Normal Scene

The 18 percent gray card is the standard. It may seem odd, but the camera's reflective light meter is designed to provide a proper exposure recommendation when one depresses the shutter button halfway when—and only when—one composes on the 18 percent gray card or a scene that reflects the same amount of light. These are both "normal" scenes as far as the camera meter is concerned.

What is this "normal" scene? A normal scene is one that includes several subjects or objects. Some of these subjects/objects are light-toned, some are dark-toned, and some are midtoned. Some have various colors and various hues of different colors. What these most frequently photographed scenes have in common, however, is that they all tend to reflect approximately 18 percent of the light striking them toward the camera. Normal scenes are very much like 18 percent gray cards.

Because these are the types of scenes one most frequently photographs, the light meter is most often correct when it recommends a particular exposure combination. For the most part, the exposure meter can be trusted to do its job well. However, because we sometimes compose on a scene that does not reflect 18 percent of the light striking it, we must recognize these times, and learn compensations that have to be made to properly expose these non-normal scenes.

Non-normal Scenes

Crime scene photographers regularly encounter non-normal scenes—often enough that we sometimes have to be prepared to make adjustments other than what the camera's light meter is recommending. These non-normal scenes tend to fall into one of four common situations.

Overly Light Scenes

At outdoor crime scenes that are located on snowy or sandy areas, the meter is best not trusted. How do these crime scenes differ from normal crime scenes? They typically reflect much more light than normal crime scenes. What is the usual result if the camera's light meter is used in order to determine the exposure for this kind of scene? The result is invariably an underexposed photo. Why?

If a scene is snowy and is also relatively well lit, the snow can reflect approximately 80 percent of the light that strikes it back toward the camera. How does the meter deal with this amount of light? The meter is expecting 18 percent light; the meter is expecting its operator to aim the camera at a normal scene. Designed to provide a proper exposure for a scene reflecting 18 percent of the light, and now detecting 80 percent light, it calculates that recommending an exposure setting to the photographer that underexposes that scene by just one stop is not sufficient to result in a proper exposure. Remember, exposure stops are in increments of halves and doubles. If a scene reflecting 80 percent light is reduced by one stop, that is the equivalent of changing the lighting received to 40 percent. But this is still too much light! Reducing the exposure by one more stop in effect reduces the light received by the camera to 20 percent. And 20 percent is so close to 18 percent that the meter is satisfied it has done its job properly. A crime scene with snow covering most of the ground will cause the camera's meter to recommend an exposure combination that effectively underexposes that scene by two stops. In these situations, if you trust the camera's meter and select the exposure recommendation it suggests, the result is invariably "dirty snow", or underexposed snow, or snow that appears to be gray. The same situation occurs with sand as well, because crystalline sand reflects much more light than normal scenes.

Underexpose snow or sand by two stops and it will resemble a scene reflecting approximately 18 percent gray. Therefore, you'll have to be smarter than the camera's meter and intentionally overexpose the snow or sand by about two stops.

FIGURE 2-52
Snow as metered

FIGURE 2-53
Snow with a +1 exposure

FIGURE 2-54
Snow with a +2 exposure

Overly Dark Scenes

If a victim wearing a black shirt or blouse has been stabbed, composing a close-up on the area with the cut through the fabric will be necessary. In effect, black fabric is filling the frame, although there is some blood in the field of view also. How is the camera's light meter going to deal with this situation? Black fabric may reflect approximately 5 percent of the light that strikes it. The meter is expecting 18 percent light; the meter is expecting its operator to aim the camera at a normal scene. Designed to provide a proper exposure for a scene reflecting 18 percent of the light, and now detecting 5 percent light, the meter calculates that recommending an exposure setting that overexposes that scene by just one stop is not sufficient to result in a proper exposure. Remember, exposure stops are in increments of halves and doubles. If a scene reflecting 5 percent light is increased by one stop, that is the equivalent of changing the lighting received to 10 percent. But this is still too little light! Increasing the exposure by one more stop in effect increases the light received by the camera to 20 percent. And 20 percent is so close to 18 percent that the meter is satisfied it has done its job properly. A crime scene with black fabric covering most of the field of view will cause the camera's meter to recommend an exposure combination that effectively overexposes that scene by two stops. In these situations, if you trust the camera's meter and select the exposure recommendation it suggests, the result is invariably an overexposure. Overexposed black objects appear to be gray.

Intentionally underexpose black fabric by two stops and it resembles black fabric. The camera's light meter is designed to provide the photographer with properly exposed 18 percent gray subject matter, not properly exposed black subject matter.

FIGURE 2-55
Black fabric as metered *(courtesy of J. Wreh, GWU MS student)*

FIGURE 2-56

Black fabric with a —1 exposure *(courtesy of J. Wreh, GWU MS student)*

FIGURE 2-57

Black fabric with a —2 exposure *(courtesy of J. Wreh, GWU MS student)*

Large Areas of Sky in the Background

At the beginning of major crime scenes, the neighborhood and the exterior of crime scene buildings are often photographed first because there is often the need to secure a search warrant for interior areas, so the exterior areas, in which there is usually no expectation of privacy, are photographed first. With these exterior overall photographs, there is frequently a large amount of sky in the background. Because the sky is not critical to documenting the crime scene, it is usually not important to include large amounts of sky in the background. However, the crime scene photographer must always be aware of the sky and how both film and digital sensors react to the blue of the sky. Both are overly sensitive to this blue. In other words, the sensors will react to blue sky similar to how they react to white areas of the scene. White areas reflect more than 18 percent light towards the camera, so they all tend to cause underexposures. This underexposure happens with blue skies as well.

When taking exterior overall photos, including too much sky in one's composition usually results in other areas being underexposed. Unfortunately, this means that the building we really wanted to document properly is now underexposed, particularly if the side of the building being photographed is already the shady side of the building.

FIGURE 2-58
As metered with the sky in view

The solution to this tendency to underexpose buildings when a bright blue sky is in the background is simply to eliminate the sky from the viewfinder when the exposure reading is taken. Briefly lower the camera until the sky is no longer in view. Take a meter reading and set the camera for that exposure. Then recompose your shot and include the sky to the extent that the image seems properly balanced, take that photo, and the building will be properly exposed rather than underexposed. Rather than lowering your camera to exclude the sky from the field of view, there are two other tricks to avoid underexposure from the sky. One is to select a spot meter setting, center the spot of interest on the shady side of the building, take a meter reading, and expose with those settings. Remember, however, to reset your exposure meter back to the matrix metering option immediately after taking this photo. Another trick is to zoom your lens to its most telephoto setting, thereby reducing the field of view. Then compose the shot so that the lens includes just the shady side of the building, take your meter reading and set the camera for that, readjust your focal length, and take the picture.

FIGURE 2-59
Metered without the sky in view, then recomposed with the sky in view

Backlit Scenes and High-Contrast Scenes

When there is a large difference in the range of lighting in any particular scene, the light meter sometimes has a difficult time determining the proper exposure. As mentioned previously, when a person is backlit by the sun or other bright light, the matrix metering capability of some cameras often makes the correct adjustment to properly expose what you wanted properly exposed. However, there will be times when some backlit subjects aren't properly exposed because the computer chip in the camera did not have your particular composition in its data bank. In this situation, the meter may not guess correctly what is really important to the photographer. Should the brighter area of the composition be properly exposed, or should the darker area of the photograph be properly exposed?

For example, consider a brightly lit scene with dark shadows within the scene, such as a car in the middle of the day. The car will be sunlit, and under the car there will be dark shadows. Now consider that in one crime scene, a gun is under the car in the shadows, and at another similar crime scene, the gun lies just outside the shadows and is now also brightly sunlit. Fill the frame with a scene that includes both dark shadows and brightly sunlit areas. How is the meter to decide which area should be properly exposed?

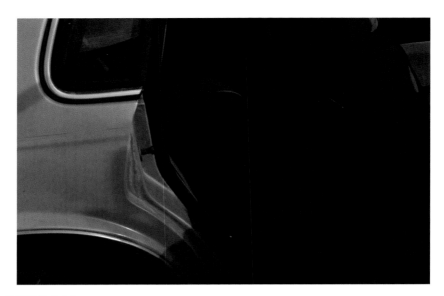

FIGURE 2-60
Sun and shade in the scene, exposed for the sunny area, underexposes the shady area *(courtesy of S. Keppel, GWU MS student)*

FIGURE 2-61
Sun and shade in the scene, exposed for the shady area, overexposes the sunny area *(courtesy of S. Keppel, GWU MS student)*

Compromising by suggesting a meter reading that averages all the light is also faulty. For example, consider a crime scene at which the brightly sunlit area requires an exposure combination of ISO 100, 1/60-second shutter speed, and f/22; the shady area under the car would require an exposure setting of ISO 100, 1/60, and f/5.6. Averaging f/22 with f/5.6 results in an f/11, halfway between them both. However, the f/11 would overexpose the area in the sun by two stops because this area required an f/22. And it would underexpose the area under the car by two stops because this area required an f/5.6. Averaging both areas merely leads to an improper exposure for both areas.

What to do in these situations? The solution is to use fill-in flash. This technique will be more fully explained in Chapter 4. But for now, set the camera to properly expose for the bright sunlit area, then add enough light from the electronic flash to throw some light into the shadows so that objects can easily be seen there without overexposing the already sunlit areas.

FIGURE 2-62
Sun and shade in the scene, the camera meter set to properly expose the sunny area and fill-in flash set to properly expose the shady area *(courtesy of S. Keppel, GWU MS student)*

TOOLS FOR DETERMINING PROPER EXPOSURES WITH TRICKY SCENES

There will be times that you'll forget whether it is proper to give snowy scenes more light or to reduce the light. When photographing a tire that has been slashed, does one increase the light or reduce it? Some scenes are just confusing. What can be done in these situations?

Meter the 18 Percent Gray Card

If you've thrown an 18 percent gray card in your camera bag, you're in luck. Simply ensure that the 18 percent gray card is lit the same as your scene of interest (i.e., if the scene of interest is sunny, ensure that the 18 percent gray card is sunny; if the scene of interest is in the shade, put the 18 percent gray card in the shade). Fill the frame with the 18 percent gray card, set the camera for this exposure, compose on your crime scene, and take the picture. The crime scene will be properly exposed, even though it is not a normal scene.

Meter Green Grass

Have a problematic crime scene but no 18 percent gray card handy? Look around for an area that has green grass. Green grass reflects approximately 18 percent of the light that strikes it. If the crime scene is sunlit, fill the frame with an area of sunny grass and take a meter reading. If the scene of interest is in the shade, fill the frame with a grassy area in the shade and take a meter reading. Your crime scene will be properly exposed, even though it is not a normal scene.

Meter Well-Traveled Asphalt

No green grass around? Look for well-traveled asphalt. Well-traveled asphalt reflects approximately 18 percent of the light that strikes it. Newly laid asphalt, however, is very dark. Once it has been weathered a bit and driven on by numerous cars, it approaches the reflectivity of an 18 percent gray card. Remember to have the lighting of the asphalt approximate the lighting of the crime scene.

Meter Your Palm

No 18 percent gray card, no green grass, and no well-traveled asphalt nearby? There is still a handy (pun intended!) ever-present object you can use to obtain a proper exposure when you encounter a problematic crime scene and don't know whether to trust your camera's light meter.

Meter your own palm, making sure that it is lit that same as the crime scene in question. Regardless of race, the palms of most humans reflect approximately 36 percent of the light striking them. Because this is more than the 18 percent the meter is expecting, the meter will recommend an exposure combination that underexposes the scene by 1 stop. Knowing this, take an exposure reading of your palm, open up 1 stop, compose on your crime scene, and take your photograph. If the crime scene is a non-normal scene, the exposure will be correct. When have you ever forgotten to bring your palm with you to a crime scene?

EXPOSURE MODES

Many cameras provide the photographer with at least four exposure modes to choose from. The four most frequently used by crime scene photographers will be explained: Manual exposure mode (M), Aperture Priority exposure mode (Av), Shutter Priority exposure mode (Tv), and Program exposure mode (P).

FIGURE 2-63
Exposure modes

Manual Exposure Mode (M)

The **Manual** exposure mode is the one most often recommended for students who are first learning photography because it requires users to manually set each of the camera's exposure variables, making them responsible for the resulting exposures. The photographer must manually set the ISO setting, the shutter speed setting, and the f/stop setting. Because the Manual exposure mode does not allow the camera to automatically control any of the exposure variables, the photographer more quickly learns how each exposure variable will affect images.

Aperture Priority Exposure Mode (A or Av, Aperture Value)

In **Aperture Priority** exposure mode, the photographer can manually set the aperture setting on the camera and the camera will automatically adjust the shutter speed setting to provide a proper exposure for the lighting of the particular scene. At first glance, this appears to be a perfect exposure mode for those wanting to maximize the depth of field. Because the depth of field is frequently controlled by selecting small apertures, all one has to do is select an f/22 or an f/16, and the resulting image should always have a well-exposed image that also has a terrific depth of field! Unfortunately, that doesn't always happen. Why not?

If the photographer begins exposure determination by selecting the f/stop for a great depth of field, when the lighting isn't bright the camera will be forced to select a shutter speed that is slow enough to guarantee a proper exposure, and that can be slower than the 1/60th of a second that permits the camera to be handheld. Arbitrarily setting small apertures first often produces this result.

Is Aperture Priority exposure mode ever the right choice of exposure mode? Yes! Whenever the camera is on a tripod, a series of images is to be captured of an item of evidence, and the situation calls for examination-quality images, then this exposure mode is perfect. In such a case, small apertures can be used for the best depth of field, and slow shutter speeds are irrelevant because the camera is on a tripod and steady at any shutter speed.

Shutter Priority Exposure Mode (S or Tv, Time Value)

The **Shutter Priority** exposure mode enables the photographer to set the shutter speed desired, and then the camera will automatically select the aperture for the lighting at the scene. Is this exposure mode recommended? Consider this: in both Manual exposure mode and Shutter Priority exposure mode, the photographer sets the ISO manually. In both exposure modes, the photographer next sets the shutter speed. In both exposure modes, the photographer next composes on the scene in question and then depresses the shutter button halfway to take a meter reading of the light being reflected from the scene. Now comes the only difference. In Manual exposure mode, the meter recommends a particular f/stop setting and the photographer has to manually set the recommended f/stop. In the Shutter Priority exposure mode, the camera automatically sets the f/stop required for the lighting coming from the crime scene. Is there a difference? With both modes, the same f/stop is eventually set on the camera. The difference is that in Shutter Priority exposure mode, that same f/stop is automatically set by the camera, requiring one less manual setting by the photographer. Does this automation take any choice away from the photographer? No. It just makes the exposure determination and settings more efficient. The photographer saves time and ends up with the same f/stop he or she would have set if doing so manually. This exposure mode is highly recommended!

Program Exposure Mode (P)

With the **Program** exposure mode, the camera automatically sets both the shutter speed and the f/stop to arrive at a proper exposure for the scene. Is this good or bad? Definitely bad! The idea of automatically arriving at a proper exposure without having to manually set f/stops and shutter speeds seems like a proper way to allow "smart" cameras to do their job. Unfortunately, there are two negative results. In Program exposure mode, the camera's computer chip invariably chooses shutter speeds that are unnecessarily fast. When hand-holding a 50mm lens, it is usually optimal to select a 1/60-second shutter speed to avoid blur caused by holding the camera. Using any faster shutter speed requires exposure compensation of another type, usually in the form of a wider aperture. This sort of setting degrades the depth of field range.

At most crime scenes, the evidence is lying on the floor or ground. There is no need to freeze its motion with a faster shutter speed. Program exposure mode frequently selects 1/125 or 1/250 at its preference. This setting, in turn, usually requires f/5.6 or even f/4. Both of these f/stops produce limited depth of field. In order to ensure proper exposures quickly, the program exposure mode uses faster shutter speeds than necessary for the subject matter and wider apertures than desired for good depths of field.

Program exposure mode should be used only by those who do not yet know how to properly set the camera's controls to obtain optimal results. Faster shutter speeds are available when stopping motion is critical; smaller apertures are available when maximizing the depth of field is a priority.

With that said, there is one time when the Program exposure mode is perfect for the crime scene photographer. After finishing the photography at a crime scene, and when packing the camera up, set the camera to the Program mode and automatic focus. If your next scene is one that is still active, such as a serious accident scene where victims are still being recovered from vehicles and carried to ambulances, you might want to try photographing the victims before they are put into the ambulance. But because treatment is a first priority, you cannot stop them to get a photograph. You'll have to do the best you can while walking alongside of them. If your camera has been preset to the program exposure mode and auto focus, all you have to do is to turn on the camera and begin taking pictures. The faster shutter speeds will help freeze any motion, and a proper exposure is almost guaranteed. The depth of field won't be able to cover long distances, but these shots are usually just of particular subjects, not deep crime scenes. Once the urgency of removing the injured is over, you can then select other exposure modes and manual focus to get better depths of field.

BRACKETING

At times, particularly when doing examination-quality images, it is advisable to **bracket** one's shots: to intentionally vary exposures of a particular subject while taking additional photos of the evidence from the same viewpoint.

Does use of this technique mean that the photographer doubted the proper exposure for an initial shot? Sometimes yes, and sometimes no. If getting any particular image is critical, and there is any doubt about the original exposure, it is only wise to take additional pictures of it using different exposure settings. To do otherwise would be foolish. In this case, the series of photographs is usually expressed as taking a sequence of 0, +1, and −1. In this case, the 0 is the exposure considered "optimal" or what is believed to be correct. Then, just in case, the photographer will "bracket that shot by taking another photograph set to be one stop brighter and a third shot set to be one stop dimmer than the original shot.

Exposure doubt is just one good reason for taking a series of brackets. Even when one is confident that an original exposure is accurate, there are times—especially with examination-quality photos—that brackets make sense. Consider a shoe print or tire track in dirt. These will invariably be captured using an oblique flash. The electronic flash is a very bright light source, often producing very dark shadows or "hard" shadows. Hard shadows are so dark that one cannot see details within them. To ensure that more detail is captured in each photograph, a bounce card or reflector is used to bounce some light back toward the impression, thereby lightening the areas in hard shadows. This technique theoretically adds sufficient light to these areas so that the examiner can see the details in the shadow areas necessary to make identifications.

However, to provide the examiner every opportunity to see what they must see to effectively do comparisons, a series of brackets are routinely done. In this way, areas that may still be a bit dark will receive more light with the +1 bracket, and areas initially a bit overexposed will receive less light with the −1 bracket. Brackets can be regarded as an insurance policy, helping to ensure that the details present within the impression are eventually able to be seen by the examiner or analyst.

Must all brackets be in sequence of 0, +1, and −1? No. When one knows that additional exposures need to be in only one direction, it makes sense to bracket in just that direction. For instance, when the shape of the knife wound penetrating Caucasian skin is an issue, we have already learned that the exposure meter will automatically recommend an exposure that underexposes the image by one stop. Therefore, there is no need for a −1 bracket at all. In this case, as the presumed correct exposure is a +1 from what the meter recommends, you could take brackets around this by taking a meter reading and then take your brackets by adjusting the original meter reading by a 0, followed by a +1, followed by a +2.

Likewise, if the same knife punctured a vehicle's tire, we know that the exposure meter will tend to recommend an exposure that overexposes the image by approximately two stops. It may be wise, therefore, to bracket this series of tire photos with a −1, followed by a −2, followed by a −3.

Of course, instead of a three-shot series of brackets, you can also choose to do four or five brackets of a particular image if appropriate.

Manual Exposure Mode Bracketing

When using Manual exposure mode, bracketing is most frequently accomplished by changing either the shutter speed or the f/stop. One must always remember to not select a shutter speed that makes hand-holding the camera a problem or select an f/stop that makes retaining a good depth of field a problem. Remember, motion control and maximizing the depth of field are just as important as maintaining good exposure.

With digital cameras, one can also change the ISO setting. With film cameras, this was usually not an option; with digital cameras, the option of changing the ISO setting is always an option. As mentioned earlier, those of us who have done years of work with film cameras constantly have to remind ourselves that changing the ISO is now a possibility.

Automatic Exposure Mode Bracketing

If you are currently using either Aperture Priority exposure mode or Shutter Priority exposure mode, bracketing is not accomplished by changing f/stops or shutter speeds.

If you are using Aperture Priority exposure mode and are currently set at an f/11, does changing to an f/8 provide a +1 exposure? No! With any f/stop selection, the camera will attempt to set a shutter speed that provides a proper exposure. So, instead of a +1 exposure, the result will be another reciprocal exposure. For example, if the original f/11 resulted in the camera automatically selecting a 1/125th of a second shutter speed, then changing to an f/8 would result in the cameras selection of a 1/250th of a second shutter speed. Both combinations result in the same exposure—a reciprocal exposure.

If you are currently using Shutter Priority exposure mode and have selected 1/125 as your shutter speed, would changing to 1/60 result in a +1 exposure? No! With any shutter speed selection, the camera will attempt to set an f/stop that provides a proper exposure. So, instead of a +1 exposure, the result will be another reciprocal exposure. For example, if the original 1/125 resulted in the camera automatically selecting an f/11, then changing to 1/60 would result in the camera now selecting 1/250th of a second shutter speed. Both combinations result in the same exposure—a reciprocal exposure.

So, how does one bracket in these automatic exposure modes? Conveniently located near the exposure controls is an exposure compensation button or dial. It usually is labeled with a $+/-$ indication, as in Figure 2-64. Or, your camera may allow the user to select from -2 to $+2$, with increments between full stops usually: $-2 \ldots -1 \ldots 0 \ldots +1 \ldots +2$, as can be seen in Figure 2-65. In this case, thirds of a stop increments can be selected. In both of the automatic exposure modes, bracketing is achieved by selecting the desired bracketing amount on the exposure compensation dial/button.

FIGURE 2-64
Exposure compensation button indicated by the $+/-$ button

FIGURE 2-65
Exposure compensation indicated by a $+2$ to -2 continuum

Caution! After your set of brackets has been taken, it is critical to reset the exposure compensation dial/button back to 0! Otherwise, all your subsequent images will also be under- or overexposed to the same degree.

The exposure compensation dial/button does not affect the exposure in the Manual exposure mode.

Flash Bracketing

When using an electronic flash, it is also possible to change the output of the flash unit, which offers the photographer a third way to bracket a series of photographs. The full explanation of this method is provided in Chapter 4. This short note is inserted here as a reminder that there are multiple options for bracketing.

THE F/16 SUNNY DAY RULE

Experienced photographers frequently find themselves taking photographs under reoccurring lighting conditions—so much so that an exposure combination can often be anticipated even before a meter reading is taken. It is sometimes suggested that the seasoned photographer can sometimes "smell" the light, evaluating its intensity from experience, knowing what exposure combination is normally the "correct" exposure combination under various lighting conditions.

However, it is not just experience that can lead a photographer to being able to anticipate a proper exposure combination. Following several guidelines about exposures is likely to result in a proper exposure even for the novice. They are the F/16 Sunny Day Rule and its corollaries.

An F/16 Sunny Day Produces Hard Shadows

Walk outside on a bright sunny day, between the hours of 10:00 a.m. and 3:00 p.m., and look at the shadows being produced by the sun. If the shadows have sharp, well-defined edges, that is a classic f/16 kind of day. Hold up your hand and you can count your fingers in the shadow that is made. See Figure 2-66. On such a day, set your camera to f/16. Whichever ISO your camera is currently set at, convert that ISO number to a fraction, and determine the closest shutter speed to that fraction (or the shutter speed nearest this fraction that is "faster"). This guideline can economically be restated as "Convert ISO to shutter speed." Set the camera to that shutter speed. This combination of ISO, shutter speed, and f/stop will provide a proper exposure under this lighting condition.

FIGURE 2-66
An f/16 sunny day shadow, with sharp outlines

A caveat. The F/16 Sunny Day Rule and its corollaries are exposure recommendations only! Remember that crime scene photographers always have multiple needs pulling us in different directions. Not only do we want a proper exposure, but at the same time we often want to maximize the depth of field while managing at least one kind of motion blur (hand-holding the camera). The F/16 Sunny Day Rule will provide the photographer with one possible reciprocal exposure combination. The wise crime scene photographer will sometimes be required to seek a different reciprocal exposure for the optimal exposure when taking a photo under this lighting condition.

For example, on a bright sunny day, a photographer notices that the camera is currently set to ISO 100. (For the sake of this example, and to simplify things, we'll consider only whole shutter speed numbers, not increments in thirds or halves.) ISO 100 converts to 1/100, and the nearest shutter speed to this is 1/125. The photographer then sets to f/16 and arrives at an exposure combination of ISO 100, 1/125, and f/16. Take the picture? Let's think. If this is really just one reciprocal exposure, are there any others we may want to consider?

FIGURE 2-67
An f/11 shadow, with nondistinct edges

What guides do we have? We always have three needs: (1) a proper exposure, (2) motion control, and (3) the need to maximize the depth of field. With these three exposure variables, we notice that the f/16 can be changed to an f/22 to obtain a better depth of field. But this option results in a −1 exposure. We can either change the ISO to 200 for a +1, which balances the −1, or we can change the shutter speed to 1/60 for a +1. Is either approach preferable? In this case, either will be fine.

An F/11 Partly Cloudy Day Produces Soft Shadows

Walk outside in the middle of the day when it is partly cloudy and notice the shadows. The shadows are often present but less well defined. They have soft edges. Hold up your hand, and you can barely even see a shadow of your arm, much less see your fingers. This is the classic f/11, soft shadow kind of day. Under these conditions, convert ISO to shutter speed and set the camera to f/11. If the beginning ISO was 100, then the resulting exposure combination is ISO 100, 1/125, and f/11. Should you take the photograph with this exposure combination?

This combination would result in a proper exposure, but is it the optimal exposure combination for this lighting? As we usually seek to maximize the depth of field, changing the f/11 to f/22 is desirable but results in a −2 exposure. If hand-holding a 50mm lens, the 1/125 shutter speed can be changed to 1/60 for a +1, still requiring another +1 from somewhere. The ISO of 100 can be changed to ISO 200 for this remaining +1, and the resulting optimal exposure combination of ISO 200, 1/60, and f/22 has been achieved.

An F/8 Overcast Day Produces No Shadows

Walk outside on an overcast day, hold up your hand with five fingers extended, and your body doesn't cast any shadow at all. No tree shadows, no lightpole shadows, no shadows anywhere! In such conditions, convert the ISO to the shutter speed and set the camera to f/8. If your beginning ISO was 100, the result is an exposure combination of ISO 100, 1/125, and f/8. A proper exposure, certainly, but should you take the photo with this exposure combination?

Wanting a good exposure while maximizing the depth of field would require us to change the f/8 to f/22, resulting in a −3 exposure. With a 50mm lens on the camera we are hand-holding, we can change the shutter speed to 1/60 for a +1. Changing the ISO from ISO 100 to ISO 400 provides a +2, resulting in the exposure we take the photo with: ISO 400, 1/60, and f/22.

COMMON FILTERS

A variety of filters are commonly used by crime scene photographers, and sometimes these filters can affect the exposure by blocking out different increments of light.

Polarizer Filter

A **polarizing filter** or **polarizer** should be readily available to every crime scene photographer. It may not have to be in every crime scene photographer's camera bag, but it should be quickly available when needed.

Sunglasses for the Lens

One feature of the polarizer lens is that it absorbs light. In Figure 2-68, the fabric beneath the filter is darker because the filter is absorbing light. The filter is adjustable. Once it is screwed on the lens, it can still rotate around the lens. As it rotates, its ability to absorb light changes. The amount of light absorbed can vary from 1.3 stops to 2 stops of light. Recall the elimination of falling snow mentioned previously? A 2- to 3-second shutter speed was required to do this. Having the shutter open this long lets in a tremendous amount of light. When

FIGURE 2-68
A polarizer filter absorbs light

using the smallest aperture of the lens still produces an overexposure, using a polarizer may be sufficient to prevent that overexposure.

Reflection Elimination

The primary use for a polarizer filter is to remove the reflections from glass and water. Occasionally, it is necessary to take a photo of evidence on the other side of glass or beneath water. Both glass and water can act like a mirror and reflect the surrounding environment, and these reflections frequently make it difficult to see the evidence through them. In these cases, having the ability to eliminate these reflections is a great benefit.

Unlike other filters, which can be screwed onto the end of a lens, once the polarizer is screwed onto the lens tightly, it can still be rotated without over-tightening it. One ring on the frame of the polarizer is used for affixing the filter to the lens; another ring is used to rotate the filter to optimize the amount of reflection being eliminated.

The other key to eliminating reflections from glass and water is to orient the camera at a 34-degree angle to those surfaces. Viewing either surface at other angles may not result in the reflection's total elimination. It is usually easy to view either surface at an initial 45-degree angle. Once that angle is established, with water, just take a step or two farther away from the water to approximate a 34-degree angle. With glass, once the 45-degree angle has been approximated,

FIGURE 2-69
The polarizer filter removing a reflection from glass

step a bit closer to the surface the glass is in—not closer to the evidence behind the glass, closer to the surface to the left or right.

From that position, view the reflection on either surface, and begin to rotate the filter counter-clockwise. It is very important to *not* rotate the polarizer filter clockwise; this may effectively unscrew the filter from the lens! While viewing the reflection through the polarizer filter, rotate the filter until most of the reflection is eliminated. Further rotation will cause the reflection to return to the surface. Once the maximum amount of reflection has been eliminated, if it has not been entirely eliminated, the final step is to try stepping a bit to your left or right. In case you had not originally arrived at exactly 34 degrees, moving a bit laterally may be all that is needed to find the correct viewing angle.

From the position that results in the maximum elimination of reflections, take a new meter reading and set the camera for that exposure. You'll notice that the polarizer filter is tinted a bit gray, like sunglasses. Just affixing the filter to the lens reduces the amount of light entering the lens by about 1.3 stops. Rotating

FIGURE 2-70
The polarizer filter removing a reflection from water

the filter to the point that reflections are totally eliminated increases the light being absorbed to 2 stops. If you don't take the meter reading after the reflections have been eliminated, an underexposure is usually the result.

Enriching Color Saturation

At times, sun glare can cause colored objects to be overwhelmed by the glare, which causes colors to look less vibrant. When it is critical to capture the accurate colors of evidence, a polarizing filter can help. For instance, at a fatal hit-and-run accident, green paint from one car may have been transferred to a blue car. When it is necessary to accurately show the green paint on the blue car, if those two paints are in direct sunlight, the sun glare may mask the true colors of both paints. Use the polarizer filter from the right viewpoint and both colors will be captured as you saw them.

Skid Marks

Many crime scene photographers also take photographs at vehicular accidents. At many accident scenes, there are skid marks and scuff marks. Sun glare may wash out these tire marks, just as sun glare can wash out colors. Sometimes these tire marks are also faint. Combine faint tire marks with sun glare, and the

FIGURE 2-71
The polarizer filter capturing the true color of adobe tiles

tire marks may be very difficult to photograph. The polarizer can again help eliminate this sun glare, making the tire marks darker and easier to see. Make sure to view tire marks from both ends, because sometimes the polarizer filter works better from one direction rather than the other.

Linear and Circular Polarizer Filters

There are two kinds of polarizer filters. The linear polarizer is designed for older lenses that do not have autofocusing capability. For newer lenses that can be autofocused, you must buy a circular polarizer.

Neutral-Density Filters

Another filter type that looks like sunglasses is the neutral-density filter. These filters are available in different strengths, blocking one stop, two stops, or three stops of light. They do not eliminate reflections on glass or water. Their primary use is to help attain a proper exposure when the lighting conditions and the exposure settings would otherwise result in overexposures. Recall that the way to eliminate falling snow from being captured by the camera is to use a 2- to 3-second shutter speed? In these conditions, one can use a polarizer filter or neutral-density filter to lower the exposure.

FIGURE 2-72
The polarizer filter reducing sun glare and darkening skid marks on the top image

FIGURE 2-73
A two-stop neutral-density filter

UV/Haze/1-A/Skylight/Protection Filters

Five other filters are used by many photographers on almost all lenses. It is not the effect that these filters have on the final image that is the consideration. It is the protection these filters provide to the end of the lens that makes them valuable. Many crime scene photographers run around their crime scene with their cameras hanging from their necks by camera straps. As they perform other duties within the crime scenes, their cameras swing in various directions. Inevitably, the camera will impact something hard. This happening is not a case of "if," it is only a case of "when." It will happen at some time or another. When this happens, one of two things will happen: (1) the outer ring of the lens or the outer element of the lens will sustain damage, dents, or breakage, or (2) the filter mounted to the end of the lens will sustain the damage. What would you prefer—replacing the lens or replacing the filter? That is an easy answer!

Environmental contaminants can also adversely affect the outer element of the lens. These filters help avoid that problem, too. That being said, there are photography purists out there who will claim that any additional filter over the lens adversely affects the quality of the image. Strictly speaking, this may be true. However, I've had to replace several such filters over my career because of dinged, scratched, or broken glass elements. My lenses themselves did not have to be replaced . . . so I use these filters!

These five filters are all clear filters that don't affect exposures at all. Although they do have other specific purposes, their main use by crime scene photographers is to protect their lenses. If you're doing vast scenic photography, both the UV and haze filters will help cut through atmospheric haze and the

FIGURE 2-74
A dented UV filter saved its lens!

tendency of these shots to look a bit blue. If the blue of the sky is critical to your landscape images, a skylight filter might not wash out the sky as much.

After the digital camera revolution, a protection filter also made its way into the market. It is solely created to protect the outer lens element. Hopefully, these two images will make you a believer.

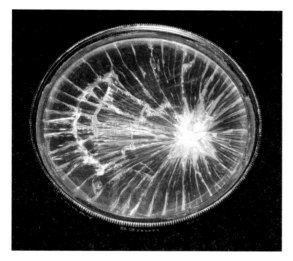

FIGURE 2-75
This UV filter took the punishment so that the lens did not have to!

It worked for me!

CHAPTER SUMMARY

This chapter should make you confident to begin capturing images with exposure settings you have intentionally chosen to produce the effect you want. There should be no need to rely on the program mode anymore. You now know what the exposure variables are, and you know the effects they produce. When you want to, you can freeze motion within the crime scene. You know which f/stops are best for producing long depth of field ranges. (This subject is discussed at length in Chapter 3.) You know when to trust the camera's exposure meter and when it will recommend an incorrect exposure. Better yet, you now know how to compensate for the erroneous exposure recommendations of the meter. You can make rain and snow disappear. When it is necessary to capture a sequence of bracketed images, you know how to do this. You can remove reflections from glass and water. Rather than having the camera provide you with images you had no control over, your images are now composed and exposed in ways that you chose for specific reasons.

You are becoming the master, and the camera is becoming your tool you use to get the job done.

Discussion Questions

1. What are the four variables that affect exposure? Why does changing one of them require an adjustment to one of the other exposure variables? What are the two main reasons for changing exposure variables while maintaining the *same* exposure?
2. How do different lights affect the tints present in an image?
3. What is the meaning of "exposure latitude"?
4. Shutter speeds affect motion. Which kinds of motion are affected?
5. In order to determine a proper exposure, some standard must be used. What is this standard? Explain "normal" and "non-normal" scenes. Presented with a non-normal scene, how can the proper exposure be determined?
6. There are various methods for determining proper exposures. Name and explain the different exposure modes.
7. Explain the different methods to bracket an image.
8. Explain the F/16 Sunny Day Rule and its corollaries.
9. Explain the various filters commonly used by photographers and their effects on images.

Practical Exercises

The following are composition and exposure exercises only. As such, issues of focus, depth of field, and flash techniques are not considered. You may use an SLR set to autofocus. Composition and exposure are the only issues in these exercises.

1. Determine the proper exposure for one item that is totally sunlit, and photograph it.
2. Determine the proper exposure for one item that is totally in the shade, and photograph it.
3. Freeze a subject walking parallel to the film plane 10 feet from the camera.
4. Fill the frame with a sheet of white paper on which you have written your name. Photograph it after determining the proper exposure for it. Bracket +1 and −1.
5. Fill the frame with a black object. Photograph it after determining the proper exposure for it. Bracket +1 and −1.
6. Photograph a building façade that is in the shade.

7. Place an interesting object on your vehicle dashboard, and photograph it through the windshield using a polarizing filter to eliminate the reflections.
8. From this same position, photograph the same object without the polarizer.
9. Place something in a shallow puddle and photograph it through the water using a polarizer to eliminate the reflections.
10. From this same position, photograph the same object without the polarizer.

Suggested Readings

Polarizer Filter

Baines, H. 1976. *The Science of Photography*. New York: Halsted Press.

Siljander, Raymond P., and Darin D. Fredrickson. 1997. *Applied Police and Fire Photography*. Second Edition, Springfield IL: Charles C. Thomas.

Mitchell, Earl N. 1984. *Photographic Science*. New York: John Wiley & Sons, Inc.

Theory of Reciprocity

Davis, Phil. 1995. *Photography*. Seventh Edition. Boston: McGraw Hill.

Exposure Latitude

Davis, Phil. 1995. *Photography*. Seventh Edition. Boston: McGraw Hill.

Upton, Barbara London, with John Upton. 1989. *Photography*. Fourth Edition, Glenview, IL: Scott Foresman and Company.

Burning and Dodging

Hedgecoe, John. 1998. *New Introductory Photography Course*. Boston: Focal Press.

F/16 Sunny Day Rule

Larry S. Miller & Richard T. McEvoy Jr. *Police Photography*. Sixth Edition. Cincinnati OH: Anderson Publishing Co.

Miscellaneous Exposure Topics

Mannheim, LA. 1970. *Photography Theory and Practice*. London & New York: Focal Press.

Focus, Depth of Field, and Lenses

KEY TERMS

Automatic focusing
Barrel distortion
Close-up filters
Depth of field (DOF)
Depth of field scale
Extension tubes
Focal length
Focal length multiplier
Focus

Hyperfocal focusing
Macro lenses
Magnification with a 1:1
    ratio
Manual focusing
"Normal" lens
Pincushion distortion
Prefocus
Resolution

Rule of Thirds
SWGFAST
SWGIT
SWGTREAD
Telephoto lenses
Wide-angle lenses
Zone focusing

LEARNING OBJECTIVES

Upon completion of this chapter, you should be able to:

- Explain how to hyperfocal focus on a scene by using a depth of field scale
- Explain how to hyperfocal focus on a scene without using a depth of field scale
- Explain how to zone focus on a scene by using a depth of field scale
- Explain how to zone focus on a scene without using a depth of field scale
- Explain the three factors that affect depth of field
- Explain the techniques to maximize depth of field
- Explain the various designations of lenses: focal length, "fast" or "slow," and the widest aperture of the particular lens
- Explain what a reference to a "normal" lens means
- Explain the effects on a photograph produced by telephoto lenses
- Explain the effects on a photograph produced by wide angle lenses
- Explain the magnification ratios related to macro lenses
- Explain the difference between pincushion and barrel distortion

155

FOCUS

Most nonprofessional photographers who are not using autofocus cameras consider the act of focusing their camera to be relatively easy. Just rotate the focus ring until the subject being photographed appears to be "sharp" or "in focus" in the viewfinder. This technique is adequate as long as there is just one subject in the field of view to be concerned with. For example, when photographing a close-up image of a pistol at a crime scene, it is just necessary to focus on the top of the pistol when the film plane is parallel to it.

FIGURE 3-1
A single object is easy to focus on

However, crime scene photographers frequently have to focus on areas instead of single objects. If a crime scene is located on the lawn outside a residence, the area of concern might include the sidewalk, the lawn between the sidewalk and the residence, and the front façade of the residence. All three should be in focus in the same image. New techniques have to be learned so that an area, not just one object, appears to be in focus.

The terms "in focus" or "sharp" are sometimes confused with the term "resolution." We are all aware that digital cameras are available with different numbers of megapixels. It is common to find digital cameras with 8 MP, 10 MP, and 12 MP. It is sometimes said that these digital cameras have an 8-MP resolution, a 10-MP resolution, or a 12-MP resolution. But what does "resolution" really mean?

To be precise, the term "resolution" means the ability to resolve, or distinguish, black and white line pairs. As alternating black, white, black, white, black, and white lines become thinner and closer together, there will come a time when one can no longer distinguish the difference between adjacent black and white lines and they seem to blend into gray. Therefore, a higher-resolution digital camera will be able to detect individual adjacent black and white lines further into the continuum as they get thinner and closer together. With more resolution, the camera's ability to distinguish fine details becomes greater.

Resolution Standards and Guidelines

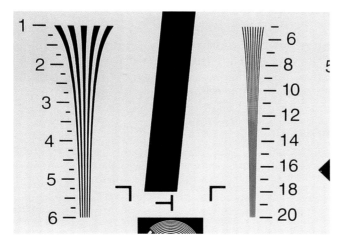

FIGURE 3-2
A resolution chart's black and white lines getting thinner and closer together

Digital camera resolution is frequently expressed by a camera's total resolution; for example, the Nikon D 7000 camera has 16.2 MP. Sometimes the resolution is expressed by the number of horizontal and vertical pixels on the digital sensor: the Nikon D 7000 camera features 4,928 × 3,264 pixels. And sometimes a digital camera is explained as having the ability to put a certain number of pixels over an inch, or "ppi," meaning pixels per inch. The Nikon D 7000 can place 1,000 ppi over an area of 4.928 × 3.264 inches. The Nikon D3000, however, has 10.2 MP, with 3872 × 2592 pixels horizontally and vertically, and can place 1,000 ppi over an area of 3.872 × 2.592 inches. It can correctly be said that the Nikon D 3000 has less, or lower, resolution than the Nikon D 7000.

Why does this matter? For crime scene photographers, there are well-defined standards for digital cameras intended to be used for general crime scene documentation, for digital cameras to be used to capture fingerprints at crime scenes, for digital cameras capturing images of footwear, and for digital cameras capturing images of tire tracks. SWGIT, SWGTREAD, and SWGFAST have all issued recommendations on the minimum resolution that digital cameras should have to do certain jobs.

SWGIT recommends that general crime scene photographers should have at least 6 MP cameras to document crime scenes. SWGTREAD recommends that crime scene photographers intending to photograph shoe prints and tire tracks should have at least an 8 MP camera to adequately do those jobs. And SWGFAST recommends that if one is about to photograph fingerprints or palm prints, it is necessary to have a digital camera that can put a minimum of 1,000 ppi over the area in question.

Having a digital camera with less than these minimum resolutions is taking a risk of capturing images with inadequate sharpness, making it more difficult for experts when trying to compare crime scene images with known shoes, known tires, and known fingerprints.

Manual Focusing

Presuming that you're working with a digital camera that has adequate resolution: for every image, the camera must be focused. Manually focusing the camera does have an optimal time when it is to be used: as mentioned earlier, that is when the sole job of the crime scene photographer is to focus on just one surface that is the same distance from the photographer. Consider a rifle lying on the ground. If the muzzle is the same distance from the photographer as the shoulder stock, then manual focusing on the rifle would be appropriate. If, however, the muzzle is closer to the photographer than the shoulder stock, then focusing on one end of the rifle or the other end of the rifle may not ensure that both ends of the rifle are in focus at the same time. In this case, a different method of focusing must be learned to ensure that the entire rifle will be in focus. (The method is called zone focusing, which is explained later in this chapter.)

Actually, Figure 3-3A has two problems. First, the focus was set on the muzzle. Second, the camera was put into the program exposure mode, which selected an f/4 as its aperture of choice. It is hoped that Figures 3-3A and 3.3B discourage the reader from doing either of these things in the future, either individually or together.

When there is just one object or subject to be photographed and it is all the same distance from the photographer, then it is time for manual focusing. See Figure 3-5.

When both the muzzle and stock are equidistant from the photographer, it is easy to have both in focus at the same time. This means that for most of the close-up photographs that will be taken at a crime scene, manual focusing will be the optimal focusing technique.

FIGURE 3-3A
Focusing on the muzzle ensures that the muzzle is in focus

FIGURE 3-3B
The stock is out of focus

FIGURE 3-4A
Zone focusing ensures that everything is in focus

FIGURE 3-4B
The stock is in focus

FIGURE 3-5
When both ends of a long object are the same distance from the photographer it is easy to have everything in focus *(courtesy of I. Walker, GWU MS student)*

Automatic Focusing

Most of today's modern digital cameras feature an automatic focusing capability. Because a camera that offers automatic focusing usually costs more than one that only has manual focusing, this suggests that autofocusing is somehow "better" than manual focusing. It is certainly an "upgrade" to a camera offering only manual focusing. Well, if it is considered an "upgrade" and costs more, doesn't that prove that it is "better"?

Most photography instructors usually want their students to learn manual camera controls, both manual exposure and manual focusing. Doing so forces the student photographer to think about each available option. Relegating a personal choice to camera automation early in a photographer's learning process is not usually recommended. However, there will be times when autofocusing a camera will be appropriate and will not result in a poor-quality image.

When to Use Auto-Focus

Again, when there is just one subject of concern in a particular image, and it is all the same distance from the photographer, then autofocusing will get the job done.

The issue is this: there are frequently multiple objects in the field of view, or just one object in the field of view but with its various parts at different distances from the photographer. In these situations, the camera's autofocusing capability might not focus on the one part of the scene that needs to be in focus. An example will clarify this idea. At a homicide scene, where the victim has had his throat cut, a crime scene photographer set the camera to autofocus and then tried to take a photograph of the wound to the neck. Having the camera in autofocus usually guarantees that one part of the scene will be in focus, but it does not necessarily guarantee that the specific part needing to be in focus will in fact be in focus. After the photograph was captured, it was noticed that the autofocus camera did its job: it did focus on one thing. It had the chin of the victim in perfect focus, but the neck wound was out of focus. The camera worked as designed. The photographer just failed to ensure that the camera autofocused on what the photographer wanted to be in focus.

Had the camera been in manual focus mode, the photographer would have ensured that the neck wound was in focus before depressing the shutter button. Beware! The author has seen too many photographs out of focus because the autofocus mode was used. Try to keep to manual focus mode, and more photographs will be successful. It is not a solution to say that if the focus is not as you intended, you'll immediately see the out-of-focus image when you check out the image on the back of their digital camera and you'll take another image. Stick with manual focusing and you won't have to retake so many images.

Difficult-to-Focus Subjects for Autofocus

There are other common situations in which an autofocus mode will not function particularly well. When there is a lack of strong vertical or horizontal lines present in a particular scene, autofocus may not work at all. For instance, if you want to photograph a bullet hole in a wall from several feet away and the image that is composed is just the wall and bullet hole, the autofocus mode may not be able to focus the camera. You may hear the camera "searching" for something to focus on as it roams through its full focusing range and then back again. Many of today's cameras will not allow you to capture the image unless the camera's focusing mode has locked onto something. Depress the shutter button, and nothing will happen, because the camera was unable to focus on anything.

Another example, unrelated to crime scene photography, is trying to focus on a particular cloud formation in the sky. Without a well-defined vertical or horizontal edge in the field of view, the camera may not be able to focus.

A third example of when the autofocus may not function as desired is when there are two different well-defined objects at different distances in the field of view, and the camera decides it wants to focus on the nearer or farther object, when you wanted the other one to be in focus. For example, you might intend to photograph a fingerprint on a window, but the camera decides to focus on something outside the window. Or, you might want to photograph someone through a window with venetian blinds, but the camera decides to focus on the venetian blinds.

In each of these cases, switch over to manual focus, and focus on what is important to you.

Focusing with a Zoom Lens

Many digital cameras are now sold with a lens that offers the photographer a choice of various focal lengths. For instance, your primary lens might be an 18—55mm lens or a 28—105mm lens. Many years ago, the most frequently encountered lenses were called **prime lenses**, or lenses with just one focal length, such as a 50mm lens. Today, zoom lenses seem to be the norm.

With different focal lengths to choose from, is there one that is best to use when focusing? Or should one focus the camera after the focal length has been selected?

Consider the effects of the different focal lengths. If there is an object that is 30 feet away from the photographer, how does it look when viewed through the viewfinder with different focal lengths selected? Any of the wide-angle selections will make the object appear farther away; the focal lengths in the middle of the zoom range will tend to make the object appear to be the same distance from the photographer as the photographer sees it with his or her eyes; and the telephoto focal lengths will make the object appear nearer to the photographer. Focusing on the object with any of the focal lengths, and one is focusing at the same 30 feet. However, set the focal length to the extreme telephoto setting and the object appears to be very close to the photographer. If it appears to be closer to the photographer, then it is easier to focus on. Isn't that the point?

So, when using a lens featuring different focal lengths, focus when zoomed out to the furthest telephoto setting, and then reset the camera to the desired focal length for any particular shot. Your focusing will be more precise this way.

Prefocus

Some of the less expensive cameras, such as the use-once cameras sold in many drugstores, do not even offer the photographer the ability to focus the camera. The camera is preset to a certain range. On the camera's exterior, it may state that nothing closer than 4 feet should be photographed with that camera. In this case, the camera is prefocused to ensure that everything between 4 feet and infinity will be in focus. Anything closer than 4 feet will be out of focus.

Our more expensive digital SLR cameras, and the various lenses that can be put on those camera bodies, also have a minimum focusing distance. Get any closer than that minimum distance, and the camera and lens cannot focus on anything. Put the camera and lens precisely at its minimum focusing distance, and the camera and lens will be in focus, and the object will appear the largest it can possibly appear while still being in focus. Move the camera and lens any farther away, and one will have to refocus the lens on the subject, but the object will now look farther away and smaller.

When is prefocusing the camera at its closest focusing distance the optimal way to use the camera equipment? When you are using a macro lens, and you want to fill the frame with a relatively small item of evidence, then prefocusing the camera is the most efficient method of focusing the lens.

FIGURE 3-6
A macro lens

FIGURE 3-7
The macro lens prefocused at 1:1 so that an item of evidence the size of a fingerprint will fill the frame

A bit of explanation about macro lenses is necessary here. Most "normal" lenses will not permit both focusing on small objects and filling the frame with that small object. For instance, most normal lenses, which have various focal lengths to choose from (say, 18–70mm), cannot both fill the frame with three fingertips and focus on them at the same time. Try this with your normal lens. Rotate the focus ring to the lens's closest focusing distance. Then, set the lens to its longest telephoto setting if you have a zoom lens. While looking through the viewfinder, move your three middle fingers nearer and farther from the camera until they are in focus. For some, the three fingers may never be in focus. For others, when the fingers do appear to be in focus, they don't appear to be also filling the frame.

At crime scenes, you'll often need to fill the frame with a single-digit fingerprint. The normal lens cannot do this job.

FIGURE 3-8
1:1 magnification ratio

FIGURE 3-9
1:2 magnification ratio

FIGURE 3-10
1:3 magnification ratio

Many macro lenses offer the photographer the option of composing on areas from 1:1 to 1:10. What does this mean? For a second, think of the colon in 1:1 as a fraction, or 1/1. And 1/1 also means 1, or full size. Taking a picture with a macro lens set to 1:1 means that the full size of the object will fill the frame. A single-digit fingerprint will fill the frame when the macro lens is set to 1:1. Two fingerprints, side by side, will fill the frame vertically when the macro lens is set to 1:2. Or, on a full-sized digital sensor, a printed image of two vertical fingers side by side, without being enlarged in any way, will appear to be 1/2 their real size, as is shown in Figure 3-9.

If the job at hand is to both focus on and fill the frame with three adjacent vertical fingerprints, then the macro lens should be preset to 1:3. Put the camera on a tripod, and move the camera on the tripod closer and closer to the fingerprints until they come into focus. Prefocusing the macro lens to the desired size gets the camera to the precise distance from the fingerprints that will both have them in focus and filling the frame, as in Figure 3-10.

Consider the alternatives. The photographer can inadvertently set the camera on the tripod too close to the surface with the fingerprint(s), and the camera will never focus. The camera is too close to focus. Or, the photographer can set the camera farther than optimal, and focusing can be done, but when focus has been achieved, the finger(s) don't fill the frame, and they are smaller than optimal.

Hyperfocal Focusing

Hyperfocal focusing is the method to maximize the depth of field (DOF)—one of our cardinal rules—when infinity (∞) is in the background. The need for hyperfocal focusing usually occurs when capturing exterior overall photographs for a large scene. We normally regard infinity as a very large number. But consider the placement of the infinity symbol on the lens in Figure 3-11. It lies just to the right of the 10-meter distance (the white 10) in Figure 3-11.

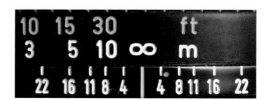

FIGURE 3-11
Focused on infinity: ∞

Notice that in this figure, just to the left of the 10-meter mark is the 5-meter mark. The infinity symbol is as far to the right of the 10-meter mark as the 5-meter mark is to the left of it. However, the distance from 3 meters to 5 meters is longer than the distance from 5 meters to 10 meters, so these distance changes are *not* proportional! For practical purposes, one can consider the infinity symbol to be the equivalent of about 80 feet and beyond. How does this help us?

The need for hyperfocal focusing occurs when one composes on a large outdoor scene, and in the background there is something 80 feet or farther away. In these cases, if you've included something in the background of your composition, it is reasonable to expect that it will also be both properly exposed and in focus. Hyperfocal focusing is a focusing technique to help ensure not only that the background is in focus, but also that as much of the foreground as possible is in focus. In other words, hyperfocal focusing helps us maximize the DOF.

How can one ensure the background is in focus? The naïve way to ensure the background of a large scene is in focus is to actually focus on infinity, as Figure 3-11 depicts. The orange line is the focusing line, and the distance scale has been rotated so that the infinity symbol aligns with the orange line. But how much of the scene, besides the background, will also be in focus when the image is captured? That is the same as asking how you can determine the DOF range.

The answer used to be relatively easy when most lenses also included what was called a **depth of field scale**. Notice the pairs of f/stop numbers placed to the left and right of the orange focusing point in Figure 3-12.

FIGURE 3-12
The pairs of numbers on either side of the orange focusing line are the depth of field scale

Figure 3-12 includes the depth of field scale. Unfortunately, current lens manufacturers do not seem to be including them on their lenses. Nevertheless, once the idea of determining one's DOF range with the depth of field scale is understood, this text will provide you with easy-to-remember rules of thumb for determining the DOF ranges for large outdoor crime scenes.

Look at Figure 3-12 again. Notice that the "22" to the left of the orange focusing line is approximately aligned with the 3.5-meter mark (white numbers) or where 12 feet would be on the green number sequence. This tells us that if the daylight on the crime scene is bright enough to require an f/22 for a proper exposure, the DOF range will be 12 feet to infinity when the lens is focused on infinity. Also notice that the "8" to the left of the orange focusing line is approximately aligned with the 10-meter mark (white numbers) or the 30-foot mark (green numbers). This tells us that if the daylight on the crime scene is dimmer and requires an f/8 for a proper exposure, the DOF range will be 30 feet to infinity when the lens is focused on infinity. The depth of field scale was very handy to have when trying to determine the DOF range.

On the depth of field scale, there are the same numbers on both sides of the orange focusing line. How are they used? Whenever any individual item is focused on, the orange focusing line will be aligned with the distance that object is from the camera. In addition to that object, there will also be some area in front of that object that is also in focus and some area behind that object that is also in focus. The depth of field scale shows us this range for every f/stop combination.

Look at Figure 3-13. In this case, the infinity symbol has been aligned with the 22 on the far right of the depth of field scale. Now, the distances between the two 22s on the depth of field scale represent the DOF range. What distances are opposite the two 22s? The right 22 is aligned with infinity and the left 22 is aligned with 6 feet. In other words, in order to maximize the depth of field when infinity is in the background, take a meter reading, and if the meter indicates that f/22 is required for a proper exposure, align the right 22 with the infinity symbol and the distances between the two 22s will now be in focus when the image is captured.

FIGURE 3-13
The infinity distance aligned with the right "22"

Focusing naïvely on the infinity symbol resulted in a DOF range of 12 feet to infinity. With hyperfocal focusing (by putting the right 22 across from the infinity symbol), the resulting DOF range is now 6 feet to infinity. Hyperfocal focusing maximizes the DOF when infinity is in the background by extending the DOF range in the foreground.

Now, notice the point of exact focus when you are hyperfocal focused with an f/22. The orange focusing line is aligned with 12 feet, or twice the short end of the DOF range. This setting works for each of the DOF ranges when different f/stops are used for different lighting at the crime scene.

Rather than methodically working through each f/stop, as was done with an f/22 in the previous example, the text will now provide the rules of thumb for hyperfocal focusing when different f/stops are required for the particular lighting of a scene (these are worth memorizing):

- F/22 provides a DOF range of 6 feet to ∞, when focused at 12 feet.
- F/16 provides a DOF range of 8 feet to ∞, when focused at 16 feet.
- F/11 provides a DOF range of 12 feet to ∞, when focused at 24 feet.
- F/8 provides a DOF range of 15 feet to ∞, when focused at 30 feet.

Therefore, even if your lens does not have a depth of field scale, you will still be able to hyperfocal focus. Determine the f/stop for the lighting at the crime scene. Focus at the distance indicated above for that f/stop. You will then have the DOF range indicated when the image is captured. Any other focusing technique will result in a shorter DOF range!

FIGURE 3-14
When infinity is not in the background, zone focusing should be employed

If all the evidence for your crime scene is lying in front of such a wall, then hyperfocal focusing does not apply because infinity is not visible in the background. A different focusing technique is required to maximize the DOF for an area like this: zone focusing.

Zone Focusing

Zone focusing is the optimal focusing technique to use for scenes when infinity is not in the background. This setup usually means there is some barrier, like a wall, preventing a view of anything beyond it. Or it could include a scene in which the camera is aimed down enough so that the top of the viewfinder does not include infinity in the field of view, like in Figure 3-15. This scene includes photos of indoor areas. The essential element is that infinity is not in the background.

FIGURE 3-15
When infinity is not in the background, zone focusing should be employed

In order to explain zone focusing, it is necessary to understand that when the DOF range is considered, the distance behind the plane of exact focus is not the same as the distance in front of the plane of exact focus. An old photography rule of thumb indicates that within the DOF range, there is approximately 1/3 of the DOF distance in front of the plane of exact focus and 2/3 of the DOF range behind the plane of exact focus.

 ## *RULE OF THUMB 3-1*

The DOF extends 1/3 in front of the point of exact focus and 2/3 behind the point of exact focus.

This rule is sometimes mentioned as the **Rule of Thirds**. Simplistically, this rule can mean that if you are viewing a scene that does not have infinity in the background, as in Figure 3-15 the best way to ensure that most of the scene will be in focus is to focus 1/3 of the way into the scene while using the smallest aperture possible for the lighting that also ensures proper exposure.

This method is easy to describe but difficult to use in practice. Trying to determine the precise distance that is 1/3 of the way into a composed scene is very difficult for most photographers. The purpose of this text is to try to make complex concepts relatively easy to implement in our crime scene photographs. To do this, I've composed several scenes, varying the background distances, and then placed a pen within each scene at exactly 1/3 of the distance from the front of the scene to the back of the scene. When you view the resulting series of images, there is something about the placement of the pens that should be immediately apparent.

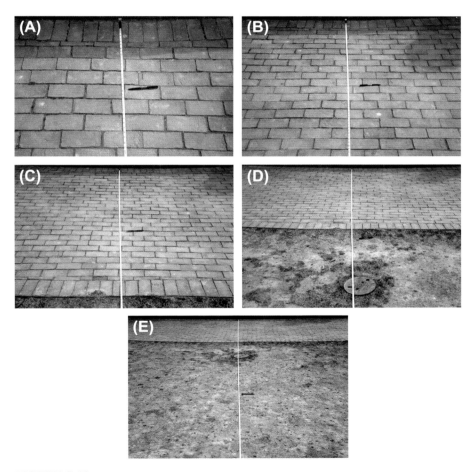

FIGURE 3-16
A, B, C, D, and E, Notice the locations of the five pens as viewed from the top to the bottom of each image

In these five images, all the pens appear to be approximately halfway between the bottom of the image and the top of the image. That is not halfway into the perceived scene; it is halfway between the bottom of the viewfinder and the top of the viewfinder. Estimating 1/3 of the way into a composed scene is tricky; determining halfway from the bottom of the viewfinder and the top of the viewfinder is easy: there is invariably a focusing rectangle in the middle of the viewfinder!

 ## *RULE OF THUMB 3-2*

When attempting to maximize the DOF with crime scenes ranging from 5 to 30 feet, the most effective way to do this is to focus at a distance that appears to be midway between the top and the bottom of the composed image.

For all crime scene area images that do not have infinity in the background, the optimal focusing technique to maximize the DOF is to use the smallest aperture the lighting will allow and then focus at the plane that is closest to the middle of the viewfinder when considered as half the distance between the bottom and the top of the viewfinder. This trick makes zone focusing relatively fast and easy to do.

DEPTH OF FIELD (DOF)

Depth of field is the variable range, from foreground to background, of what appears to be sharp and in focus. This range can be relatively small, as when just one item in the field of view appears to be in focus, with everything in front of it and behind it out of focus. Or the DOF range can include almost everything in the field of view. With today's modern digital SLR cameras and their various controls, the photographer usually can ensure exactly what they want is in focus when the image is captured.

Factors Affecting DOF

There are three camera variables that directly affect the depth of field. By being aware of the variables that affect the DOF, the photographer can choose to maximize the DOF for most shots and, on occasion, to minimize the DOF when that helps get the job done.

F-Stop Selection

The major variable that affects the DOF is the f/stop selection. As mentioned previously, the best f/stops to use when one wishes to maximize the DOF are f/22, f/16, f/11, and f/8. When one takes a meter reading and the exposure meter recommends any other wider f/stops, consider using one of these choices so that smaller f/stops can ultimately be used, resulting in better DOF:

1. Use a slower shutter speed so that you can use a smaller aperture. However, if the slower shutter speed is slower than 1/60th of a second, you will have to put the camera on a tripod to avoid blur from hand-holding the camera.
2. Use a higher ISO setting so that you can use a smaller aperture. This method is reasonable up to ISO 800. After that, a higher ISO selection may result in increased digital noise.
3. Add light in the form of an electronic flash. By making the scene brighter with a flash, a smaller aperture can be used for a proper exposure and a better DOF.

Lens Choice (Focal Length Selection)

Many cameras are sold as a kit that includes one or more lenses. These lenses are increasingly frequently zoom lenses featuring a variety of focal lengths the photographer can choose from, such as a zoom lens featuring focal lengths of 18mm, 28mm, 35mm, 50mm, and 80mm. Many years ago, photographers once sought out prime lenses with just one focal length, such as a 50mm lens, because at the time, prime lenses could boast superior optics, resulting in higher-quality images. Because today's zoom lenses have improved in quality, they are now almost universally included as the normal lens with most camera kits.

Of these various focal lengths, which provide a better DOF? Generally speaking, wide-angle lenses have the best DOF when compared to the other lens types, and the normal lens has a better DOF than any telephoto lens. Why is this?

Remember that the term "f/8" is really an expression of the relationship of the f/stop number, "8," to the focal length currently being used. For example, if one is using a zoom lens with a focal length range of 18–80mm, and the camera is currently set to f/8, as one changes between the various focal lengths, the aperture will also be changing:

- 18/8 = a 2.25mm diameter of the diaphragm (DOD)
- 28/8 = a 3.5mm DOD
- 35/8 = a 4.375mm DOD
- 50/8 = a 6.25mm DOD
- 80/8 = a 10mm DOD

The smallest DOD produces the best DOF. The wide-angle focal lengths (18mm, 28mm, and 35mm) produce smaller DODs and better DOFs than either the normal focal length (50mm) or the short telephoto focal length (80mm). And the normal focal length (50mm) produces a smaller DOD and a better DOF than the short telephoto focal length (80mm).

Unfortunately, this section on the focal length of a lens affecting the DOF merely states the fact that wider focal lengths produce better DOF ranges than normal or telephoto focal lengths. The proof of these statements is quite complicated and involves the term "circles of confusion." In an effort to make this text more easily readable, I'm intentionally omitting that complex discussion here because it is beyond the scope of this introductory text. If your curiosity compels you to look into this concept more, begin your search with "circles of confusion."

Camera to Subject Distance

Recall that an f/22 can produce a DOF range of 6 feet to ∞ when focused at 12 feet, it is a bright sunny day, and one uses the hyperfocal focusing technique. As the point of exact focus gets shorter than 12 feet, the DOF range begins to shrink as well. When focused at approximately 9 feet, the DOF range is about 5 feet to 30 feet (see Figure 3-17A). As the point of exact focus gets closer and closer to the photographer, the DOF range gets smaller and smaller (see Figures 3-17B through 3-17D).

FIGURE 3-17A
DOF range of 5 feet to 30 feet with an f/22

FIGURE 3-17B
DOF less than 15 feet with an f/22

FIGURE 3-17C
DOF less than 10 feet with an f/22

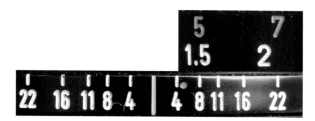

FIGURE 3-17D
DOF less than 7 feet with an f/22

Finally, when using that same f/22, the DOF range will not reach from the top of a .45 caliber casing to the surface the casing is on when using a macro lens and filling the frame with the casing. As the distance from camera to subject decreases, the DOF also decreases. As the distance from camera to subject increases, the DOF also increases.

Tips to Maximize the DOF

Maximizing the DOF is frequently a major concern of the crime scene photographer (it is not often that the crime scene photographer wishes large areas of their images to be out of focus).

 RULE OF THUMB 3-3

When choosing camera variables, the crime scene photographer should lean in these directions.

- *Use the smallest f/stop available that provides a proper exposure.*
- *Use the slowest shutter speed that allows the camera to be handheld.*
- *Use faster ISOs to help obtain small apertures, when necessary, but not as rule of thumb.*
- *Add light from an electronic flash to obtain smaller apertures.*

Use the slowest shutter speed available that will allow you to hand-hold the lens currently selected. Using a faster shutter speed can also result in a proper exposure, but it would usually require using a wider aperture, which in turn reduces the DOF. If using the slowest shutter speed to hold the lens does not result in the smallest f/stops including f/22, f/16, f/11, and f/8, then consider using an even slower shutter speed. However, if the slower shutter speed is slower than 1/60th of a second, you will have to put the camera on a tripod to avoid blur from hand-holding the camera.

Use a higher ISO setting so that you can then use a smaller aperture. This advice is reasonable up to ISO 800. After that, a higher ISO selection may result in increased digital noise. With each new camera you work with, before using it at a crime scene, take a series of properly exposed images using faster and faster ISOs, such as 800, 1600, and 3200. Determine at which ISO setting you can obviously notice digital noise. That will let you know your limit when considering faster ISOs.

Add light in the form of an electronic flash. By making the scene brighter with a flash, a smaller aperture can be used for a proper exposure and a better DOF.

LENSES

Lenses are known by various descriptors: focal length, speed, aperture width, magnification, angle width, and other factors. Let's examine the more frequently encountered lens descriptions.

Focal Length

As mentioned previously, lenses are known by their focal lengths (18mm, 28mm, etc.). What does the focal length of, for instance, 50mm really mean? Although any lens may have multiple glass elements inside the lens barrel, there is usually a point that the lens manufacturer regards as the "optical center" of that lens. A definition of a lens's **focal length** is the distance between the optical center of the lens and the sensor plane when the camera is focused on infinity. At one time, as one focused a lens, the outer element of the lens would extend outward as the focusing shifted from infinity to closer and closer distances. Today, many lenses focus internally, so their actual length does not change. In either case, there would be 50mm in distance between the optical center of the lens and the plane of the sensor when the lens is focused on infinity.

This is why most wide-angle lenses are relatively compact and most telephoto lenses get longer and longer as one considers 100mm, 200mm, and 300mm lenses.

"Fast" and "Slow" Lenses

Most lenses used with SLR camera systems do not have "speeds" or any components that are speed related, but they do have a variable f/stop range. Because a 50mm lens can have various apertures as its widest f/stop, and wider apertures let in more light, the lens with the widest aperture requires a faster shutter speed to balance the exposure of the same scene as a lens with a narrower aperture. For example, a 50mm f/1.7 lens would let in more light than a 50mm f/2.8 lens. If both cameras are used to photograph the same scene when not using an electronic flash unit, the 50mm 1.7 lens will be required to use a faster shutter speed than the 50mm f/2.8 lens. The 50mm f/1.7 lens, then, would be called "faster."

Many professional photographers value having a "faster" lens. It might enable them to photograph a child blowing out the candles on their birthday cake without needing to use an electronic flash to properly light the scene. Crime scene photographers, however, do not typically place a value on "fast" lenses, as we normally seek to maximize the DOF with small apertures. "Fast" lenses also typically cost more than "slow" lenses. So if a crime scene photographer is shopping for any particular lens, console yourself by knowing you can buy the less expensive "slow" lens option without compromising your photographic priorities.

Lenses Designated by Their Widest Apertures

Because of the concept of "fast" lenses, lenses are normally labeled by their maximum aperture so they can be clearly compared. On the carton and on the lens, a lens can be marked as a 50mm 1:2.8 lens, indicating that its widest aperture is f/2.8.

A zoom lens, however, will usually be marked as an 18—80mm, 1:3.5/5.6 lens. When two different f/stops are indicated, that means the widest focal length (18mm) has as its widest f/stop the first f/stop mentioned, and the extreme telephoto focal length (80mm) has as its widest f/stop the second f/stop aperture mentioned. Some higher-quality zoom lenses list just one focal length throughout its full focal length continuum, such as a 28—105mm, 1:3.5 lens.

The "Normal" Lens

With film cameras and digital cameras featuring a "full"-sized digital sensor (24mm × 36mm; the same size as the film negative), the **"normal" lens** was regarded as a 50mm lens. In theory, this meant that when you looked at the crime scene with your eyes and then looked at the same area through the camera's viewfinder, the relative spacing and layout of objects in the scene looked the same. Objects closer to the photographer looked the same distance from the photographer when looking above the camera and when looking through the viewfinder. Objects farther from the photographer looked the same distance from the photographer when looking above the camera and when looking through the viewfinder. In each case, the world looked the same, or "normal."

 RULE OF THUMB 3-4

The 50mm lens is normally the focal length of choice when it is our intention to offer the photograph of the scene in court and maintain that the photograph is a "fair and accurate representation of the scene."

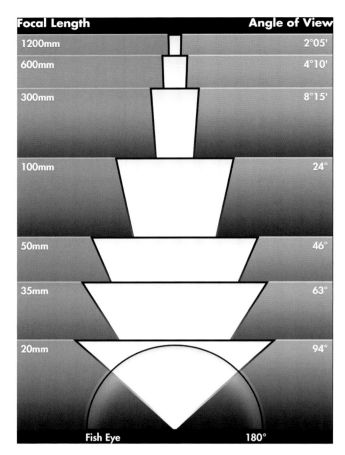

FIGURE 3-18
Focal lengths and their angles of view *(courtesy of scamper.com)*

The 50mm lens features a 46-degree view of the world. Other lenses show wider views of the world or narrower views of the world. Figure 3-18 is a representation of the areas of view of different lenses available today.

With digital cameras, however, the concept of a normal lens takes on a new-meaning. In order to save money on the construction of digital sensors, many digital sensor manufacturers created digital sensors that are smaller than the film negative had been. There are digital sensors that are the same size as the film negative had been, but these are typically used on the more expensive digital cameras in any manufacturer's camera lineup.

The smaller digital sensor is called an APS-C-sized sensor, which stands for the Advanced Photo System, type C, film size used with those film cameras. This

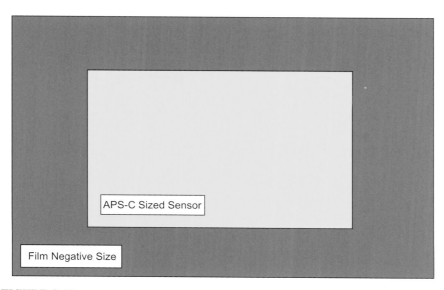

FIGURE 3-19
The relative sizes of a film negative and an APS-C-sized digital sensor

film negative was smaller than the full-sized 24mm × 36mm film negative, and was approximately 22mm × 15mm. Why all the concern?

The 35mm film negative provided an image with a certain size, similar to the blue area in the above figure. Because a digital APS-C-sized sensor was smaller than the film negative, it captures just a portion of what was captured by the film negative or full-sized digital sensor. It captures a smaller field of view, as if the image obtained from a film negative were cropped to a smaller size. Less of the field of view is captured on a smaller digital sensor.

Cameras with the APS-C-sized sensors are said to have a **focal length multiplier**. Depending on the manufacturer, the focal length multiplier is said to be the equivalent of a 1.5 or 1.6. This smaller field of view is the equivalent of the film camera/digital camera switching from the normal 50mm lens to either a 75mm (50 × 1.5) or 80mm (50 × 1.6) lens.

Thus, a photographer wishing to see the same scene through a digital camera with an APS-C-sized sensor as a film camera sees or a digital camera with a full-sized digital camera sees, would have to use a focal length of 50/1.5 (33.33mm) or 50/1.6 (31.25mm). For photographers with an APS-C-sized digital sensor, the **new normal** focal length is either 33.33mm or 31.25mm, depending on the focal length multiplier of their digital camera! Check the specification data of your camera for this information.

FIGURE 3-20
The relative size of an APS-C digital sensor with a 33mm focal length on the left and an APS-C digital sensor with a 50mm focal length on the right *(courtesy of M. Hur and J. Buffington, GWU MS students)*

Telephoto Lenses

A **telephoto lens** is considered any focal length that is larger than the normal lenses' focal length. For a film camera or a digital camera with a full-sized digital sensor, this length ranges from 70mm to 1200mm. For a digital camera with an APS-C-sized digital camera, it includes 50mm to 1200mm. That is because the 50mm lens will be acting like a 75mm lens (50×1.5) or an 80mm lens (50×1.6).

The focal length multipliers of APS-C digital sensors actually act to the benefit of those using telephoto lenses. Their nominal focal lengths are dramatically increased for no extra cost. Usually, longer focal length lenses are more expensive.

FIGURE 3-21
An 800mm lens *(courtesy of AFOSI)*

Apparent Magnification

One of the effects of using a telephoto lens is apparent magnification. If you captured an image of a single distant object with both a 50mm lens and a 300mm lens and then had both the single objects printed to the same size, the object would be more clear, or better resolved in the image captured with the 300mm lens. If one cannot get closer to an object or person but still wanted to see them more clearly, using a telephoto lens is the solution. During surveillance photography, it is possible to use a telephoto lens to better see a subject and his or her activities while remaining at a safe distance.

FIGURE 3-22
A white pickup truck 500 feet away, photographed with a 50mm lens on the top, and a 960mm lens on the bottom

FIGURE 3-23
A student standing 400 feet away in the center of the top image; below left is an enlargement from the original image; below right is an image from the same distance, taken at night, with an 800mm lens

Narrower Field of View

Telephoto lenses take in a narrower view of the world, excluding areas to the left and right of the central object that a normal lens would have captured. And by capturing a narrower area, all the pixels of the digital camera can be placed over a smaller area, dramatically improving the resolution of everything within the narrower field of view.

Compression of the Foreground and Background

If the distant object now looks larger because a telephoto lens was used, a viewer of this image could interpret this fact to mean that the photographer was actually closer to the subject/object at the time the image was captured. For crime scene photographers, who usually strive to have their images convey a "fair and accurate representation of the scene," this effect of using a telephoto lens has to be carefully monitored. Images taken with a telephoto lens may be deceiving as to the relative distance between the foreground and the background. One does not want to mislead the jury viewing a photograph taken with a telephoto lens. And although crime scene photographers must be constantly vigilant to avoid this problem, they must also be watchful of the images offered as evidence by the defense to ensure that those images are not misleading for the same reason.

FIGURE 3-24

The same double yellow lines photographed with a telephoto lens on the left, a normal lens in the center, and a wide-angle lens on the right *(courtesy of S. Lingsch, GWU MS student)*

How can telephoto lenses be used for one of their strengths—apparent magnification—while at the same time avoiding this possible tendency to mislead by making the distant background appear closer than it really was? If the photographer intentionally composes the image so that the compressed foreground to background distance is not in the field of view, then a telephoto lens does not deceive.

For instance, imagine the inside of an arson scene with a V-shaped burn pattern on the opposite wall but the floor in the middle of the room weakened by the fire. One wants to fill the frame with the wall with the V-shaped burn pattern, but it is not safe to stand at a distance needed to do that with a normal lens. One way to solve the problem is to stand at the opposite wall and fill the frame with the V-shaped burn pattern with a short telephoto lens, intentionally making sure to remove from the composition the intervening floor, ceiling, and side walls. In this way, the wall with the burn pattern is filling the frame, but there are no visual clues to suggest how far away the photographer was standing when the image was captured. Had much of the floor or ceiling been included in the field of view, the distance from photographer and the opposite wall would appear closer than it really was, and if the jury were told the photographer stood at the opposite wall, the conclusion the jury could form was that the room was much smaller than it really is, misleading them about a fact that might ultimately be important to the case.

Narrower Depth of Field

As explained earlier, the DOF ranges of telephoto lenses are shorter than any of the other lenses for the same f/stop. Consider a series of images taken with an f/16, but with different focal lengths. Because FLL divided by f/stop = DOD:

- 100/16 = 6.25mm
- 50/16 = 3.125mm
- 24/16 = 1.5mm

The smaller the DOD, the better the DOF.

Wide-Angle Lenses

A **wide-angle lens** is considered any focal length that is smaller than the normal lenses's focal length. For a film camera or a digital camera with a full-sized digital sensor, this length usually ranges from 8mm to 35mm. For a digital camera with an APS-C-sized digital camera, these same lenses provide a narrower field of view than their full-framed counterparts because the 8mm lens will be acting like a 12mm lens (8 × 1.5) or a 12.8mm lens (8 × 1.6).

The focal length multipliers of APS-C digital sensors actually act as a negative for those using wide-angle lenses. Their nominal focal lengths are dramatically increased, making them act less like what their owners purchased them for. Very wide-angle lenses are quite expensive. With an APS-C-sized digital sensor, the benefits of super wide-angle lenses are lost.

Wider Field of View

A wide-angle lens will take in more to the left and right compared to what a "normal" lens captures. This is often a distinct advantage for the crime scene photographer tasked with the responsibility to photograph wide areas or wide walls. A wide-angle lens is also particularly suited for photographing smaller spaces like the inside of a garage or small room such as a bathroom. When the space is small, the photographer frequently cannot get far enough away from an opposite wall to have much of it in the field of view with just a normal lens. The wide angle lens captures more to the left and right in any one image.

Elongation of Foreground and Background

There is a price to pay for the benefit of being able to capture more to the left and right than a normal lens would capture. The negative aspect of using a wide-angle lens is that the perceived distance between foreground and background will appear to be stretched or elongated. Why is this a negative aspect? It makes the area being photographed appear larger than it really is. Images going to court as evidence need to be "fair and accurate representations of the scene." If a wide-angle lens is used, the scene will appear to be larger than it looked to the photographer, thereby misleading the viewer of the photograph, which can include jury members. There are times that an issue being contested during a trial is the relative size of the crime scene area or the distance apart between two object or two individuals. If the use of a wide-angle lens makes the relative distance between objects or individuals appear to be longer than it appeared to the photographer's eyes, then the images can be held to be inadmissible by the judge.

For instance, what if a witness claims to have been able to recognize a particular defendant from a certain point of view and from a certain distance? If the crime scene photographer stands where the witness claims to have been standing and takes images from that position toward where the defendant allegedly stood, those images can be evaluated by the jury to help them decide whether recognizing someone at that distance is possible. However, if different focal lengths are used to photograph the area in question, the relative distance between the witness and the defendant can radically change. See Figures 3-25 and 3-26. If Figure 3-25 was taken with a normal lens, then it truly depicts the distance from the photographer to the front of the building where the defendant was supposedly recognized. Figure 3-26 was taken from the same location as the witness stood, but this time a wide-angle lens was used to suggest that the building is farther away and that making the identification would be more difficult.

How can a wide-angle lens be used as a benefit, by being able to capture wider areas, without being constrained by their negative aspect and tending to stretch out the foreground to background distance? The photographer must consciously compose the image so that it includes just the wider aspect of the scene without including in the field of view large areas of the foreground in view. For instance, if it is necessary to photograph an exterior wall of a wide building, the wide-angle lens is perfectly suited for this job. However, the photographer must intentionally eliminate from the field of view large expanses of the foreground in front of the building because the foreground will appear longer in the image than it did to the photographer. Ensure that the bottom edge of the viewfinder includes the bottom of the building but not a lot of landscaping of the building between the photographer and the building.

Increased Depth of Field

One of the three aspects that affects the DOF is the selection of the focal length. A wide-angle lens has a better DOF than either a normal lens or a telephoto lens. However, for crime scene photographers, this aspect of wide-angle lenses is rarely utilized, because to benefit from an increased DOF, you must be careful not to

FIGURE 3-25
The true distance between the photographer and the building being accurately depicted by using a normal lens *(courtesy of K. Kinsie, GWU MS student)*

FIGURE 3-26
A wide-angle lens makes the perceived distance between the photographer and the building seem to be greater *(courtesy of K. Kinsie, GWU MS student)*

FIGURE 3-27
Including the foreground in view suggests that the photographer was a particular distance from the building

FIGURE 3-28
When the foreground is excluded, it is unclear where the photographer was when the image was captured; they may have been relatively close, but using a wide-angle lens

capture in the image expanses between the foreground and the background. As just explained, when using a wide-angle lens properly, crime scene photographers seldom include large areas of the foreground to background in their images. Many other professional photographers may be able to capitalize on this benefit of a wide-angle lens, but it is seldom a benefit to the crime scene photographer.

Macro Lenses

If a telephoto lens can make distant objects appear larger, is it the ideal lens to also use whenever it is necessary to make anything larger? No. Telephoto lenses excel at making distant objects appear larger and easier to see, but the optimal lens to use to make small objects larger in the field of view is the **macro lens**. As mentioned earlier when discussing prefocusing the camera, the macro lens is the best lens suited to enlarge evidence that is smaller than your hand. Because the crime scene photographer frequently encounters small evidence, having a macro lens, or one of the equivalents discussed shortly, is a must-have for a crime scene photographer.

Magnification with a 1:1 Ratio

In Figure 3-29 are two images of a black talon bullet that has passed through a body and mushroomed as designed. One can see that the jacketing itself has separated into six sharp sections, which is intended to inflict more damage than other ammunition. Figure 3-29A is not adequately filling the frame; Figure 3-29B, a close-up with a partial scale in view, does an excellent job of filling the frame. In order to compose Figure 3-29B, a macro lens set to a 1:1 magnification ratio was used. A 1:1 magnification ratio enables an item of evidence the size of a film negative or full-sized digital sensor to fill the frame.

FIGURE 3-29A
A black talon bullet not filling the frame properly

FIGURE 3-29B
A black talon bullet properly filling the frame

Figure 3-29A was probably set to a 1:2 magnification ratio. Whenever it is possible to fill the frame with the evidence, it is better to do so. Why place a majority of your digital pixels on the surrounding pavement, like Figure 3-29A does? If the image on the left were to be enlarged to the same size as Figure 3-29B, it would quickly be seen that the resolution of the image is not as sharp as the image on the bottom because there are more pixels covering the bullet in Figure 3-29B.

Figure 3-30A is an enlargement of Figure 3-29A; Figure 3-30B is an enlargement of Figure 3-29B. These two images should convince you of the value of filling the frame with your subject matter. As more digital pixels are placed on the subject of interest, it has more resolution, which is extremely important in case an examiner should wish to enlarge any area to more closely inspect a detail of interest.

FIGURE 3-30A
An enlargement of Figure 3-29A

FIGURE 3-30B
An enlargement of Figure 3-29B

The best way to obtain 1:1 magnifications of small evidence is to use a macro lens. Having a macro lens provides the sharpest images, but it is also the most expensive option. Nikon has several excellent macro lenses with the prime focal lengths ranging from 40mm through 200mm. Each of these macro lenses offers 1:2 to 1:1 magnification ratios. What is the practical difference if most will produce a 1:1 magnification ratio? Each can also be used as a regular lens featuring its prime focal length. Select the focal length that you use most frequently and you'll also have macro capabilities whenever they are required.

Extension Tubes

Adding **extension tubes** between your primary lens and the camera body effectively makes your primary lens longer, and when the optical center of the lens is farther from the sensor, the result is magnification. See Figures 3-31A and 3-31B. Typically, extension tubes come in two or three sizes providing different magnification strengths individually, but many are designed so that they can be stacked, increasing the possible magnification.

Used with a zoom lens, as in Figure 3-32 the extension tube provides magnification with each different focal length, creating many possibilities. This lens has a 28—105mm zoom range. With the 105mm focal length and the extension tube, the magnification ratio is almost 1:1.

FIGURE 3-31A
A camera without the extension tube, courtesy of Ron Taniwaki, Nikon Professional Services

FIGURE 3-31B
Adding the extension tube between the camera body and the lens results in the optical center of the lens being further from the digital sensor, which allows greater magnification, courtesy of Ron Taniwaki, Nikon Professional Services

FIGURE 3-32
An extension tube used with a zoom lens

Close-Up Filters

With a very restricted budget, a **close-up filter** set is another option. This set typically comes with three filters in different powers: +1, +2, and +4, and they can be stacked to produce different magnification ratios, as shown in Figure 3-33B.

FIGURE 3-33A
A set of close-up filters

FIGURE 3-33B
Close-up filters showing different amounts of magnification when stacked

With a 50mm lens used without any of the close-up filters, at the lens's closest focusing position, seven nickels will be stacked vertically, from the bottom of the image to the top of the image, and be in sharp focus. This setup can be expressed as a 1:7 magnification ratio. With all three close-up filters stacked together, a +7, the result is a ratio of approximately 1:1.8. It is important to remember that if one wishes to combine the filters to increase the magnifying capability, the highest filter number is supposed to be placed on the prime lens first and the lowest filter number placed on the lens last.

Many photography purists will remind you that the effective clarity of an image is downgraded as one increases the number of filters on a lens. This guideline is undoubtedly accurate, so you shouldn't use more than two of these filters at any time.

Lens Distortion

If most of your images are captured when using the normal focal length, you cannot usually see noticeable lens distortions. But as you use very wide-angle focal lengths or very long telephoto focal lengths, the instances of lens distortions increase. To a certain extent, these lens distortions cannot be avoided altogether, but sometimes they can be minimized or eliminated with software corrections.

Barrel Distortion

When using a wide-angle lens to photograph exterior overalls of wide buildings, a distortion known as **barrel distortion** can often be seen. Like a barrel bows out from the sides, the straight lines of the sides of the building or any straight lines near any of the sides of the image will appear to bend slightly outward. As can be seen in Figure 3-34A, the same metal railing will bend out different directions, but always toward the sides of the image.

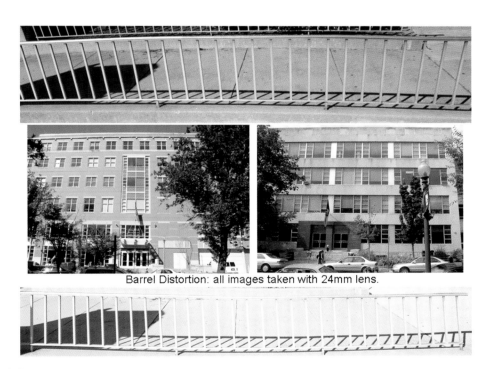

Barrel Distortion: all images taken with 24mm lens.

FIGURE 3-34A

Barrel distortion: wide-angle lenses tend to have straight lines near the sides of the image bend outward

FIGURE 3-34B
Photoshop can correct barrel distortion

Figure 3-34A also shows two buildings with rooflines that appears bowed outwards. This is the normal result of using a wide-angle lens to capture images. Perhaps it is consoling to know this distortion can easily be corrected with software such as Adobe Photoshop, as is shown in Figure 3-34B. Not only is the barrel distortion removed, but the building also appears more upright, rather than seeming to lean backward, as is shown in Figure 3-34A.

Pincushion Distortion

If barrel distortion is produced with wide-angle lenses, some might expect the opposite type of distortion to be caused by using a telephoto lens. This expectation is correct! Pincushion distortion has the effect of the outside walls appearing to be bent inward.

The same building was photographed with a wide-angle lens in Figure 3-35A, producing barrel distortion, and with a telephoto lens in Figure 3-35B, producing pincushion distortion. With a bit of Photoshop tweaking, both of these distortions can be corrected (Figure 3-35C).

Neither barrel distortion nor pincushion distortion affects vertical or horizontal lines in the center of the image. But as straight lines get closer to any of the sides of the image, the effects get more and more pronounced.

FIGURE 3-35A
A building with barrel distortion because a wide-angle lens was used

FIGURE 3-35B
A telephoto lens causing pincushion distortion

FIGURE 3-35C
Photoshop can correct most distortions

CHAPTER SUMMARY

In this chapter, the various techniques used to control and maximize your DOF were explained. You have also learned how the different lenses will affect an image.

Having read the first three chapters, you are now able to properly compose on the subject of interest, whether that is a single object or an area of different sizes. Regardless of what your primary subject is, you should also be able to ensure that it is properly exposed and that brackets of that image are taken when needed. And now, in addition to properly composing on the subject and properly exposing that subject, you also know the proper method for focusing on the primary subject, whether this is a single object or various-sized crime scenes, so that the DOF covers the area from the foreground to the background. When it is a bright sunny day, you should have complete confidence that your images will turn out great.

But what about photography at dusk and dawn? What about nighttime photography? And what about indoor photography? To be successful in these situations, you'll have to learn about supplementing the ambient light with an electronic flash. Chapter 4 explores all the flash-related techniques to produce examination-quality photographs at any time of the day and in any location.

Discussion Questions

1. Automatic focus has difficulties locking on some types of scenes. Explain two situations in which it may be better to use manual focusing.
2. Explain hyperfocal focusing. Include an explanation of how to use the technique when you do have a depth of scale on your lens and when you don't.
3. Explain zone focusing. Include an explanation of how to use the technique when you do have a depth of scale on your lens and when you don't.
4. Explain the camera variables that affect depth of field, that maximize depth of field, and that minimize depth of field.
5. Explain which focal length of lens is most appropriate for most crime scene photography and why this is so.

Practical Exercises

1. Create a single-digit fingerprint on an outside surface that is fully sunlit. Place the camera on a tripod, prefocus the lens so that it will produce a 1: 1 or 1:2 magnification ratio, include a scale, and take a set of three exposures at 0, +1, and −1.
2. Hyperfocal focus on a large outdoor scene where infinity is in the background.
3. Zone focus on an area in front of a building façade that is 30 feet from the camera.
4. Zone focus on an area in front of a building façade that is 20 feet from the camera.
5. With the widest aperture of the lens, focus on an object 20 feet away. Use a 50mm lens.
6. With the smallest aperture of the lens, focus on the same object 20 feet away. Use a 50mm lens.
7. With the smallest aperture of the lens, focus on the same object 20 feet away. Use the widest angle lens available.
8. With the smallest aperture of the lens, focus on the same object 20 feet away. Use the longest telephoto lens available.
9. Place a coin on the sidewalk with the mint designation or date as large as possible. With the camera on a tripod, determine the best exposure using an f/22.

Suggested Readings

Ditchburn, R.W. 1991. *Light*. New York: Dover Publication.

Landt, Artur. 1998. *Lenses for 35mm Photography* the Kodak Workshop Series. Rochester NY: Silver Pixel Press.

McDonald, James A. 1992. *Close-Up & Macro Photography for Evidence Technicians.* Second Edition. Arlington Heights, IL: Phototext Books.

Paduano, Joseph. 1998. *Wide-Angle Lens Photography.* Amherst, NY: Amherst Media, Inc.

Sheppard, Rob. 1997. *Telephoto Lens Photography.* Buffalo NY: Amherst Media, Inc.

Walls, H.J., and G.G. Attridge. 1977. *Basic Photo Science: How Photography Works.* London: Focal Press Limited.

Electronic Flash

KEY TERMS

Aperture priority mode
Automatic flash
   exposure mode
Dedicated/TTL flash
   exposure mode
Fill-in flash
Guide number

Hard shadows
Inverse Square Law
Manual flash mode
Negative dust print
"Normal" room
Oblique flash
Positive dust print

Remote flash cord
Snow print wax
Soft shadow
Sync speed
TTL

CONTENTS

LEARNING OBJECTIVES

Upon completion of this chapter, you will be able to:

- Explain the meaning of flash guide numbers.
- Explain the meaning of the flash sync speed.
- Explain why it is important for the flash head to duplicate the camera and lens viewpoints.
- Explain the basics of the Manual flash exposure mode, and explain some of the drawbacks with the Manual flash exposure mode.
- Explain the Inverse Square Law related to light. Explain how flash intensities can be determined when the distance the flash travels is known. Explain how the f/stop numbers are derived from these different flash intensities.
- Explain the various ways in which the flash output can be reduced to provide for precise flash control at different distances.
- Explain the basics of the Automatic flash exposure mode.
- Explain the basics of the Dedicated/TTL flash exposure mode.
- Explain the benefits these modes have over the Manual flash exposure mode.
- Explain how to bracket in all three flash exposure modes.

- Explain how to utilize fill-in flash to obtain proper exposures with various lighting conditions.
- Explain how to take photographs using the oblique flash technique.
- Explain what kinds of situations would benefit from the use of bounce flash.
- Explain how to compensate for the light loss resulting from the use of bounce flash.
- Explain how to use the Aperture Priority mode to ensure that a large dimly lit crime scene is properly exposed.

When the ambient lighting begins to dim, an electronic flash can add supplemental light to help you achieve proper exposure. During the night, or in areas without any lighting, an electronic flash can be the sole source of lighting. And even in the middle of a sunny day, an electronic flash still has uses. The bright sun will create areas of dark shadows, and if it is necessary to capture an image of an area that is both sunlit and shady, the electronic flash can add sufficient light to the shady area so that details in those areas are easy to see.

In addition to adding light to areas with insufficient light, an electronic flash can also "cure" problems that may occur because the quality of the ambient lighting can otherwise create objectionable color tints. As mentioned previously, indoor fluorescent tubes produce greenish tints, and the tungsten filaments in many household lightbulbs result in a yellowish tint on the scene. An electronic flash can provide the right quality of light for the scene to have all the correct colors as our eyes see them.

There are various flash exposure modes, just as there were several nonflash exposure modes.

MANUAL FLASH EXPOSURE MODE

Having acquired an understanding of how the exposure meter in the camera body helps us determine proper exposures, it is now time for you to learn a new exposure method. The Manual flash exposure mode does not use the camera's exposure meter at all to determine a proper exposure.

Our task is now to determine the proper amount of light coming from the flash for the distance between the flash and the subject. We will always try to determine the right light for the distance.

The Manual flash exposure mode has some very basic fundamental ideas it is based on, as explained in this section. The full manual flash burst of light is everything the flash is capable of. The flash output cannot be any greater than full manual flash. The full manual flash will be fired regardless of the distance between the flash and the subject. Whether the primary subject is 37 feet from the flash, 27 feet away, 18 feet away, or 13 feet away, the full flash is being fired. So how does the photographer control the exposure at these different distances to ensure a proper exposure? When using the manual flash mode, the exposure is controlled by the choice of f/stops. At 37 feet, a longer distance, the full manual flash can produce a proper exposure only if a wider f/stop is used. As the distance between the flash and the subject decreases, the photographer must use progressively smaller f/stops to avoid overexposures.

Consider the images in Figure 4-1 for a particular flash unit. The flash unit tells the photographer the necessary f/stop for each distance, when the ISO and focal length are known.

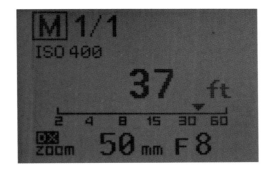

FIGURE 4-1A
F/8 will light 37 feet *(courtesy of M. Halter, GWU MS student)*

FIGURE 4-1B
F/11 will light 27 feet *(courtesy of M. Halter, GWU MS student)*

FIGURE 4-1C
F/16 will light 18 feet *(courtesy of M. Halter, GWU MS student)*

FIGURE 4-1D
F/22 will light 13 feet *(courtesy of M. Halter, GWU MS student)*

Guide Numbers

Electronic flash units offer different intensities. The relative intensity of an electronic flash, or its output power, is expressed by its guide number. At one time, it was critical to know the guide number of your flash. Before today's modern flash units with built-in LED screens that tell the photographer the distance that the flash will properly light based on the other camera exposure variables (ISO setting, f/stop, shutter speed, and lens focal length), early flash units had to determine the proper f/stop to use for a particular shot by dividing the flash guide number by the distance between the flash and the subject:

$$GN/distance = f/stop$$

The photographer had to do some mental math to determine the proper f/stop to use for any flash shot. For example, if the guide number for a particular flash unit was 120 (this will eventually be explained), and the current flash to subject distance was 11 feet, then the f/stop required to proper light the subject with that particular flash unit was f/11:

$$120/11 = f/11$$

Different electronic flash units featured various guide numbers. For instance, flash units with guide numbers of 56, 80, 120, and 160 were not uncommon. If each of these flash possibilities were used when 10 feet from a particular subject, the necessary f/stop to be used for each flash would be:

$56/10 = f/5.6$

$80/10 = f/16$

$120/10 = f/12$

   (but, back then, f/stops were available only in whole f/stop numbers,

   when halves of an f/stop and thirds of an f/stop were not available,

   so this ended up being an f/11)

$160/10 = f/16$

Because the larger guide number flash produced more intense light at the same distance as other flash units, it would result in being required to use a smaller aperture for a proper exposure. Because maximizing the DOF is a major priority of crime scene photographers, law enforcement agencies usually provided their crime scene investigators (CSIs) with the stronger flash units, usually either a 120 or 160 guide number (GN) flashes.

Guide numbers also varied according to the ISO of the film (yes, once upon a time, film cameras were the norm for crime scene photography) and the focal length of the lens being used. But to simplify matters, whenever guide numbers were compared, it was usually the convention that ISO 100 and a "normal" (50mm) focal length were presumed.

As the guide numbers went up, the cost of the flash increased. To ensure most CSIs could use smaller apertures in order to obtain good DOFs, most agencies seemed to use 120 or 160 GN flash units.

Don't know your flash unit's effective guide number? Because GN/distance = f/stop, then changing this equation a bit can provide us with the guide number. A modification of this equation is GN = (f/stop) (distance). Again, if using an ISO other than 100 and/or a focal length other than 50mm, the result may be different than the expected 120 or 160 GN. For instance, a flash with a GN of 120 with a 100 ISO film will have a GN of 240 with a 400 ISO film.

Manual Flash: The Right Light for the Distance

When previously determining the proper exposure for nonflash images, the main tool used was the camera's reflective light meter. At times, this light meter could be fooled, resulting in an overexposure or underexposure unless the photographer intentionally compensated for the erroneous recommendation made by the light meter and selected an exposure combination other that what was currently being recommended. The manual flash exposure mode does not suffer from these errors.

The manual flash exposure mode sends out the right light for the distance of the subject, and it does not matter whether the subject has a white tone, a medium gray tone, or a black tone. This is a significant improvement to our exposure determination choices. Why is the manual flash exposure mode immune to the mistakes made by the camera's light meter? The manual flash exposure mode does not utilize a sensor that is affected by the different amounts of reflected light coming from differently toned subjects. If the subject matter being photographed is black, the light reflected from that subject is less than the light being reflected from a gray-toned subject. And the light being reflected from a white-toned subject is greater than both the black- and gray-toned objects. The black object reflects less light and will be darker; the gray object reflects more light and will appear to be gray; the white object reflects much more light and will appear to be white. Three objects adjacent to each other—one black, one gray, and one white—will all appear to be properly exposed with one flash burst.

Whenever it is critical to properly expose an object and you don't want to make exposure adjustments, or don't remember how to make exposure adjustments, select the manual flash exposure mode. However, whenever something has a strong positive aspect, some negative aspects may lurk beneath the surface.

Problems with the Manual Flash Exposure Mode

The Manual flash exposure mode was the first flash exposure mode, so at one time it was the only option. Several aspects of the manual flash mode were perceived as negative qualities.

Flash Recycle Times

When the full manual flash was fired, it would throw out all the light it was capable of. Therefore, the flash unit would need to recharge itself before the flash could be used again. As all its power had been expended, it would have to recharge for zero to 100 percent. This process took time. If the batteries in the flash were new, the flash would be ready almost immediately. But, when the batteries became weaker and weaker from use, the recycle time of the flash unit would become longer. It might seem like crime scene photographers could spend as much time waiting for their flash units to recharge as they spent actually taking pictures. Because of the long delays that might occur, many agencies used a rule of thumb to replace the batteries in their flash units when the recycle time exceeded 30 seconds.

 ## RULE OF THUMB 4-1

If the flash recycle time exceeds 30 seconds, it is time to replace the flash batteries.

Other solutions were to use supplemental battery packs, which almost guaranteed quick flash recycling times even after several hours of photography, or to use rechargeable batteries.

Battery Replacement

Because manual flash kicked out all the light it could with each flash picture, the manual flash mode developed a reputation of "eating" batteries (consuming them at unbelievable rates). Someone in the agency had to replace them when they died, and even rechargeable batteries have fixed life spans. Having to replace them in the middle of a crime scene, or having to replace them with newly recharged batteries, took time away from the real need of capturing crime scene photographs.

Frequent F-Stop Manipulations

Because the full power of the flash was emitted with each shot and the photographer was frequently at different distances from their subject matter, the method for controlling the exposure was to alter the f/stop for the varying distances between the flash and the subject. This meant that for almost each shot, the f/stop would have to be manually changed by the photographer. Although a necessity, this was also viewed to be a negative aspect of the manual flash exposure mode. Eventually, other flash exposure modes were developed, in part to solve these three issues.

Flash Sync Speed

With nonflash photography, the selection of the shutter speed was a true exposure control, in addition to being a means to control or "freeze" motion. When using an electronic flash, the shutter speed takes on a different role. Each camera body has a designated synchronization, or "sync," shutter speed. For the flash to work properly, it must be fired when the shutter is completely open. The sync shutter speed is what the manufacturer of the camera recommends for use with all flash photography.

Having the shutter speed set to either faster-than-sync or slower-than-sync settings can have disastrous effects. If the shutter speed is set to faster-than-sync, then the shutter opens normally, and then begins to close before the flash is electronically fired, which will result in a part of the shutter actually covering a portion of the film or digital sensor when the flash fires. A portion of the image will be dark because the shutter was partially covering the sensor. Some newer cameras will not function if inadvertently set to a faster-than-sync shutter speed. Other cameras may allow faster and faster shutter speeds to be set, resulting in the shutter blades covering more and more of the digital sensor when the flash is fired.

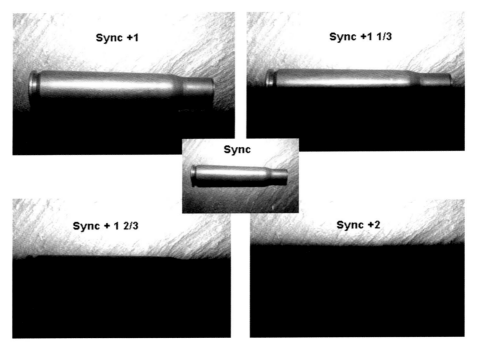

FIGURE 4-2
Faster-than-sync shutter speeds causing the shutter blades to be covering the scene *(courtesy of D. Sedig, GWU MFS student)*

If a slower-than-sync shutter speed is set, then the shutter opens, the flash is fired, and the shutter will remain open for longer than necessary. If there is any appreciable ambient lighting in the area, this may allow extra light to reach the sensor, tending to cause an overexposure. Or, under the right conditions, a "ghost" can be created.

How is a ghost created? If there is motion in the scene, the brief duration of the flash burst of light usually freezes any motion. However, if there is a relatively

FIGURE 4-3
Being able to see through someone makes them a "ghost" *(courtesy of S. Keppel, GWU MS student)*

strong light source behind the moving object/subject, something else happens. Consider a situation in which a subject in a dim room is walking in front of a window, and the exterior scene is brightly lit. When the flash goes off, the moving subject is "frozen" by the brief flash burst of light. However, if the shutter remains open after the flash has fired, and the subject is moving laterally across the window area, as the subjects moves, he or she now reveals an area of the scene outside the window that his or her body had covered when the flash went off. Because this outside area is brightly lit, it can now be partially exposed on the sensor. If the resulting image shows at the same time both the body in one position, lit by the flash, and an area outside the window, lit by outside lighting, it appears as if the body is semitransparent. One can see the body and the outside area through the body at the same time. A semitransparent body looks like a ghost.

It is not recommended to set the shutter speed at either faster-than-sync or slower-than-sync shutter speeds when using a flash. There is, however, one exception to this rule. At one time, most cameras' sync shutter speeds were 1/60 of a second. Today's newer cameras have advanced to the point that many cameras are now offering sync shutter speeds of 1/125 and 1/250 of a second. If you know your camera's sync shutter speed, then by all means use it. However, if for any reason there is the need to use a camera you are unfamiliar with, it is perfectly okay to set the camera to a 1/60 of a second shutter speed as your sync shutter speed. As most crime scene photography does not involve objects/

subjects in motion, when they are also backlit, it is better to risk a slightly slower-than-sync shutter speed than a faster-than-sync shutter speed.

Previously, it was mentioned that flash photography no longer depends on fast shutter speeds to freeze motion. This is so because the flash duration itself is very brief, and this short burst of light now freezes motion. How fast is a typical flash burst of light? Depending on the flash manufacturer, the flash duration can begin at 1/750 of a second or 1/1000 of a second. If it is relatively dark in the area where the flash is being used, this fast flash duration is equivalent to very fast shutter speeds in their motion-stopping capability.

Direct Flash

Manual flash exposure mode also presumes that the flash head is aimed directly at the subject of interest. Remember, manual flash is the right light for the distance between the flash unit and the subject being photographed. This is the shortest distance between the flash and the subject. Why is this important? The light reflected off a subject that is directly lit by the flash will be brighter than if the flash were positioned differently, and this is what the manual flash exposure mode presumes. If the flash is positioned from any other angle, the light being reflected from the subject back toward the camera will be less, which will result in an underexposure. The flash's calculator will provide the recommendation for the f/stop to be used for a particular distance between the flash and the subject *only* when the flash is aimed directly at the subject. Thus, any time one intends to use the manual flash exposure mode for angled, bounce, or oblique flash situations, some other method of determining the correct f/stop likely to produce a proper exposure will be required. Just checking the flash LED screen's f/stop recommendation will invariably lead to underexposures.

The "Normal Room"

The Manual flash exposure mode also presumes the flash is being used in a "normal" room. Flash manufacturers have done extensive research into the conditions in which their equipment will be used and have designed the flash equipment to work as anticipated when it is used under conditions in which the public most frequently uses an electronic flash. This happens to be in a normal living room. What are the characteristics of a "normal" living room? It is a room about 10 × 10 feet or 10 × 12 feet in size, typically has a ceiling about 8 to 9 feet high, and the ceiling and walls are painted white.

How does this presumption of being used in a normal room affect the image? Previously, it was mentioned that the manual flash exposure mode presumes that direct flash is being used because this method most effectively lights the primary subject. Even though the direct flash does send out most of its light directly toward the primary subject, there is still quite a bit of light that is also going up toward the ceiling and out toward the walls. Both the white ceiling and white walls will reflect some of this light back toward the primary subject. In fact, the manual flash exposure mode presumes that this additional light will reach the primary subject, and if this extra light is not reaching the primary subject, then the f/stop recommendation of the flash's LED screen will be inadequate for a proper exposure.

What does this mean? Determine the proper exposure with the manual flash exposure mode when taken in a normal room, set the camera for that f/stop, and the result is a proper exposure. Take the manual flash outside, position an object/subject at exactly the same distance away, use the same f/stop, and the result will be an underexposed image because the anticipated extra light coming from the white ceiling and white walls is no longer present.

 ## RULE OF THUMB 4-2

Manual flash mode used outside is at least one f/stop less bright than the suggestion from the flash LED screen.

And if you are using the manual flash mode in a larger-than-normal room, you must again compensate for the lack of light being reflected from closer white walls and a closer white ceiling. If the manual flash photo is taken in a smaller-than-normal room, the result tends to be an overexposure.

If the walls and ceiling are not painted white, anticipate two effects. Less reflected light will cause a tendency toward an underexposure. And if the walls and ceiling are colored, then the scene may begin to record a color tint because of the reflected light from colored surfaces.

Make exposure corrections by following these suggestions. Outside or in a larger-than-normal room, increase the exposure from what the flash LED screen recommends by +1 or more. In a smaller-than-normal room, like in a kitchen or bathroom, decrease the exposure from what the flash LED screen recommends by around −1 or more.

The Flash Head
There are several aspects of the rectangular electronic flash head that might not be completely obvious initially. These will now be explained.

On-Camera versus Off-Camera Flash
The camera body has a hot-shoe, and the electronic flash has an electrical connection on the bottom that is specifically designed to fit onto the hot-shoe. This feature does not seem to merit much discussion, right? Okay, do you

remember what the first image is that you'll capture at each new crime scene? It's the photo identifier. Whether that is a 4 × 6-inch card with the right information printed on it, or your agency uses an 8 × 10-inch version of the photo identifier, the photograph of the photo identifier will follow some basic photographic principles. Fill the frame with the photo identifier, whatever its size is, and make sure it's properly exposed.

Remember that the camera captures images of the world on a rectangular sensor. Previously, this was a film negative; now it is most frequently a digital sensor. Both of these sensors are rectangular. The electronic flash head is also rectangular, and it emits light that is shaped like a rectangle. As long as the rectangle of light from the flash gets superimposed on the same rectangle of the world that is being imaged on the digital sensor, there are no problems. It is when the rectangle of light from the flash does not get superimposed on the same rectangle of the world being imaged on the digital sensor that problems occur.

When the flash unit is mounted on the camera's hot-shoe, there will be times when the light emitted from the flash will not superimpose on the scene being imaged by the camera. This will happen every time when the camera is relatively

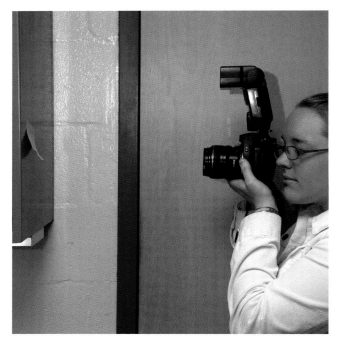

FIGURE 4-4
When you're close to the subject and the flash is on the hot-shoe, it is aimed a bit above the area being captured by the lens *(courtesy of T. Nelson, GWU MFS student)*

close to the subject being photographed. In these situations, the flash will be aimed a bit higher than the area being viewed by the camera's lens. See Figure 4-4. The result will be that the top of the image will be well lit, but there will be a noticeable area at the bottom of the image that is not receiving adequate lighting, and this area will appear to be underexposed. See Figures 4-5A and 4-5B.

FIGURE 4-5A
When the flash is close and aimed high, the lower part of the scene is underexposed *(courtesy of S. Keppel, GWU MS student)*

FIGURE 4-5B
An even exposure when the flash is 6 feet away *(courtesy of S. Keppel, GWU MS student)*

 ## RULE OF THUMB 4-3

When you're 5 feet or closer to your subject matter, remove the flash from the camera's hot-shoe so that it can more properly be aimed at the target.

Flash manufacturers are aware of this issue, and many of them have designed a feature into their flash units to try to compensate for this problem. In addition to the flash head being able to be raised at different angles until the flash head is aimed directly overhead, some flash units can also be aimed down one notch while the flash is mounted on the camera's hot-shoe. See Figures 4-6A and 4-6B. This feature is designed to help the light from the flash superimpose over the same area being imaged by the camera. But at a very close distance, even this flash head position will not adequately cover the same area being imaged by the camera.

Because our very first image is affected by this problem, many photographers have chosen to avoid the issue altogether by mounting their flash units onto a remote flash cord and then connecting the other end of the remote flash cord to the camera's hot-shoe. In this way, the photographer has the ability to aim the flash head at the area of interest rather than hope that the flash mounted directly on the hot-shoe is aimed in the right direction.

Once the flash is mounted on the remote flash cord, many photographers find that subsequently removing the flash from the remote flash cord to put it on the hot-shoe and going back and forth from the hot-shoe to the remote flash cord is just too bothersome. Just leave the flash on the remote flash cord for every photo.

FIGURE 4-6A
The flash with the normal flash angle *(courtesy of S. Keppel, GWU MS student)*

FIGURE 4-6B

The flash head tilted down one notch *(courtesy of S. Keppel, GWU MS student)*

FIGURE 4-7

The flash connected by a remote flash cord *(courtesy of S. Keppel, GWU MS student)*

Red-Eye

One issue related to the flash head being close to the lens is red-eye. If the flash head is positioned close to the lens when capturing images of people, the result is frequently red-eye. This visual effect is caused by the light from the flash going directly into the eyes, bouncing off the blood vessels at the back of the inside of the eye, and being reflected directly back to the camera. The cure for red-eye is to remove the flash from the general vicinity of the camera's lens by mounting the flash on the remote flash cord and holding the flash unit away from the camera. This is also one of the persistent problems associated with using the camera's built-in flash.

Built-in Flash Units

Many cameras today feature built-in flash units. See Figure 4-9. Press a button and they pop up, ready for use. These built-in flash units should not be used as the primary flash for most images for several reasons. In the first place, as mentioned earlier, they usually produce red-eye.

Second, they are relatively weak flash units, typically with a guide number of 35. This means that at a distance of 10 feet they require an f/3.5 for a proper exposure. With such a wide aperture, you would expect the DOF to be minimal, and that kind of DOF is not recommended by this text.

Another problem with the built-in flash is that direct flash is frequently not an attractive light. Often it produces an objectionable glare. For these reasons, most crime scene photographers do not use the built-in flash at all.

FIGURE 4-8A

With the flash near the lens, red-eye is frequently the result when photographing people *(courtesy of Jenna Stanners)*

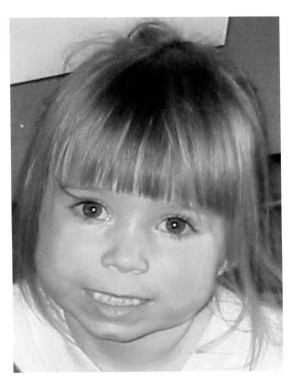

FIGURE 4-8B
Remove the flash head from close proximity of the lens and red-eye is eliminated *(courtesy of Jenna Stanners)*

FIGURE 4-9
A pop-up flash *(courtesy of S. Keppel, GWU MS student)*

Flash Head Never Closer than 2 Feet to the Subject

The idea of always having the flash unit mounted on the remote flash cord is reinforced by the idea that most flash units are not intended to ever be used when closer than about 2 feet to the subject. All electronic flash units will state in their manuals the closest distance they should be to the subject. As this varies a bit with different flash manufacturers, this book simplifies these variations and just calls this distance 2 feet.

Because every item of evidence will have a sequence of multiple close-up photos captured and many of these will require the camera to be relatively close to the evidence in order to fill the frame with the object, having the flash unit on a remote flash cord helps to properly light the subject without getting the flash unit closer than 2 feet to the subject. In order to maintain the minimum 2-foot distance, it is often recommended that when taking close-up photographs of evidence, the flash should be held with the elbow locked straight. If that is done, the flash cannot ever get closer than the distance of the photographer's arm.

FIGURE 4-10A
The Canon Macro Ring Lite MR-14EX *(courtesy of Canon, USA)*

FIGURE 4-10B
The Nikon R1C1 Close-up Speedlight *(courtesy of R. Taniwaki, Nikon Forensic Services)*

Of course, there are always exceptions to every rule. There are specialty flash units made for very close photography. There are currently two variations of these flash units designed for close-up photography. See Figures 4-10A and 4-10B. Canon makes a Macro Ring Light and Nikon makes its R1C1 Close-up Speedlight. Both units can have either side of the flash set at different intensity increments if desired, and the Nikon R1C1 can change the angles of each flash head—and each flash head can swivel around the ring encircling the lens too.

Flash Head and Camera Orientation

There will be times when the photographer chooses to use a vertical camera composition for a particular image. In these circumstances, it is imperative that the flash head also be held vertically. It is essential for both the camera

FIGURE 4-11A
Camera held vertical; flash held horizontal *(courtesy of S. Keppel, GWU MS student)*

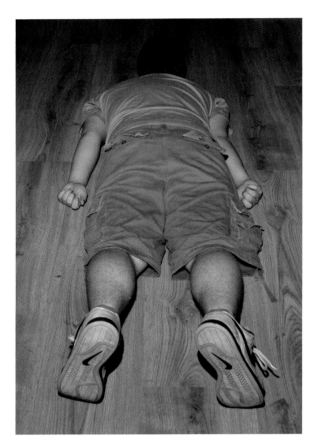

FIGURE 4-11B
Both camera and flash head held vertical *(courtesy of S. Keppel, GWU MS student)*

body and the flash head to be held horizontally or both the camera body and the flash head to be held vertically. If this is not done, the light emitted by the flash head will not properly light the scene being viewed through the view-finder or captured by the sensor. The two different rectangles always need to be aligned.

Flash Head and Focal Length Variations
The remote flash cord does more than just electronically fire the flash when the camera's shutter button is depressed. Most remote flash cords also share information about the camera's settings. The flash unit will "know" which ISO has been selected on the camera body, which f/stop has been selected, and which focal length lens has been selected. This latter exchange of information is

important if the flash head is to properly emit light over the same scene being viewed by the camera. For example, one can take a series of three images at different focal lengths, and if the flash head does not adjust to these changes, the lighting will not properly cover the different scenes being imaged. When the lens is set at a normal focal length, the flash head must emit light that will cover this area. If a zoom lens is changed to a wide angle setting, then the flash head must also adjust to throw light for the wider scene being imaged. If the lens is then changed to an 80mm setting, the flash head must again adjust its flash width to correspond to the camera's 80mm field of view.

With the flash on a remote flash cord, try changing the focal lengths on a zoom lens, then push the shutter button halfway, and you should notice that the flash head makes an adjustment for each new focal length.

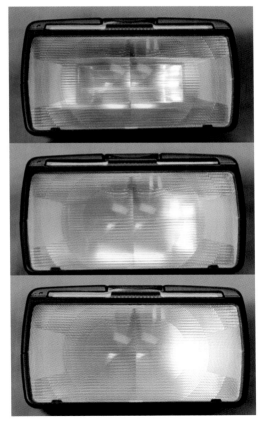

FIGURE 4-12
Internal flash head adjustments for different focal lengths

Many flash units will also offer the photographer the option to override these automatic flash focal length adjustments. The flash head can be set to manual focal lengths. In these cases, the photographer can creatively select a flash head focal length that does not correspond to the actual focal length of the lens being used. These uses of the flash do not usually apply to normal crime scene photography.

What does need to be understood, however, is that when the flash head is throwing light wider than a "normal" lens needs, the trade-off is that the light will not be quite as bright directly in front of the flash. If the full manual flash kicks out all the light it is capable of when it goes off, and it is forced to spread part of this light wider, this light has to come from somewhere. It will be dimmer straight ahead. Of course, the LED screen on the flash head, indicating the distance the light can be used for any particular f/stop selection, will make the necessary distance modifications necessary.

If a telephoto lens is selected, the flash head will adjust the width of the flash throw, which will in turn affect the intensity of the light going straight out. The light will be more intense directly in front of the camera.

Bracketing in the Manual Flash Mode

With nonflash photography, there were occasions when bracketing was necessary. Therefore, there also has to be some way for photographers using Manual flash mode to also bracket their shots.

+1 Brackets

What are the options for bracketing with a +1 when using the manual flash mode?

One option is to consider switching to a faster ISO setting. When using a digital camera, it should always be remembered that changing the ISO speed is an option. It wasn't with film, but it is an option now with a digital camera. This approach does have its limits, however. Many agencies feel that using ISOs of 50, 100, 200, and 400 can be done at any time when used as exposure controls. There are two issues to consider at all times, though. First, if a particular image is being captured as an examination-quality photograph, one should lean toward the slower ISOs of 100 and 50. Both of these choices will allow enlargements with greater detail. Second, each camera will have limits on its ability to produce high-quality images at different fast ISOs of 800, 1600, and 3200. Each time you are issued a new camera, it is wise to capture an image of the same item at each of these ISO settings, balancing the other exposure variables to arrive a proper exposure. Then, enlarge each image to an 8 × 10-inch image. Critically examine each one to see where there is an obvious loss of quality. You'll know ahead of time your camera's limit when it comes to deciding whether you truly have the option of bumping the ISO up from 400 to 800, or from 800 to 1600 to achieve a +1 bracket.

Is switching to a slower shutter speed an option for a +1 bracket? Not with flash photography. Remember that with flash photography, the shutter speed selected should be either the known synchronization (sync) shutter speed of your particular camera or 1/60 of a second as the default sync shutter speed when using a camera you are unfamiliar with.

How about switching to a wider f/stop to get a +1 bracket? This is probably the choice most often made by most crime scene photographers. But, again, there should be a limit. Changing from an f/22 to an f/16 should always be an option for a +1 bracket, as should be changing from an f/16 to an f/11 and changing from an f/11 to an f/8. Remember, f/stops are both exposure controls and DOF controls, so although there is an exact +1 exposure achieved with each of these changes, there is also a progressive narrowing of the DOF range. Therefore, if you're currently using an f/8 and you want a +1 bracket, before changing to an f/5.6—which begins to significantly shorten the DOF range—consider the other options you might have. If the image about to be bracketed is on a flat plane, where DOF is unimportant, then the option of using an f/5.6 does not appear to be a bad choice. But if DOF is critical, consider another option.

What options are there if the current photo was captured with ISO 400 (and your camera suffers noticeably when ISO 800 is selected), sync shutter speed, and an f/8, where there is texture or depth in the subject requiring a concern for DOF? How can you create a +1?

This chapter will shortly discuss the Inverse Square Law, which basically states that as light goes farther, its intensity diminishes. Conversely, if the distance between the flash and the subject decreases, the light will be brighter. Is there a way to determine the exact distance change required for the result to precisely be +1? Yes. And the way will soon be discussed.

−1 Brackets

After first capturing an image that was properly exposed, and following that with a +1 bracket, now it is necessary to capture a −1 bracket. What are your options?

It may be possible to use a "slower" ISO setting. Change from ISO 400 to ISO 200 or from ISO 200 to ISO 100. Many cameras have an ISO 50 as an option, but that choice may be found only in your camera's menu options. It may not be readily obvious that an ISO 50 is an option. Check your camera's manual for specifics.

Again, changing to a faster shutter speed than sync is not possible on some cameras and is not recommended for those who can do it. Doing so causes the shutter blades to begin closing when the flash fires, and the shutter blades will then block the light from reaching the sensor in areas of the crime scene.

Frequently, photographers create a −1 bracket by closing the aperture (using a smaller f/stop). That means changing from an f/8 to an f/11 or from an f/11 to an f/16 or from an f/16 to an f/22. Smaller apertures mean better DOF, and SWGIT recommends smaller apertures for examination-quality photographs.

As is discussed shortly, the Inverse Square Law tells us that if we move the flash farther from the subject, the light will be dimmer when it gets there. And it is possible to precisely determine what the change of distance needs to be for a −1 bracket.

The Inverse Square Law (ISL)

The Inverse Square Law is one of the foundations for manual flash. It is also the explanation for the derivation of the f/stop numbering sequence. Just where did this sequence come from? The sequence is: 1, 1.4, 2, 2.8, 4, 5.6, 8, 11, 16, and 22.

Now it is finally the time to explain these numbers! Even though they don't look like it, changing from one of these numbers to its adjacent number either halves or doubles the exposure. That is why changing from f/16 to f/22 results in a −1 exposure and changing from f/11 to f/8 results in a +1 exposure.

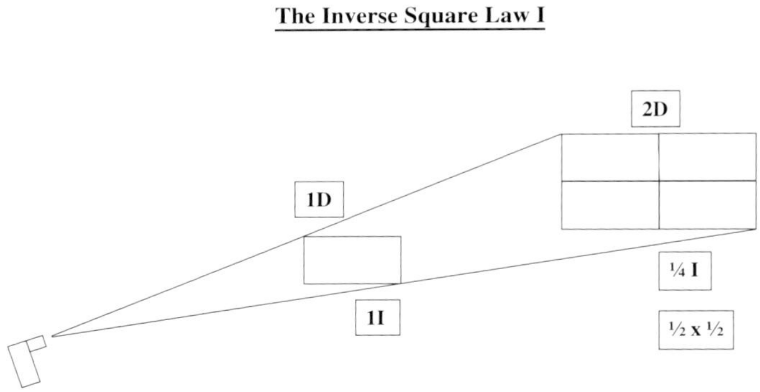

The Inverse Square Law I

The **Inverse Square Law** shows the relationship between the **Distance** light travels and the **Intensity** of the light at different distances. As the **Distance** light travels is doubled, its **Intensity** is quartered. The light at 2D covers four times the area as at 1D, therefore the light is ¼ as bright at any single point. To determine this, take the distance change, 2, and invert it (make it a fraction). 2 becomes ½. Square that (½ x ½), and the result is the **Intensity** of the light (¼ I) at that new **Distance** (2D). The **Intensity** of light at any **Distance** change can be expressed by this equation: $\mathbf{I = 1/ D^2}$.

FIGURE 4-13
The Inverse Square Law

Perhaps the most frequent statement derived from the Inverse Square Law is this:

Double the distance, quarter the light.

The Inverse Square Law is a mathematical relationship between the changes of distance light can travel and the intensity of the light at those different distances. When light travels away from its source, as the distance it travels is doubled, its intensity is quartered.

We need to work with some specific numbers to make sense of this. For the sake of discussion, although this will work with any distance, let's begin with a situation in which the flash is exactly 10 feet from some object being photographed. If the flash were set so that it would properly expose the object 10 feet away, what would happen to the flash's intensity if we now took a flash image of an object 20 feet away without changing anything on the camera or flash unit? Well, the Inverse Square Law gives us the answer: the object 20 feet away would receive one-quarter the light as the object 10 feet away. And because exposure stops are in increments of halves and doubles, we now know that an object lit with 1/4 the light (1/2 × 1/2) will be two stops underexposed.

How do we prove that fact using the Inverse Square Law? How do we prove that doubling the distance quarters the light? The Inverse Square Law begins by noticing the distance change; in this case, changing from 10 feet to 20 feet is like moving from $1D$ to $2D$, where D = 10 feet. The distance change is 2, or a doubling of the distance. Next, invert the distance change. Basically, that means to switch the numerator with the denominator of a fraction. The number "2" made into a fraction is 2/1. Switching the numerator and denominator results in 1/2. Now we square that number: 1/2 × 1/2 = 1/4. Because the Inverse Square Law shows a relationship between distance changes and the intensity of the light at those distance changes, we can now feel confident that when the distance change doubles, the intensity of the light at the new distance is quartered.

If we know the distance change, it is easy to determine the new intensity of the light. But what if we know just the intensity change and need to determine the distance change? How would one "undo" an Inverse Square? Let's look at an example for which we already know the answer: if we knew the intensity change was 1/4, how could we determine the distance change if we didn't already know that answer was 2? The answer is to find the Inverse Square Root of the intensity change. Invert 1/4 and the answer is 4/1 or just 4. The square root (a number multiplied by itself) of 4 is 2.

We are now just a couple of steps away from determining the entire f/stop sequence. It just isn't obvious yet.

It might be reasonable to ask that if at 1*D* (distance) the intensity of the light were 1I, and at 2*D* the intensity of the light was 1/4*I* or (1/2 × 1/2)*I* (where *I* is intensity), then at what *D* would the intensity of the light be just 1/2*I*? See Figure 4-14. The answer is not as simple as it sounds. Most readers want to jump up and shout that they already know the distance halfway between 10 feet and 20 feet and that it is 15 feet or 1.5*D*. But they are wrong! Let's do the math.

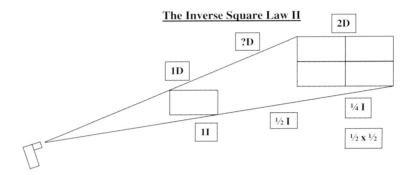

If the light at 2D is 1/4th as bright, we now realize this is a 2/stop diminishing of the light. Each 1/stop decrease of the light is half the light of the original. A 2/stop diminishment of the light is ½ x ½, or ¼ of the light. The question now is "At what **Distance** would there only be a 1/stop decrease of the light: ½ the light?" If, for example, 1D is 10 feet from the flash, and 2D is 20 feet from the flash, at what **Distance** would the light be just ½ the **Intensity** as at 10 feet? We want to say 15 feet, don't we? But is this correct?

This is how to determine the **Distance** when the **Intensity** of the light is known. Assume we knew the **Intensity** was ¼th as bright at a certain point, and we needed to determine the **Distance** that corresponded. Pretend we don't already know the answer: 2D. Beginning with the **Intensity** change, ¼, invert it (make it a fraction). The result is 4/1 or 4. Take the square root of 4, and that is the distance change, or 2. The **Distance** change would be 2D, but we already knew that. Well, if this works with an answer we know, it will also work when we don't know the answer. So, consider ½ I. Invert the ½ and that is 2/1 or 2. Take the square root of 2, and that will be the new **Distance**. **D = √1/ I**. In this case, it will be 1.4 D, or 14 feet. The progression from 1D to 1.4D to 2D is a curious one, to be sure!

FIGURE 4-14
When the intensity is 1/2*I*, what is the *D*?

We are being asked to determine the inverse square root of 1/2. The inverse of 1/2 is 2/1 or 2. Find a calculator, and punch in the square root of 2, and you will notice it is 1.414 (for the sake of convenience, this figure is most often written as just 1.4).

Notice now that we have a sequence of 1*D*, 1.4*D*, and 2*D*. These can be explained in some ways you are already familiar with. Changing from 1.4*D* to 2D would result in the light's intensity being 1 stop underexposed (where the light is just half as bright). Changing from 1.4D to 1D would result in the light's intensity being precisely 1 stop overexposed (where the light is doubled).

One more example and all will be clear, if it isn't already. We now know the distance change when the light is 1/2I, and when the light is (1/2 × 1/2)I. Let's now determine at what distance change the light is (1/2 × 1/2 × 1/2)I or 1/8I. The inverse of 1/8 is 8/1 or 8, and the square root of 8 is 2.828 (for the sake of convenience, this is most frequently written as just 2.8).

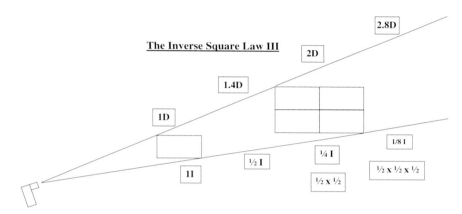

Now, lets ask ourselves at what **Distance** would the **Intensity** of the light be 3/stops less bright or 1/8th as bright? Take the inverse of 1/8 and that is 8/1 or 8. Determine the square root of 8, and that is 2.8. So, at 2.8D, or 28 feet, the **Intensity** of the light would be just 1/8th as bright. Does the sequence 1D, 1.4D, 2D and 2.8D look familiar? It should. Maybe one more example will make it more apparent.

FIGURE 4-15
When the intensity is 1/8I, what is the D?

Our new distance continuum is 1D, 1.4D, 2D, and 2.8D! Surely those numbers ring a bell. Look back to the Reciprocal Exposures in Figure 2-45. We now know the derivation of the f/stop numbers. The f/stop numbers can be thought of as precise distances at which light will be either one stop brighter (twice as bright) or one stop dimmer (half as bright).

Look at is another way. If one is standing 11 feet away from a subject, with the manual flash mode being used, and the current camera and flash settings result in a proper exposure, how can +1 and −1 brackets be captured without changing any camera or flash controls? This can now be done by simply moving to 8 feet (+1) and then to 16 feet (−1).

Halve the Distance, Quadruple the Light

Just as the Inverse Square Law (ISL) can explain the diminishing intensity of light from a flash unit as it has to travel farther, now we need to examine the situations in which the flash is moved closer to the subject, or precisely how much the intensity of the light is increased because the flash is getting closer.

The Inverse Square Law IV

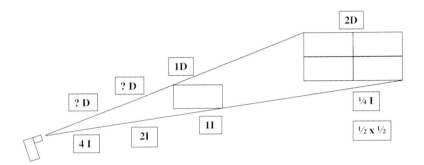

Now, rather than having the **Intensity** of the light diminishing, let's look at two examples of the light becoming brighter than the beginning point. At what **Distance** would the light be twice as bright as at 10 feet? Or, at what distance would the light be exactly 1/stop brighter? Find the inverse of 2, which is ½, or .50. Find the square root of .50, and that is 0.7. 0.7D is 7 feet.

At what **Distance** would the light be four times as bright as at 10 feet? Or, at what distance would the light be exactly 2/stops brighter? Find the inverse of 4, which is ¼, or .25. Find the square root of .25, and that is 0.5. 0.5D is 5 feet.

Notice one other thing. Doubling the original **Distance** quarters the light **Intensity**. Halving the original **Distance** quadruples the light **Intensity**.

FIGURE 4-16
The ISL (Inverse Square Law) as the flash distance gets closer

Consider any beginning distance, when the distance is $1D$ and the Intensity is $1I$. At what distance would the intensity of the flash be doubled, or $2I$? To find that distance, find the inverse square root of the intensity change. The intensity change is 2, or 2/1. The inverse of 2/1 is 1/2. What is the square root of 1/2? For most, thinking of 1/2 as a decimal will make it easier to determine the square root. The decimal equivalent of 1/2 is 0.50. What is the square root of 0.50? What number multiplied by itself results in 0.50? Even without a calculator, many of us will remember that $7 \times 7 = 49$. To be precise, the square root of 50 is 7.07. This number is usually rounded off to just being 7, so $0.7 \times 0.7 = 0.50$. The new distance is $0.7D$, and as we started at 10 feet from the subject, $0.7 \times 10 = 7$ feet.

It is interesting to notice that the f/stop numbers seem to progress in increments of 1.4 (really, 1.414): $1 \times 1.414 = 1.414$. **(1.4)**; $1.414 \times 1.414 = 1.99$ **(2)**; $2 \times 1.414 = 2.828$. **(2.8)**; $2.828 \times 1.414 = 3.99$ **(4)**; $4 \times 1.414 = 5.656$ **(5.6)**; and so on. We can see that as the intensity of light progressively increases by precisely one stop, the distance change is half of 1.414 or 0.707. This means that if you were presented with any f/stop number and did not know any of the other f/stops numbers, you could derive them all by either multiplying the original f/stop number by either 0.707 or 1.414 and then continuing to do that to each number obtained.

Next, ask yourself at what distance would the intensity of the flash be quadrupled, or $4I$? The answer is the inverse square root of 4, or 4/1. The inverse of 4/1 is 1/4, or 0.25. The square root of 0.25 is 0.5. A distance of $0.5D$ results in a light intensity that is quadrupled or 2×2. Each doubling of the light is a one-stop exposure change. If we began at 10 feet, then $0.5D$ is 5 feet, where the light is two stops brighter (2×2) than at 10 feet.

+1 and −1 Manual Flash Mode Revisited

It was previously stated that when set to full manual flash, all the light the flash is capable of is emitted when the shutter button is depressed. Can you have more than "all"? The Inverse Square Law states that as the flash is moved closer to the subject, its intensity gets brighter. Using the f/stop numbers as a guide, you now know that moving the full manual flash from 22 feet to 16 feet, 16 feet to 11 feet, 11 feet to 8 feet, 8 feet to 5.6 feet, 5.6 feet to 4 feet, 4 feet to 2.8 feet, and 2.8 feet to 2 feet all result in a +1 exposure. In like manner, moving the full manual flash from 2 feet to 2.8 feet, 2.8 feet to 4 feet, 4 feet to 5.6 feet, 5.6 feet to 8 feet, 8 feet to 11 feet, 11 feet to 16 feet, and 16 feet to 22 feet all result in a −1 exposure.

In Manual flash mode, there is another way to arrive at incremental flash intensities. The manual flash intensity can be reduced in one-stop increments by setting the flash head to 1/2 power, 1/4 power, 1/8 power, and so on. Many flash units can have their intensities reduced all the way to 1/128 power. As the manual flash intensity is incrementally reduced, the flash will also indicate the new distance that is appropriate for that new reduced intensity. See Figures 4-17A through 4-17F.

With this particular flash unit set to full manual flash, an f/22 will be the right light when you are 13 feet from your subject. (Because your flash guide number may vary, this distance may be different with your particular flash.)

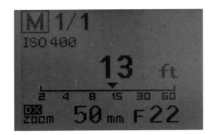

FIGURE 4-17A
Full manual flash provides light for a distance of 13 feet with an f/22 *(courtesy of M. Halter, GWU MS student)*

So 13 feet may be okay for a midrange image, but if you then want to capture some close-up shots of the item of evidence, you cannot do that from 13 feet away. So you begin reducing the flash intensity increments until you are close enough to fill the frame with the evidence. Figures 4-17B through 4-17F show the amount of flash intensity reduction necessary to get the flash unit to a 2.2-foot distance to the evidence. Manual flash mode set to 1/32 power will be required. This means that the flash head must be at 2.2 feet. The camera can be held closer to the evidence, but the flash head on a remote flash cord must be held 2.2 feet from the evidence with the arm held straight and the elbow locked (unless you are using a ring light flash or the R1C1 Close-up Speedlight).

After several close-ups (as is, with a fully labeled scale, with a partial scale), it is time for brackets. When beginning at 1/32 power, the +1 can be done by changing the flash intensity to 1/16 power, and the −1 can be done by changing the flash intensity to 1/64 power.

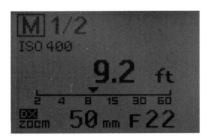

FIGURE 4-17B
Manual flash provides light for a distance of 9.2 feet with 1/2 power *(courtesy of M. Halter, GWU MS student)*

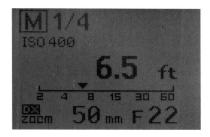

FIGURE 4-17C

Manual flash provides light for a distance of 6.5 feet with 1/4 power *(courtesy of M. Halter, GWU MS student)*

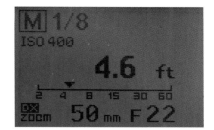

FIGURE 4-17D

Manual flash provides light for a distance of 4.6 feet with 1/8 power *(courtesy of M. Halter, GWU MS student)*

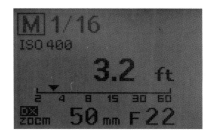

FIGURE 4-17E

Manual flash provides light for a distance of 3.2 feet with 1/16 power *(courtesy of M. Halter, GWU MS student)*

FIGURE 4-17F

Manual flash provides light for a distance of 2.2 feet with 1/32 power *(courtesy of M. Halter, GWU MS student)*

AUTOMATIC AND DEDICATED/TTL FLASH EXPOSURE MODES

Because manual flash has three perceived negative aspects, attempts were made to develop alternate flash exposure systems that provide improvements. The improvements should:

■ Provide quicker flash recycle times.
■ Reduce the need to replace batteries as often as the manual flash mode.
■ Reduce the number of manual f/stops adjustments necessary for proper exposures.

The first advancement was the Automatic flash exposure mode.

Automatic Flash Exposure Mode

With the Automatic flash mode, the flash now has a light sensor built onto the front of the flash unit, often referred to as the **flash sensor eye**. See Figure 4-18. This sensor records the reflected light from the subject being photographed, and when the right amount of light (18%) has been received, the sensor eye cuts the flash off. The automatic flash unit can never emit more light than the manual flash mode, but it can significantly reduce the amount of light the flash has to emit to properly expose certain objects that are closer to the flash.

This is the first aspect of the Automatic flash mode that differs from the Manual flash mode. Rather than one f/stop being proper for an object which is one distance from the flash, the automatic flash unit provides a range of distances within which any f/stop will work properly.

For example, consider an example in which the manual flash properly exposes an object with an f/22 when 13 feet from the object. At any other distance, closer or further, the manual flash would require an f/stop adjustment of one sort or another to maintain a proper exposure. The Automatic flash mode

FIGURE 4-18
Auto flash sensor eye *(courtesy of S. Keppel, GWU MS student)*

typically provides a flash range of 2 feet to 13 feet with an f/22. This means that at 13 feet from a subject, using either the Manual flash mode or the Automatic flash mode would produce the exact same outcome: the full power of the flash would go off, and the subject would be properly exposed.

The difference is apparent when the photographer moves closer to the subject. As long as the photographer stays in the auto flash range, indicated on the flash LED screen, the auto flash mode can continue to be used with the same f/22. That is convenient! No need to make incremental flash intensity adjustments as long as the photographer remains 2 feet to 13 feet from the subject.

Is there any other benefit from using the Automatic flash mode? Yes! As the photographer moves closer and closer to the subject, the increased reflections from the subject are noticed by the sensor eye, and the intensity of the flash being emitted is automatically reduced more and more. For example, when the photographer moves from 13 feet to 9.2 feet, the reflection from the subject is doubled, and the flash intensity is reduced by one stop to compensate for this distance change. As the photographer moves from 9.2 feet to 6.5 feet, the reflection from the subject doubles again, resulting in the intensity of the flash unit being reduced by another stop. The photographer can move anywhere between 2 feet and 13 feet and continue to use the same f/22, and the Automatic flash mode will provide proper exposures by automatically reducing the flash intensity.

In Manual flash mode, the intensity of the flash unit could be reduced by manually changing the full flash intensity to 1/2 power, 1/4 power, and so on. In Automatic flash mode, the intensity of the flash output is reduced automatically. When less than the full power of the flash is required for a proper exposure, the auto flash mode conserves the unused flash energy to make the flash recycle time shorter. The manual flash mode would discharge all of its energy with each flash, changing from having 100 percent of its power to 0 percent of its power, thereby requiring a full flash recharge. Depending on the distance from flash to subject, the auto flash would retain 20, 40, 60 percent, or more of its unused power, making the flash recycle time much shorter and more efficient. This is the auto flash unit's second benefit over the manual flash mode.

Obviously, if the batteries are not required to fully charge the flash unit each time the shutter button is depressed, the batteries will also last longer. This is the third benefit of the Automatic flash mode over the manual flash mode. These benefits have made the Automatic flash mode preferable to many photographers.

Does this flash mode have any negative aspects? There are two issues regarding the Automatic flash mode that must be understood whenever it is used, but they might not be considered to be actual negatives.

First, because the sensor eye on the front of the flash is reading the reflected light returning from the subject in order to provide the correct amount of light for a proper exposure, it can be fooled into providing the wrong amount of light when the subject is either excessively light toned or dark toned. Therefore, the auto flash sensor eye will have the same exposure errors that the camera's light meter had with nonflash photography. In these situations, light-toned subjects will tend to be underexposed and will require a manual exposure correction, and dark-toned subjects will tend to be overexposed and will also require a manual exposure correction. Just as the camera body has an exposure compensation button/dial for manually altering exposures in the nonflash automatic exposure modes, the flash unit also has an exposure compensation button/dial for manually altering the flash exposure when in either the Automatic flash exposure mode or when in the dedicated flash exposure mode. If intentionally doing this has become a habit to the experienced photographer when taking nonflash shots, applying the same exposure compensation corrections to Automatic flash mode shots should be no major issue.

Second, it is the auto flash sensor's job to ensure that the digital sensor in the camera body receives the proper amount of light. Therefore, the auto flash sensor eye can do this successfully only when it is receiving reflected light from the subject that is very similar to the reflected light entering the camera body through the lens. For this to happen, the auto flash sensor eye needs to be relatively close to the camera lens. The flash head can still be removed from the hot-shoe and put on a remote flash cord, but the farther the flash head is removed from the camera, the less effective it will be in determining the correct lighting needed by the digital sensor in the camera body.

In particular, this means that the Automatic flash exposure mode should not be used for oblique flash photography. In such situations, the flash is emitting light that is low and oblique to the subject, and the camera's sensor is parallel to and above the subject. This makes it impossible for the sensor on the front of the flash to properly determine the amount of light needed by the digital sensor in the camera. Although auto flash is a distinct improvement over manual flash, there is still room for improvement.

Dedicated/TTL Exposure Flash

The most sophisticated flash system is a dedicated flash system. In this case, the camera body and the flash unit are designed to work together and share information. When connected by the camera's hot-shoe or by a remote flash cord, the flash will know the exposure settings selected on the camera: the ISO, the shutter speed, and the f/stop. The flash will also know the focal length currently selected. But, perhaps most important, the light meter in the camera body determines the duration of the flash based on the reflected light from the scene coming into the camera through the lens (TTL). Where best to meter the light affecting the exposure of the digital sensor? The camera body exposure meter is in the perfect position for doing this important job. Many crime scene photographers prefer the Dedicated Flash Mode for this reason.

The dedicated flash mode also indicates the flash ranges, as the auto flash mode did. See Figures 4-19A through 4-19D. There will be different flash ranges displayed for each f/stop. Wider f/stops will enable the flash to light a more distant subject; smaller f/stops will have a shorter flash range. It is important to not misinterpret the flash range indicated on the flash LED screen. This is *not* an indication that everything in the displayed flash range will be properly exposed by the flash. The flash range indicated means that a single primary subject can be anywhere in that flash range and it will receive the proper amount of light to be properly exposed. This concept is very important to understand.

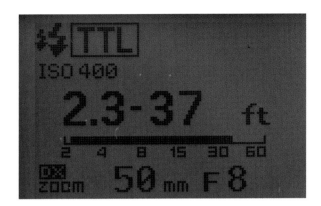

FIGURE 4-19A
TTL flash with an f/8 will light a subject from 2.3 feet to 37 feet *(courtesy of M. Halter, GWU MS student)*

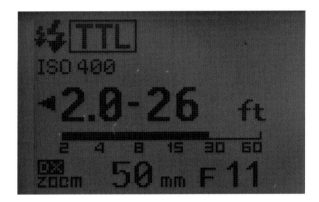

FIGURE 4-19B
TTL flash with an f/11 will light a subject from 2 feet to 26 feet *(courtesy of M. Halter, GWU MS student)*

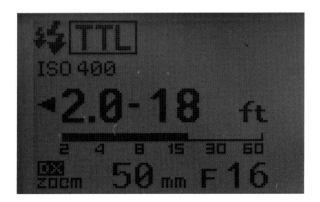

FIGURE 4-19C
TTL flash with an f/16 will light a subject from 2 feet to 18 feet *(courtesy of M. Halter, GWU MS student)*

FIGURE 4-19D
TTL flash with an f/22 will light a subject from 2 feet to 13 feet *(courtesy of M. Halter, GWU MS student)*

An example might help. If a subject is 20 feet from the photographer and the photographer wants to use the dedicated flash mode, both an f/8 and an f/11 have flash ranges that include the 20-foot distance. However, because the f/11 will provide a better DOF because it is a smaller aperture, the photographer selects it. The flash will emit its light, which will reflect off the subject 20 feet away, and the reflected light will come through the lens (TTL) and be weighed by the exposure meter in the camera body. When the exposure meter detects 18 percent light being reflected, it will shut the flash off early. The subject will be properly exposed.

However, if there is a tree trunk 16 feet from the camera in the field of view, in addition to the subject 20 feet away, how will the dedicated flash deal with this? (The auto flash mode would react the same way.) In this case, the exposure meter in the camera body might shut the flash off earlier based on the reflected light coming from the tree trunk, and the subject will be underexposed. Both the tree trunk and the subject will not be properly exposed. How can you ensure that the subject 20 feet away is properly exposed? Set the flash to the manual exposure mode that is proper for 20 feet. In this case, the tree trunk will be a bit overexposed.

Like the Automatic flash mode, dedicated flash units also rely on reflected light from the scene to determine the flash output. This means that light- and dark-toned objects or scenes will tend to cause underexposures and overexposures, respectively. Therefore, the photographer will have to make the same compensations mentioned previously. But the majority of images do not require these compensations, so the dedicated flash exposure mode is the overall preference if it is available.

Nikon makes dedicated flash units for its cameras, and Canon makes dedicated flash units for its cameras. Most camera manufacturers do this. However, there are flash manufacturers that make dedicated flash units to work with a variety of camera bodies. Although these are usually less expensive than the dedicated flash units made by the camera manufacturer, many photographers seem to have more confidence when the camera body and the flash unit are made by the same manufacturer.

FILL-IN FLASH

Recall that fill-in flash was previously recommended when there are wide extremes of light at a scene or when part of the scene is backlit. In each case, part of the scene is brightly lit and part of the scene is in the shade. If it is necessary to have both well-lit and dark areas in the same image, then fill-in flash is the solution. If it is possible to compose on just the brightly lit area or on just the shady area, it is relatively easy to expose for either area, and they will both appear to be properly exposed. But if both lighting extremes must be in the same composition, then the digital sensor is incapable of providing a proper exposure for both areas at the same time.

The solution is **fill-in flash**. I recommend Manual flash mode when doing fill-in flash, because that gives you complete control of the lighting. Your first step is to take a meter reading of the bright part of the scene while it is filling the frame. Do not meter the scene while it has both bright and dim areas in view. Position the camera so that the bright part of the scene is totally filling the frame. Take the meter reading, and then set the camera for this exposure. If you were to take the photo at this point, the bright part of the scene would be properly exposed, and the shady areas of the scene would be grossly under-exposed. But this is just the first step of the fill-in flash technique.

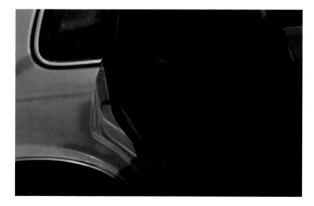

FIGURE 4-20A
Metered for the sunny part of the scene, the car is properly exposed, but not the shady area *(courtesy of S. Keppel, GWU MS student)*

FIGURE 4-20B
Metered for the shady part of the scene, the shade is properly exposed, but not the sunny area *(courtesy of S. Keppel, GWU MS student)*

Because part of the scene is very bright, the correct ISO is 100. You have probably also selected a shutter speed of 1/60. The camera's meter, then, probably suggested an f/stop of f/16 or f/22, or something very close to that, because fill-in flash most frequently is called for on bright sunny days.

Normally, when taking flash photographs, we determine the flash setting for the distance we are from the subject, and this leads to our f/stop selection. However, with fill-in flash, we already have the f/stop selected based on the meter reading of the bright part of the scene. Now, knowing the f/stop to properly expose the bright part of the scene, we take that f/stop and check the back of our flash unit's LED screen to determine the necessary distance for that f/stop. Remember, we cannot change the ISO, the shutter speed, or the f/stop, because if we do, we'll alter the exposure for the bright part of the scene. The only thing left for us to do is adjust the flash so that it is appropriate for the f/stop we already know.

But if the flash is set to be proper for the distance, that is the definition for full manual flash. In this case we want to do fill-in flash, not full flash. What is the difference?

At this point, we borrow a trick used by professional portrait photographers. They will typically use multiple light sources positioned around the subject to be photographed. But in the simplest case, there is always a key light and a fill light. The **key light** is the primary light, and it is usually high and aimed diagonally down at the subject. This light in turn produces a shadow on the opposite side of the face. The portraiture photographer does not want the **fill light** to be as bright as the key light because this produces an unpleasant look. Through trial and error, many portraiture photographers have settled on having the fill light one stop dimmer than the key light.

So, when standing at the appropriate distance for the f/stop determined by taking a meter reading of the bright part of the scene, your next step is to diminish the output of the flash unit by one stop. This can be done in many ways, but the easiest method is to adjust the full manual flash to −1 stop, or 1/2 power.

At this point, it is necessary to remind the reader that the manual flash exposure mode presumes the image is being taken in a "normal" room. Recall **Rule of Thumb** 4-2:

 RULE OF THUMB 4-2

Manual flash mode used outside is at least 1 f/stop less bright than the suggestion from the flash LED screen.

Simply by taking the full manual flash outside, where there are no white walls and a nearby white ceiling to help reflect light toward the subject, automatically diminishes the full manual flash by one stop. But inside a normal room, adjusting the flash to 1/2 power is required.

Figure 4-21 is the result of using fill-in flash outside. The bright part of the scene is properly exposed because the camera was set for an exposure based on the bright part of the scene. The area that had been in the shade is now receiving light from the flash unit, and this is enough light to reveal anything that had

FIGURE 4-21
Fill-in flash allows us to see details in the shadows *(courtesy of S. Keppel, GWU MS student)*

been in the shade. The shadow is still present, but we can now see details within the shadow.

Fill-in flash is also necessary if the task at hand is to photograph a person sitting by a window when the outside is fully lit by the sun. Again, take a meter reading of the sunny area outside, without anything else in the field of view, and set your camera for this exposure reading. This meter reading will provide you with an f/stop setting. Using the manual flash mode, determine the distance appropriate for this f/stop, and position the camera and flash at this distance. Because the flash is being used indoors in this case, the manual flash has to be set so that it is one stop less bright, which can be done by setting the manual flash to 1/2 power. The fill-in flash technique will then ensure that the outside is properly exposed *and* that the subject is properly exposed.

If for any reason, when you stand at the distance required by the f/stop needed to properly expose the bright part of the scene, you do not like the composition at this distance, you do have some options. Recall that the f/stop numbers are also distances in feet that light changes by one stop. So, if the distance you are

FIGURE 4-22A

A backlit subject, and the camera metered to properly expose the outside scene *(courtesy of Major Stutzman)*

FIGURE 4-22B
A backlit subject properly exposed with fill-in flash *(courtesy of Major Stutzman)*

currently standing happens to be 5.6 feet from the subject, or something very close to that distance, you can simply move back to 8 feet to diminish the light by one stop. In this case, you would not have to change the flash to 1/2 power because moving to this new distance will have effectively the same result. If you were positioned at 11 feet from the subject and you felt this was too far away from the subject, you could move to 8 feet and diminish the flash output by another stop. Or you could move from 11 feet to 5.6 feet and diminish the flash output by −2 stops, 1/4 of the light.

Fill-in flash gives you the control to properly expose two widely different parts of the scene that were originally both sunlit and shady.

DIRECT LIGHT

The evidence to be photographed often has some texture or depth or a 3D pattern that must to be photographed. In these cases, direct flash will obliterate the very detail needing to be captured. When light goes directly into a 3D pattern, the entire area is brightly lit, and often the result is that the pattern itself is washed out and no longer visible.

FIGURE 4-23A
The same shoe impression lit with direct light *(courtesy of S. Keppel, GWU MS student)*

FIGURE 4-23B
The same shoe impression lit with oblique light *(courtesy of S. Keppel, GWU MS student)*

OBLIQUE LIGHT: HARD AND SOFT SHADOWS

The solution is to use **oblique light**. Oblique light creates shadows, and the shadows themselves reveal the pattern of interest. However, the shadows created by an oblique flash unit are very dark, and details within the shadow area are difficult or impossible to see. These are called **hard shadows**. If the shadows are covering part of the detail that needs to be seen, then it is our flash technique itself that is responsible for hiding important details. The solution is to use a reflector or bounce surface to reflect light back toward the evidence. This bounced light will frequently add sufficient light so that details within the shadows can now be seen. These are called **soft shadows**.

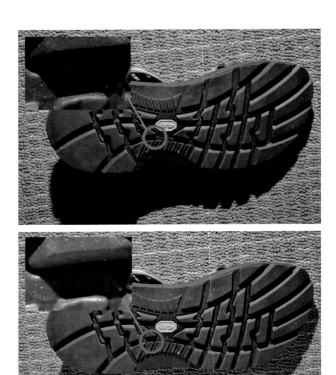

FIGURE 4-24A
"Hard" and "soft" shadows *(courtesy of S. Lingsch, GWU MS student)*

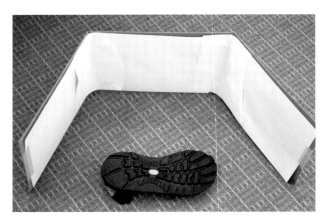

FIGURE 4-24B
The reflector that made the "soft" shadows *(courtesy of S. Lingsch, GWU MS student)*

In a classroom, it is easier to photograph shoes rather than impressions in dirt. The technique is exactly the same. In Figure 4-24, the upper image was photographed without a reflector, and the results are hard shadows, which hide part of the wording "Non-Marking." By using a reflector, the N of "Non-Marking" can now be seen. Figure 4-24B shows the reflector used to create the soft shadows. It folds flat for easy transportation. Figure 4-25 shows the same reflector used outdoors with a real shoeprint in dirt, and the results obtained. As SWGIT and SWGTREAD indicate, a reflector is essential photographic equipment.

The variations for shoeprint photography range from the impression being in dark-colored dirt at midnight, without ambient lighting in the area of the impression, to a light-colored impression in sand or soil, at noon on a sunny day. Of course, there will be some variations in the exposure variables selected,

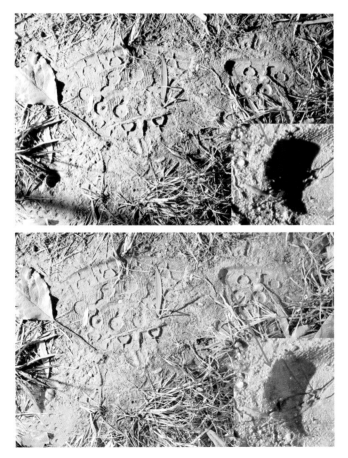

FIGURE 4-25
A reflector used on a shoeprint in dirt *(courtesy of S. Lingsch, GWU MS student)*

but still incorporate as many of the guidelines offered by SWGIT and SWGTREAD as possible.

The Oblique Flash Sequence

Recall SWGIT and SWGTREAD's recommendations for examination-quality photography. This is the perfect time to repeat their key recommendations, with emphasis added as needed:

Examination-quality photography equipment recommended by SWGIT:

- A professional film or digital SLR camera system, with a minimum of **8** megapixels resolution.
- Use a detachable electronic flash unit, with a **6-foot** remote flash cord. (SWGTREAD indicates that "the flash should be held **4 to 5 feet away** from and directed at the impression." Does this conflict with SWGIT's recommendation to use a 6-foot remote flash cord? No. You need a 6-foot remote flash cord to hold the flash 4 to 5 feet away from the impression. Some flash units even permit remote use without being connected by a remote flash cord.)
- Use a macro lens, capable of **filling the frame** with the footwear impression, when doing examination-quality photography.
- Use **a remote shutter release cable.** Or use your camera's **delayed shutter release** capability, usually set to a 10-second delay.
- Use a sturdy **tripod** mount, and position the camera so that the **film plane is parallel.**
- Use **suitable digital storage media.**
- Use **flat rigid scales.**
- Use a **photo memo form.**
- Use a **reflector.**
- If necessary, use a device for **blocking ambient lighting.**

Additional SWGTREAD recommendations:

- Manually focus on the bottom of the impression and close the aperture to maximize the depth of field (e.g., set the aperture to f/16 or f/22).
- If using a digital camera, set the camera to the highest resolution available, and select an uncompressed or "lossless" compression file format like RAW/NEF or TIFF.
- For a long tire impression, a series of overlapping photographs of 12 inches each should be taken.
- Multiple exposures using various settings (**bracketing**). A minimum of three images should be taken **with oblique lighting in at least 100-degree increments** around the entire impression.
- If the impression is processed in any way with powders or chemicals, **rephotograph** the impression after each process.

Oblique Light: Hard and Soft Shadows   245

Tripods

The previous recommendations include the use of a tripod. Previously, the use of a tripod has been associated with the use of slow shutter speeds to prevent blur from affecting an image when the camera is not being hand-held. How do tripods relate to examination-quality photographs?

In this case, the tripod will hold the camera steady while the photographer holds the flash unit 4 to 5 feet away from the impression. The camera will be mounted on the tripod, with the film plane/digital sensor positioned parallel to the impression. It will be best to fill the frame with the impression with either a 50mm lens or a macro lens, depending on the length of the impression. The legs of the tripod can be adjusted so that the camera is the right height to fill the frame with the impression.

Some tripods allow the center stem to be removed and reinserted from beneath the tripod, so the camera can be held between the tripod legs. This position helps you get the camera closer to the impression and helps keep the tripod legs out of the field of view. Figure 4-26 shows this setup, with arrows indicating the directions the flash will be held.

FIGURE 4-26
Tripod center stem reversed

SWGTREAD's recommendation is that the flash be held in at least 100-degree increments around the impression. This setup ensures that the flash directly lights all the surfaces of the impression to give the examiner the best view of them all. Held between the tripod legs has the flash positioned at 120-degree increments. The first photo in the series will be taken without a scale in view, so that it can be documented that where the scale is eventually placed does not have evidence of value beneath the scale. Then a scale is placed at the same level as the bottom of the impression. This may require digging a trough alongside the impression to get the scale as deep as the impression is. From each of these three 120-degree viewpoints, a series of three brackets will be taken, for a total of ten images of each shoeprint, one without a scale and nine with a scale.

If the tripod does not allow the center stem to be reversed, Figure 4-27 shows the recommended positioning of the flash. The front two tripod legs are set vertically, which helps ensure that the tripod legs are not in view. But having the camera positioned as shown makes the tripod want to fall forward, so the back leg of the tripod is counterweighted with our camera bag.

FIGURE 4-27
Tripod positioning when the center stem cannot be reversed

When the tripod is used to minimize camera movement, images should *never* be captured by depressing the shutter button, which can produce some camera movement. Whenever the camera is on a tripod, use either an electronic remote shutter cable or the ten-second-delay shutter setting on the camera.

Shoe Prints in Snow

Snow is highly reflective, so even oblique flash frequently does not produce sufficient shadows to highlight the pattern well. Figure 4-28 illustrates this issue. To increase the contrast so that detail can be seen, the impression is first usually sprayed with red Snow Print Wax from one direction. This added color acts just like shadows from an oblique flash: the pattern pops out! If Snow Print Wax is unavailable, most spray paints will also enhance the contrast of the snowy shoeprint. However, the Snow Print Wax has an additional benefit: its waxy layer helps insolate the snow from the exothermic reaction of the hardening castone, helping to preserve the details of the impression from the heat the castone will generate. Castone generally has replaced Plaster of Paris to cast 3D impressions. After the Snow Print Wax has been sprayed from one side and the impression is thoroughly photographed, the impression is again sprayed with Snow Print Wax, but this time all sides of the impression are sprayed so that every vertical part of the impression is coated. The photography sequence is repeated prior to pouring castone into the impression. The far right image of Figure 4-28 shows this more thorough spraying of the impression.

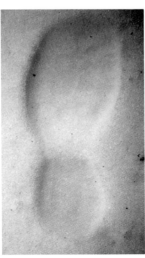

FIGURE 4-28
Shoe prints in snow need enhanced contrast to show their pattern

Remember, when filling the frame with the shoeprint in snow, before any Snow Print Wax has been applied, you will need to make an exposure compensation if using either the Automatic or Dedicated/TTL flash modes. If you don't, the result will be "dirty snow" or underexposed snow. Otherwise, ISO 100, sync shutter speed, and f/16 or f/22 are the proper camera exposure settings. Adjust the flash for a proper exposure.

Tire Tracks

The photography of tire tracks is similar to the photography of shoe impressions, but there are some added requirements. Because the tire track can be quite long, it is essential to capture the entire circumference of each tire track to be assured that all the identifying nicks, cuts, gouges, and

FIGURE 4-29A
Tire track segments *(courtesy of J. Sinex, GWU MS student)*

FIGURE 4-29B
An individual segment *(courtesy of J. Sinex, GWU MS student)*

embedded rocks in the treads have been captured. To do this, SWGTREAD advises that 12-foot overlapping increments be photographed. Unless you are dealing with monster truck tires, at least 8 feet of each tire track needs to be photographed and casted. Before these individual 12-foot increments are photographed, to help document the eventual segments it is recommended that the entire length be photographed with lettered or numbered markers and that a long tape measure be placed alongside the track to help make clear which segment is in any particular image. Figure 4-29 shows these elements.

Again, ISO 100, sync shutter speed, and f/16 or f/22 are the proper camera exposure settings. Adjust the flash for a proper exposure. Remember to use a reflector for each of the ten images of each tire track segment.

Bite Marks

Although bite marks are frequently found on skin, they can also be found on partially eaten food products and other surfaces. The American Board of Forensic Odontology (ABFO) recommends using an ABFO #2 scale with bite marks, as the three circles on the scale can help determine whether the scale was properly aligned with the camera's film plane parallel to the scale. If not, the circles are seen as ellipses, and editing software will be needed to rectify the image to its proper orientation for comparisons. Figure 4-30 shows the ABFO #2 scale.

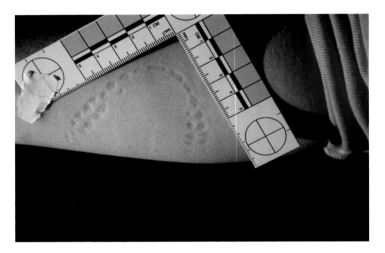

FIGURE 4-30
The ABFO #2 scale in use. *(courtesy of J. Polangcus, GWU MS student)*

In addition to being photographed, bite marks can also be documented and collected by powdering them with our regular black fingerprint powder and then tape lifted, and they can also be cast with silicone rubber products like Mikrosil. Figure 4-31 shows these three methods being compared to a castone copy of a suspect's teeth on the far left.

One aspect of bite marks to keep in mind is that when they are found on curved surfaces, after photographing both arches together to show that they were a pair at the scene, it is best to photograph them individually with a series of close-ups for each arch because they are actually each on a different plane. Figure 4-32 is a close-up "as is" of the bottom arch. Notice how difficult it is to see any detail of the other arch. When the bite mark is in a hairy area, after swabbing for saliva, the hair can be shaved if it obstructs the view of the bite mark too much.

FIGURE 4-31
Castone, Mikrosil, photo, and fingerprint powder and tape lifts

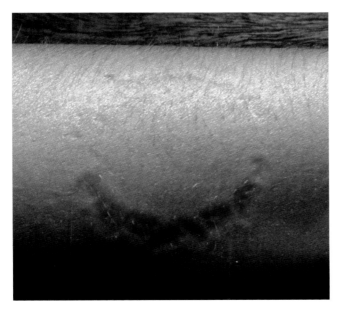

FIGURE 4-32
A close-up "as is" of the lower arch *(courtesy of J. Polangcus, GWU MS student)*

Examination-quality photographs usually require ISO 100, sync shutter speed, and f/16 or f/22 as the proper camera exposure settings. Adjust the flash for a proper exposure.

Indented Writing

Sometimes indented writing can be visualized with oblique photography if the indented writing isn't more than two or three sheets beneath the original writing. If it is deeper than that, the paper will have to be sent to the lab to be treated with an Electrostatic Detection Apparatus (ESDA), which can detect indented writing up to eight pages down. I prefer lighting the paper with an oblique flashlight rather than a camera flash because you can see the shadowing you are creating, and sometimes fine flashlight angle changes make all the difference in being able to make out the words most clearly. A second trick to this type of photography is that because there are many vertical and horizontal elements to printed and cursive writing, lighting the writing from one of the four sides tends to wash out some of the indentations. The indentations are best seen if they are lit diagonally to the written words. Figure 4-33 shows this effect well.

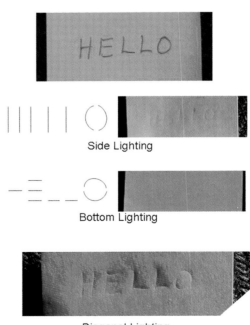

FIGURE 4-33
Indented writing is best seen when lit diagonally

With the camera mounted on a tripod and filling the frame with the paper, set the camera to a 2-second shutter speed. The flashlight is held very oblique to the paper and about 6 feet away so that you can see the indentations being produced when the room lights are turned off. During the 2-second exposure, keep moving the flashlight over the paper so that there is no flashlight streak noticed on the image. It is recommended to first photograph the entire sheet of paper and to do close-ups of any wording after that.

Dust Print Lifts

When some one walks in shoes across dusty surfaces, the shoes can pick up the dust and transfer this dust to other surfaces, which creates a "positive" dust print: the dust that has been transferred looks like a dusty residue in the shape of the shoe tread. Find where the shoe originally walked across the floor, and you'll find that the dust has been removed from the dusty surface. This void, a clean area on a dusty surface, is called a "negative" dust print. Either print can be associated to the shoe that made it and possibly identified. Figure 4-34 shows positive and negative dust prints.

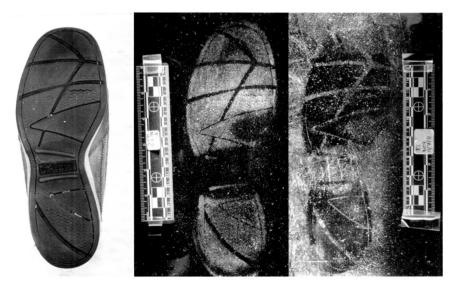

FIGURE 4-34
Positive and negative dust prints *(courtesy of J. Sinex, GWU MS student)*

Dust prints can be lifted with Electrostatic Dust Print Lifters, which transfer the light-colored dust to a black Mylar film surface for excellent contrast, as seen in Figure 4-34. The dust print lifts on the Mylar film can be photographed with either an oblique flash or oblique flashlight. I prefer using a flashlight because its angle can be controlled and the effect can be seen while the photo is being taken. The flash goes off so fast that you cannot tell whether it was aimed correctly until after the image is captured and inspected. Because the flashlight is less bright than the flash, a shutter speed of approximately 6 seconds is required to properly expose the dust print. During the 6-second exposure, keep the flashlight moving so that no flashlight streak is noticed. Of course, with this shutter speed, the camera must be mounted on a tripod to avoid blur.

The photography of dust prints needs to be done in a room as dark as possible. The Mylar film is very glossy, and if there are other lights in the room they may reflect off the Mylar film and glare may partially cover parts of the dust print.

BOUNCE FLASH

As mentioned previously, using direct flash can sometimes be counterproductive. At times it can produce a harsh hot-spot reflection, red-eye, and unattractive shadows and reflections if there are reflective surfaces within the scene. The solution is frequently **bounce flash**. Try to bounce the flash off the

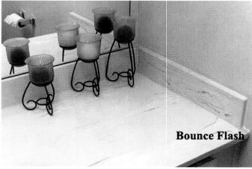

FIGURE 4-35
Strange shadows eliminated with bounce flash

ceiling at a point approximately halfway between your subject and the flash head. This is the shortest distance the light of the flash has to travel when using bounce flash. Figure 4-35 shows a mirror in the background catching the light of a direct flash and creating shadows of vertical objects in front of those objects. These shadows can be very distracting. Bouncing the flash off of the ceiling produces a very soft light and frequently eliminates these shadows.

With highly reflective surfaces in a confined area, there can be multiple undesirable effects from direct flash. Notice how the left image of Figure 4-36 has several issues that can be fixed with bounce flash. Because the direct flash was aimed at the sink, the area behind the photographer that is seen in the mirror is underexposed. With bounce flash creating a soft light coming from the ceiling, even the area behind the photographer now is better exposed. The direct flash created unattractive shadows of the soap dispenser and the sink. Recall the previous recommendation to be aware of the shadows that are in the scene? This recommendation applies not only to the shadows that are already in the scene from sunlight but also to the shadows created by the use of flash. Figure 4-36 shows the elimination of these shadows by the use of bounce flash.

If bounce flash is such a useful type of lighting, why isn't it used more often? There are two main reasons. First, because the Inverse Square Law tells us that if light has to travel farther to get to the subject, it is dimmer when it gets there. For this reason, bounce flash is not usually used over large areas when it is

FIGURE 4-36
Multiple problems solved by the use of bounce flash

necessary to have the entire scene properly exposed. Second, because the light from the bounce flash is less bright, it is frequently necessary to compensate for that by opening the aperture, which has the unwanted effect of diminishing the depth of field.

 ## *RULE OF THUMB 4-4*

When using bounce flash, if the subject of the photograph is 10 feet or farther from the photographer, the use of an f/5.6 or wider aperture may be necessary, which will diminish the DOF. Consider ways to get closer to the subject to avoid having to use wide apertures.

FIGURE 4-37
Shows both of these effects; the area properly lit by the bounce flash is relatively small, and we can see that the background quickly becomes dimmer and out of focus.

How do we compensate for the light reduction when using bounce flash? First, it is necessary to realize why the light is dimmer:

- When light has to travel farther, it is dimmer when it gets there.
- When the light strikes the ceiling, it is diffused and not all of it goes directly toward our primary subject. So it is not just direct light traveling farther; by the time the light does get to the subject, some of it has been directed elsewhere and never reaches the subject.
- When the reflective surface is textured with a pattern, or if the ceiling has acoustical tiles on it, some of the light is absorbed and is not reflected at all.

To determine a proper exposure when using bounce flash, the first step is to determine the new distance the flash has to travel. Determine the distance from the flash head to the bounce surface and then the distance from the bounce surface to the subject. In Manual flash mode, this distance will require a particular f/stop. But this is presuming that it is direct flash at this distance. Because of the other factors mentioned earlier, another exposure step is necessary. Here, experience offers some suggestions. If you're in a normal room, open the aperture two more stops. If you're in a larger-than-normal room, open the aperture three more stops from what the flash indicates for this new distance. If you're in a smaller-than-normal room, open the aperture one more stop from what the flash indicates for this new distance. Don't just set the flash to the dedicated/TTL flash mode and let the flash do all the work, because if the aperture is not wide enough, even the dedicated/TTL flash mode will produce underexposures.

APERTURE PRIORITY MODE FOR LARGE, DIMLY LIT SCENES

Many years ago, when using a film camera without an Aperture Priority exposure mode, the simplest way to light a large nighttime scene was to put the camera on a tripod and take a series of time exposures. This method was necessary because we would not see the results of any of these images until the film was developed. We had to just hope that one of the images came pretty close to a proper exposure. See Figure 4-38.

Today, with a digital camera proving an instant review of all images, the aperture priority mode is the solution of choice. Put the camera on a tripod, hyperfocal focus with an f/8, and let the camera decide when it has received enough light. Great depth of field and a proper exposure, too! If the first shot needs any tweaking, you can select the desired exposure compensation and take another shot. The results are very reliable.

FIGURE 4-38
A series of time exposures

FIGURE 4-39
The aperture priority mode lights a large dimly lit scene *(courtesy of M. Hashemi, GWU MS student)*

CHAPTER SUMMARY

When the ambient lighting of the scene is not bright enough for a proper exposure with an f/8 or smaller aperture, you can now supplement the lighting with an electronic flash. The flash can, at times, totally replace the sun as the key light for any scene. At times, the flash will act as the fill light, ensuring that areas previously in shadows receive enough light for the details of the evidence to be lit sufficiently so that an examiner can use these details for comparison purposes.

Ensuring that the flash output matches both the camera viewpoint and the focal length of the lens was emphasized.

Many flash units allow the crime scene photographer to choose from the Manual, Automatic, or Dedicated flash exposure modes. These flash exposure modes were explained, along with their relative strengths and weaknesses.

The need to use the camera's designated sync shutter speed was explained.

The Inverse Square Law, as the foundation for determining the proper exposure when using electronic flash, was explained. And the common flash exposure errors that may be encountered were pointed out.

Bracketing with flash was also explained.

Certain types of evidence are best lit with the light coming from the side. Whenever 3D texture, pattern, and similar details are present, side/oblique lighting often improves the visibility of these qualities. This chapter explained how to photograph such objects. Reflectors can also be used to soften the hard shadows cast by oblique flash and illuminate evidence hidden in the shadow area.

The benefits of bounce flash were listed and how to utilize this technique was explained.

You have reached the point at which you should be able to combine the concepts of composition, nonflash exposure, depth of field, flash exposure, and the use of various types of lenses to capture any image necessary at the crime scene. From this point on, your photography should be very different than it was before reading this text. Hopefully, this book should help make all your crime scene images stand out in court. And you will notice that all your other types of photography will have improved as well.

Discussion Questions

1. Explain the meaning of flash guide numbers. How can it be determined which guide numbers of flashes are best suited for crime scene work?
2. Is there just one sync speed a camera can use with a particular flash unit? Though most cameras designate one shutter speed as that camera's sync

speed, can faster or slower shutter speeds ever be used effectively at crime scenes?

3. Discuss the nuances of the Manual flash exposure mode, including the presupposition that the flash is used in a "normal" room and the flash is used as direct flash rather than bounce or oblique flash.

4. Indicate one circumstance under which it would be better to choose the Manual flash mode over either the Automatic or Dedicated flash mode. Why?

5. Indicate one circumstance under which it would be better to choose the Automatic flash mode over either the Manual or Dedicated flash mode. Why?

6. Indicate one circumstance under which it would be better to choose the Dedicated flash mode over either the Manual or Automatic flash mode. Why?

7. In what circumstances does fill-in flash result in distinct benefits to exposure?

8. Explain all the concerns related to tire track photography.

9. Bounce flash produces dim light on the subject. Explain why this is so, and the method to determine a proper exposure when using bounce flash.

Practical Exercises

1. Take a flash picture of any object 15 feet from the camera using the camera's sync shutter speed. If your camera will allow it, photograph the same object, from the same position, at one stop faster than sync. Also at two stops faster than sync. If your camera allows these shots, you should be able to anticipate the effects of all three different shutter speeds.

2. With the flash mounted on the hot-shoe, take a photo of any object 10 feet from the camera. Keep the flash on the hot-shoe and repeat at distances of 5 feet, 4 feet, and 3 feet. At what distance is it imperative to remove the flash from the hot-shoe for your equipment?

3. Standing 15 feet from a white (or just slightly off-white) wall, determine a proper exposure for the Manual flash exposure mode and take the picture. Using either Automatic or Dedicated flash exposure modes, from the same position, photograph the same wall without making any exposure compensations. For the third shot, in either the Automatic or Dedicated flash exposure mode, make an exposure compensation to ensure that the wall is not underexposed.

4. Fill the frame with a large black or deep navy-blue object (do not use the black or blue painted sheet metal of a car). First, photograph with the Manual flash mode. Second, use either the Automatic or Dedicated flash mode without any exposure compensations. Third, use either the

Automatic or Dedicated flash mode with an exposure compensation to prevent overexposures.

5. On a day with bright sunlight producing deep shadows (an f/16 kind of day), place an object under a car by one of the tires so that it is in deep shadow. Meter the sunny part of the scene, set the camera for that exposure, and photograph the object. Next, determine the correct fill-in flash exposure for the same object from the same position. Take that photo, and compare it to the first.

6. Sometime after 10:00 p.m., find or create a shoe print in dirt, place the camera on a tripod, and photograph the shoe print with the flash as direct as possible. Next, determine a proper oblique flash exposure, and take a second image. Compare the two.

7. In the bathroom, place several items around the sink and take a direct flash photo. Next, determine the correct bounce flash exposure for the same scene, from the same position, and take a second photo. Compare.

Suggested Readings

The Amphoto Editorial Board. 1974. *Night Photography Simplified*, Englewood Cliffs, NJ: Prentice-Hall.

Child, John, and Galer, Mark. 2000. *Photographic Lighting*, Oxford: Focal Press.

Cornfield, Jim. 1976. *Electronic Flash Photography*. Los Angeles: Peterson Publishing Co..

Frost, Lee. 1999. *The Complete Guide to Night & Low-Light Photography*. New York: Amphoto Books.

Hedgecoe, John. 2003. *The New Manual of Photography*. New York: DK Publishing, Inc.

Lefkowitz, Lester. 1986. *Electronic Flash*. Kodak Workshop Series. Rochester, NY: Eastman Kodak Company.

McCartney, Susan. 1997. *Mastering Flash Photography*. New York: Amphoto Books.

Neubart, Jack. 1988. *The Photographer's Guide to Exposure*. New York: Amphoto Books.

CHAPTER 5

Energy Filters and Sensors
Ultraviolet/Visible/Near Infrared

Gerald B. Richards

Gerald B. Richards

KEY TERMS

Absorption
Analog
Band pass filter
Barrier filter
Cut-on filter
Cut-off filter
Digital
Electromagnetic
    spectrum (spectrum
    or EMS)

Excitation filter
Fluorescence
Long-wave LWUV
Luminescence
Near Infrared (NIR or
    IR) energy or light
Phosphorescence
Pixels
Reflectance
Sensor

Shortwave SWUV
Transmission
Ultraviolet (UV) energy,
    or light
Visible (VIS) energy or
    light

CONTENTS

LEARNING OBJECTIVES

Upon completion of this lesson, you will be able to:

- Explain the parts of the electromagnetic spectrum
- Explain ultraviolet and infrared cameras
- Explain analog sensors
- Explain digital sensors
- Explain the functioning of a camera lens in the ultraviolet and infrared
- Explain filters and how they work
- Explain the process of producing reflected photographs in the UV and IR
- Explain the process of producing luminescent photographs in the UV and IR
- Explain how an object will react to various parts of the spectrum differently

THE SPECTRUM

To produce a normal photograph, two of the most basic things needed—aside from the subject—are **energy** (for example visible light energy) and a **sensor** (such as our eyes, film, or an electronic sensor). An additional, optional tool is a **filter** that reduces or limits the spectral range of either the energy source, the sensor, or both. This is also true for energy and sensors beyond the visible spectrum, such as x-rays, ultraviolet, near infrared, and so on. Throughout this chapter we will focus on this triad: energy sources, sensors, and filters. Our eyes are real-time sensors used to image visible light (energy) in the world around us. A camera is used to record or capture the same world in a fashion similar to that of our eyes.

Figure 5-1 shows the retina of one of the author's eyes. The eye contains rods that sense black and white or light. Rods are partially responsible for night vision. The eye also contains cones that are sensitive to red, green, and blue and are ultimately responsible for color vision. The rods and cones relay visible light energy via the optic nerve to the brain, which consequently processes the information and produces an image in our "mind's eye." Therefore, the images we see are a combination of energy (visible light) and a sensor (our eyes) with processing and interpretation performed by our brain.

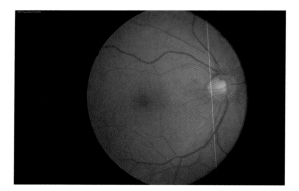

FIGURE 5-1
Right eye of author

The energy that produces the images we use in our daily lives, and particularly for crime scene photographers, can be identified and compared as a continuum called the **electromagnetic spectrum (EMS)** or the spectrum. The spectrum is an infinite continuum. It is measured in two basic ways, wavelength and frequency, although there are other methods for identifying all or part of the spectrum. The major portions of the spectrum are generally described as gamma rays, x-rays, ultraviolet rays, visible rays, infrared, microwaves, and radio/TV.

The portions of the spectrum that are of most interest to the crime scene, forensic, or law enforcement photographer can be broken down into more specific descriptive units. Hard x-ray, soft x-ray, shortwave ultraviolet, long

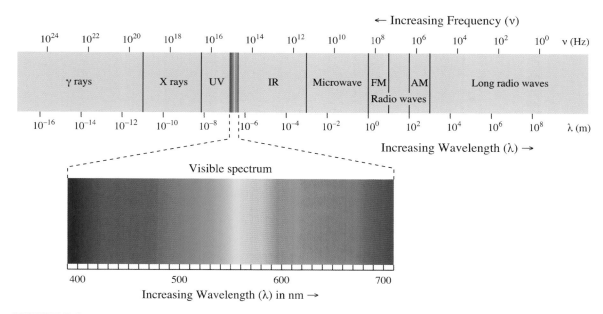

FIGURE 5-2

The electromagnetic spectrum *(Modified with permission from http://en.wikipedia.org/wiki/File:Electromagnetic-Spectrum.png)*

wave ultraviolet, visible (blue, cyan, green, yellow, and red), near infrared, medium infrared, and far (thermal) infrared.

In numerical terms, the spectrum consists of waves that are measured in nanometers (nm) from peak to peak, Figure 5-3, with a nanometer being one billionth of a meter, one millionth of a millimeter, or 25.4 millionths of an inch. Although the spectrum is also measured by wave frequency, measurement via wave length is the more popular method for the majority of photographers. The visible spectrum is the range in which our eyes can generally see and is most commonly recognized from blue, approximately 400nm, to red, approximately 700nm.

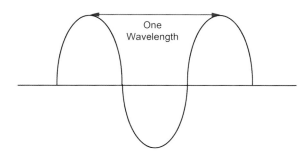

FIGURE 5-3

One wavelength

As previously noted, the range or portions of the spectrum of most interest to crime scene or forensic photographers are:

Hard x-ray (HXR)	0.01nm–0.10nm
Soft x-ray (SXR)	0.10nm–10nm
Shortwave ultraviolet (SWU)	200nm–300nm
Long-wave ultraviolet (LWU) (black light)	300nm–400nm
Visible (VIS)	400nm–700nm
Near infrared (NIR)	700nm–1000nm
Shortwave infrared (SIR)	1000nm–3000nm
Medium infrared (MIR) (thermo image)	3000nm–5000nm
Far infrared (FIR) (thermo image)	8000nm–12000nm

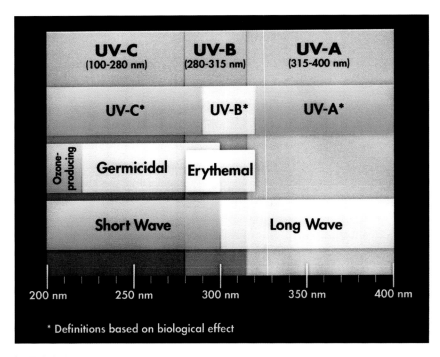

FIGURE 5-4
Breakdown of the ultraviolet portion of the spectrum *(courtesy of Jeff Robinson, scamper@me.com)*

Of course, as this is a continuum, these ranges should be considered approximates. For instance, in the visible 400nm–700nm range, many people can see less than 400nm and farther than 700nm, but 400nm to 700nm is a generally accepted as the average. Although film and digital sensors can capture more than the visible portion of the spectrum, filters are used to limit their spectral range to that of the human eye. If these filters were not placed on modern digital cameras, energy beyond the visible spectrum would make everyday images look unnatural.

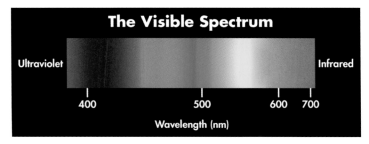

FIGURE 5-5
Visible portion of the electromagnetic spectrum *(courtesy of Jeff Robinson, scamper@me.com)*

The gap between soft x-ray and shortwave ultraviolet, approximately 10nm to 200nm, is referred to as the germicidal or vacuum ultraviolet portion of the spectrum. This portion of the spectrum is not used for crime-scene work. The near infrared and shortwave infrared are closely akin to the visible portion of the spectrum. The medium infrared and far infrared are best described as heat radiation encompassing the radiation or **emission of energy** from many objects, as well as their reflectance, absorption, and transmission of energy. Most people not familiar with the characteristics of near infrared and shortwave infrared think they emit heat that is being detected, but that is not the case. These areas of the spectrum act similar to visible light. For ease of discussion, from this point on when we use the generic term **infrared (IR)**, we will be referring only to near infrared (NIR), approximately 700nm to 1000nm.

UV/IR CAMERAS

Analog versus Digital Cameras

For 150 years, film cameras reigned as king. In the early 1990s, digital cameras moved out of the laboratory and into the commercial world. In 1991, one of the authors purchased for the government, one of the very first digital single-lens reflex (DSLR) cameras to come onto the market, which at that time was specifically targeted to the photojournalist. Kodak had reworked a Nikon F-3 35mm body and inserted a 1.3 MP sensor developed by Kodak (megapixel refers to one million picture elements, or pixels). Kodak called it the DCS; later it became known, unofficially, as the DCS 100. This camera produced solely black and white images. After a picture was taken, the camera took several seconds to record it via a tether wire to a large hard drive that hung on the photographer's shoulder. By approximately 2000, the DSLR camera had begaun to appear in the general marketplace and was produced by most of the major manufactures. Up to that point, only a few crime scene photographers had had the opportunity to try digital cameras, and it was generally decided that their limited resolution made them of little value.

From that time on, the new DSLRs that were coming onto the market from Nikon, Canon, Sony, Casio, and others began to improve resolution and processing speed at a feverish pace. These cameras now had a 2.7 MP sensor, and in less than a year, the sensor size had grown to over 5 MP. It became immediately evident that the life cycle of digital cameras was going to be far different than that of analog film cameras. It was not unusual for a film camera to come onto the market and remain virtually unchanged for ten or more years. DSLR cameras were becoming outdated in six to nine months, with that same trend continuing to the present day. In just ten years, the 35mm SLR film camera has almost entirely been replaced by the 35mm DSLR: it has truly become a digital world.

Specialty cameras have been produced and specifically designed to photograph UV and IR using the digital sensors' extended spectral range. These cameras have been produced at the factory without any type of UV/IR blocking filter or have the ability to mechanically remove the filter. These filters are used to block the UV/IR that the digital sensor can record beyond the visible spectrum.

One of the first still cameras to come on the market was the Sony 717, which had a feature called "night shot." With the night shot feature, the photographer could push a lever and remove the UV/IR blocking filter, providing the photographer with the full spectral range of the sensor. Sony also produced a number of video cameras with night shot that could produce still images as well as video. The author used a Sony DCR-TRV27 for a number of years for both still and video IR photography. The author's TRV27 was fitted with a filter holder that would retain the UV/VIS block-IR pass filter.

Although these were some of the first multipurpose cameras for those looking to venture into the infrared, they were of limited resolution and did not have interchangeable lenses.

In 2006, Fujifilm brought onto the market a purpose-built camera designed to be used not only in the visible but also in the UV and IR portions of the spectrum. The Fuji FinePix S3 Pro UV/IR SLR, a modified FinePix S3 Pro, was designed with law enforcement and UV/IR photographer enthusiasts in mind. Following closely after the S3 came the lower-end Fujifilm IS-1, a modified FinePix S9100, and the higher-end Fujifilm IS Pro UV/IR, which was a modified FinePix S5 Pro. These cameras were advantageous because they used the Nikon

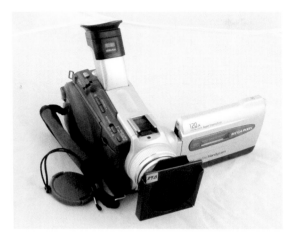

FIGURE 5-6
Sony DCR-TRV27 video camera with night shot

FIGURE 5-7
Close-up of Sony DCR-TRV27 with night shot

range of interchangeable lenses as well as the higher-resolution sensors. Unfortunately, the UV/IR line was discontinued after only a few years. Used versions of all of these cameras can still be found from time to time on the Internet and from local camera dealers.

Another option is to have a digital camera converted to UV/IR. There are Internet companies that will remove the blocking filter, replacing it either with a piece of glass, which will ultimately allow transmission of the full spectral range of the sensor, or by installing a UV or IR-pass-only filter. Additionally, most of these cameras can have the autofocus recalibrated for UV or IR. Canon

FIGURE 5-8
FujiFilm FinePix S3 Pro UV/IR single-lens reflex (SLR) camera

and Nikon are two of the most commonly converted camera models. The cost for these services is currently between $250 and $600 dollars, depending on the camera and requested alterations. One issue to consider is that any conversion will void the camera's warranty.

If you have a digital camera with a built-in filter, you still may be able to use it for limited infrared photography. To determine whether a camera is sensitive to infrared, take an ordinary remote control (television, stereo, etc.) that uses IR for transmission, point it directly at your camera, and push a button while simultaneously taking a picture. If the light from the front of the remote is visible in your picture, your camera is somewhat sensitive to IR. You can then take an IR filter, either an 88A or 89B, and start experimenting to see how various objects react differently to IR than to the visible spectrum.

UV/IR Lenses
Because the ultraviolet, visible, and infrared are at different wavelengths, they each focus at a different plane in the camera. Therefore, although the image may be in focus in the visible portion of the spectrum, it will not be in focus for the ultraviolet or infrared portions with a normal camera lens. There are several specialty lenses that have been corrected to focus in the UV, VIS, and IR. These lenses are quite expensive; however, as they are purposefully designed, they are best suited for the job.

Two of these specialty lenses have been around for years: the Nikon UV-Nikkor 55mm F/4 (1965) and perhaps one of the rarest Nikon lenses, the UV-Nikkor 105mm f/4.5 (1984). Both of these lenses are very rare and if found, will most likely sell for many thousands of dollars. More readily available is the Coastal

FIGURE 5-9
Using a stock Nikon D90, the IR energy from a TV remote can be easily seen

Optical, Coastal Opt UV-VIS-IR 60mm Apo Macro lens, which eliminates the need for refocusing in the UV and IR. However, this lens also boasts a hefty price tag of over $4,500. If a considerable amount of work is needed in UV/IR, then the convenience may outweigh the cost.

Most lenses are specifically designed to provide best focus in the visible portion of the spectrum. The average lens used for visible light photography will work quite adequately in the UV/IR for the average crime scene photographer. However, when imaging in either of these areas of the spectrum, the camera must have a filter placed over the lens that allows only UV or IR to pass to the sensor and should therefore ultimately eliminate all visible light. These filters are completely opaque, making direct visual focusing of the UV or IR image impossible. Prior to digital photography, many lenses had a small red mark on the barrow that allowed the photographer to focus in the visible range, then shift the focus to the IR. As noted in Figure 5-10, (top), the original visible focus of this lens is set on the white focus mark at the green 7-foot number. In order to have the subject in focus in the IR, the original green 7-foot number must be shifted to the red 28mm focus mark, Figure 5-10 (bottom). As this is a variable focal-length (zoom) lens, four red focus marks are available, depending on the focal length being used.

FIGURE 5-10
Top, lens focused at 7 feet (green number on white line) in visible light; bottom, lens refocused at 7 feet (green number on red 28mm line) for infrared energy

Digital cameras manufacturers go to great lengths to block IR, so most digital lenses no longer have these IR refocus marks. Therefore, other techniques can be used to determine focus for IR. If your camera has a "live view" feature wherein you can view and focus the live image, then focusing with the IR filter in place will be straightforward. If live view is not an option, an alternate method is to take a number of test images in the IR using distance markers and see what the visible foot scale on the lens reads in relation to the actual measured distance. With this data, you will be able to draw up a table to establish the IR focal length for your camera and lens. If you choose to have an online company remove the blocking filter and install an IR pass filter, in many cases you can request that the camera's autofocus be recalibrated for the IR.

Focusing in the long-wave ultraviolet range for reflectance is a little more interesting. Because the digital sensors are sensitive to only approximately 50nm below the visible (i.e., 350nm–400nm), with many lenses little refocusing is necessary, particularly when using a relatively small aperture for better depth of field. However, if refocusing is necessary, even with "live view" it is difficult to focus, due to the limited amount of energy being recorded on the sensor. Many times, I use a small ball bearing placed in the image to give a point of light to focus on, as the ball bearing will reflect both UV and IR. If you do not have live view, then a series of tests is the best way to determine the correct focus. It should be noted that the correction for UV may or may not be in the same direction as the IR correction, depending on how the lens has been manufactured for these respective portions of the spectrum.

FILM AND OTHER CAMERA SENSORS

Film comes in many forms, sizes, types, sensitivities, and resolutions. The basic structure of most film is a base as well as an emulsion(s) containing a light-sensitive material. Modern-day films can contain dozens of layers that serve a variety of functions, such as antihalation backings, anticurl coatings, and surface coatings, to name just a few. The base is a material that acts as a support for the emulsion and other layers. The most common substances used for this purpose have been glass, cellulous nitrate, cellulous acetate, and polyester. All modern film bases are polyester.

The emulsion is where the action happens. A typical emulsion is a combination of gelatin and silver halide. Silver halide crystals are distributed evenly throughout the gelatin as a light-sensitive material. The larger the silver halide crystals, the more sensitive to light they become; however, the image produced by this emulsion will appear grainy and have limited resolution. The smaller the crystals, the less sensitive to light the film becomes; however, the finer the grain appears on the image and the higher the relative resolution. Black and white film usually contains one emulsion layer. Color film contains three emulsion layers, each recording one-third of the spectrum—red, green, and blue—based on the intensity of the energy striking that layer of the film. When the film is processed and printed, these colors are combined to produce the illusion of color to our eyes.

When placed into a camera, the film becomes the sensor that is affected by the light energy or other energies. Panchromatic films are sensitive from about 700nm and less. When exposed, the energy is recorded in an **analog** manner, or as a continuum of dark to light. How much it is affected depends on a number of factors, the first of which is how sensitive it is to the light or energy that is being produced by the light source and scene. For this purpose, at least in the visible portion of the spectrum, film has been rated as to its sensitivity using several numbering systems. Older relative sensitivity numbering systems are the American Standards Association (ASA) and the German Deutsches Institute für Normung (DIN). Although from time to time you may hear the terms ASA or DIN being used, ISO (from the International Standards Organization) is the current world-wide standard and is the most widely used term. The ISO standard is also used for digital sensors and is based on its relationship to film.

The progression used by most film and digital sensor manufactures is: 50, 100, 200, 400, 800, 1,600, 3,200, 6,400, and 128,000. The ISO rating, or number, denotes the amount of light needed to produce a properly exposed image. A piece of film has only one ISO or sensitivity rating, whereas the digital sensors ISO can be changed to suit the lighting conditions. Many digital cameras have a variable range between 100 through 128,000 or higher. So, in essence, we can change the sensitivity of the sensor as we see fit. As the number increases, say from 400 to 800, the sensor is twice as sensitive to light. Inversely, as the number decreases, say from 800 to 400, the sensor is half as sensitive to light.

Most panchromatic film is sensitive to energy from the x-ray through to the red portion of the visible spectrum (approximately 0.10nm to 700nm). Panchromatic films also have special layers to reduce their sensitivity below 400nm. There are some specialty IR films that will record up to approximately 900nm. However, using films such as Kodak High Speed Infrared can be somewhat difficult, as they must be loaded in total darkness. Many manufacturers have discontinued or greatly curtailed production of the specialty films and are slowly getting out of the general film business altogether. In the near future, the range and availability of film will be severely reduced. The digital sensor is the wave of the future, and when initially produced in the factory can have a spectral range of approximately 350nm to 1100nm. That gives us a 50nm range in the UV spectrum (350nm−400nm); a 300nm range in the visible spectrum (400nm to 700nm), but even more interestingly, it extends the spectral range another 400nm in the IR spectrum (700nm to 1100nm). The total range of the digital sensor is approximately 750nm. So we can conclude that most digital sensors have some UV sensitivity, good visible sensitivity, and great IR sensitivity. And it should be duly noted that over half of the digital sensor's sensitivity is in the infrared portion of the spectrum.

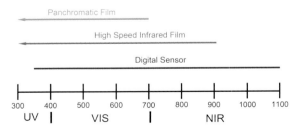

FIGURE 5-11
Spectral range of film and digital sensors

Most modern-day cameras use either film or an electronic sensor to detect light energy. Digital sensors operate and are constructed completely differently than the aforementioned analog film; they are replacing the film sensor that has been used in cameras for the past 160 years. By definition, a digital system is based on discrete numbers. So the purpose of the digital camera sensor is to convert light energy into a number.

All cameras and scanners are designed as a digital array of extremely small light sensitive sensors (photosites) called **pixels**. Each one of these light sensors acts like a little light meter, or bucket, collecting the amount of energy that strikes the sensor. The light collected by the sensor is converted to an electrical signal and then measured. The analog electrical signal is, in turn, converted to a number relative to the amount of light that was collected by the sensor. This number is usually between 0 and 255 (one byte), with 0 as pure black and 255 as pure white. All of the shades of gray are in between, from 1 to 254. These numbers are what the camera and computer use to represent a continuous-tone image.

The array can be linear, composed of a straight line of pixels, such as what is used on most scanners, or a rectangular matrix of pixels. DSLR cameras used for crime scene photography normally use a rectangular matrix that ranges from approximately 3000 × 2000 pixels (about 6 MP) up to 6000 × 4000 pixels (about 24 MP). It should be noted than the first number in the matrix usually refers to the number of horizontal pixels. The SWGIT currently recommends that the best practice for crime scene photography and most other forensic and law enforcement application is to use a digital camera that has at least 6 MP or a film camera using 35mm film.

DSLR cameras have three basic types of sensors; the **charge-coupled device (CCD)** and the **complementary metal-oxide semiconductor (CMOS)**, which are by far the most common, and the **Foveon sensor**, which is used solely by Sigma cameras. It is important to remember that all of these sensors basically record a gray scale and a method must be used to separate portions of the spectrum in order to simulate what we call color. The Foveon uses a three-layered sensor mimicking that of traditional film. Each layer filters and records the three primary colors: red, green, and blue. CCD, CMOS, and most other single-chip devices use red, green, and blue filters over the pixels and determine the color using a computer algorithm. There are twice as many green pixels (50%) as there are red (25%) and blue (25%) pixels, which mimics the human eye. This design is called a Bayer filter pattern or mosaic.

The CCD and CMOS are constructed completely differently, which is beyond the scope of this discussion, but produce similar images. Up until the last few years, most DSLR cameras used the CCD sensor; however, the

CMOS is currently dominating the market. Both sensors have positive and negative attributes, and neither is categorically a clear winner. That being said, some of the reasons the CMOS has taken over most of the DSLR market is because it has somewhat lower power requirements, lower fabrication costs, increased sensitivity to visible light and decreased sensitivity to infrared and ultraviolet, and it is systemically less complex. Some of the advantages of CCDs, particularly for crime scene and forensic photographers, are that they are very sensitive to infrared, somewhat sensitive to ultraviolet, have low system noise, and have high pixel uniformity. So in the most up-to-date DSLR, you will probably find a CMOS sensor; however, if you own an older DSLR, it is very likely to be a CCD. In either case, photographers should become well acquainted with the advantages and disadvantages of their particular sensor. Most photographers prefer the CCD for UV/IR work.

As previously mentioned, all of the DSLR sensors use a rectangular matrix composed of millions of pixels. This matrix is similar to a checkerboard (see Figure 5-12) and is usually numbered starting in the upper-left corner by rows and columns. The corner pixels in our 7×5 checker board sensor are 0,0; 0,6; 0,4; and 4,6. Therefore, each pixel—the smallest element of a picture—has three numbers associated with it, representing row, column, and light (energy) gathered. The row and column number can be any number, depending on the number of pixels, and the light (energy) acquired by a pixel is between 0 and 255. These matrices come in a variety of sizes and aspect ratios.

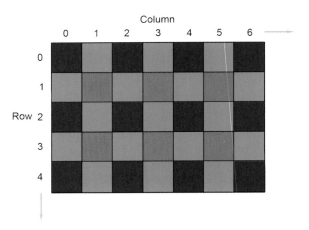

FIGURE 5-12
Illustration of how a sensor matrix is similar to a checkerboard with each square being one pixel

LIGHT (ENERGY)

The second portion of our triad is light or energy. The sensor must have some form of energy to sense or there will be no image. Stealth planes and ships use this concept by reflecting radar energy in a direction other than the sensor or by absorbing the energy, which denies the radar sensor any reflected energy in which to form an image.

In the visible portion of the spectrum, the most common light sources are natural daylight, incandescent lights, fluorescent lights, flash units, and, in more recent times, **light-emitting diodes (LEDs)**. In crime scene photography, these same energy sources can be utilized along with a wide array of specialty lights, including lasers, alternate light sources (this name was coined in the 1970s, meaning an alternative to a laser light source), UV or black lights, narrow-wavelength color flashlights, and **compact fluorescent lamp (CFL)** lightbulbs. There are literally thousands of light sources available for the photographer. They might be hand-held, in cabinets, or part of an entire system. Alternate light sources are designed specifically for the work of a crime scene photographer and provide high energy along with a wide range of specific wavelengths. However, these systems cost many thousands of dollars and must be utilized enough to justify the cost. Some of the specialty colored flashlights can also be costly; others are relatively inexpensive.

As with camera sensors, each light source has a native spectral range that may or may not be manipulated for a specific wavelength by using either excitation or barrier filters. Excitation filters are placed in front of the light to allow only the desired wavelengths of energy to pass. For purposes of this chapter, we are going to narrow our discussion to just the UV and IR energy sources. Barrier filters are used in front of the lens.

There are dozens of commercial UV light sources available in either shortwave, long-wave, or both. We will illustrate five very inexpensive long-wave ultraviolet (LWUV) light sources that can be found on the Web or at a local hardware store. The sixth light (letter "F" in the list) has been used for UV photography for many years.

All of these light sources produce long-wave UV at approximately 355nm, which is the center wavelength of the Baader BPU2 U-filter (320nm−390nm) barrier filter used for Figure 5-13.

In Figure 5-13 (top), only UV energy is seen by the camera, giving us a relative idea of the intensity of the six UV light sources. Note that UV lights A and D appear to be by far the brightest at this wavelength. When we look at Figure 5-13 (middle), which was photographed in the visible portion of the spectrum using a camera with a normal UV/IR blocking filter (400nm−700nm), all of the

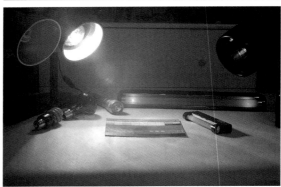

FIGURE 5-13
Top, ordinary eyeglasses, UV safety glasses, and 18A filter in the UV portion of the spectrum; middle, ordinary eyeglasses, UV safety glasses, and 18A filter in the VIS portion of the spectrum; bottom, ordinary eyeglasses, UV safety glasses, and 18A filter in the IR portion of the spectrum

light sources produce a violet/blue light. In this case, light A appears to produce the most visible energy, with light F producing the least. In Figure 5-13 (bottom), a Tiffon 87 barrier filter was used that allows only IR energy to pass. It is evident that light source B produces an extreme amount of infrared and light D shows some infrared near the location of the end heaters for the fluorescent lightbulb. Based on this test, it appears that the two cheapest UV light sources, both available at most local hardware stores, produce the most UV. Furthermore, we can conclude that light source B produces very little UV while producing a tremendous amount of IR.

A number of specialty strobes (flashes) have come and gone over time. The Nikon SB-140 Speedlight is perhaps the most well known and was specifically designed for use in both UV and IR photography. Manufacturing of the Speedlight has ceased, making them quite rare and very pricey. Quantum has recently marketed the Qflash UV/IR Wave Reflector, which replaces the standard reflector on the Quantum Qflash and provides a more powerful UV/ IR source. Note that most flash tubes provide considerable UV/ IR energy, but are limited to the visible by a UV blocking filter. However, we are not concerned with the IR as these flashes were designed for film, which is not sensitive to NIR. I've experimented with removing the front lens of a Vivitar 283 Auto Thyristor photo flash and found that it provides sufficient energy in the UV, VIS, and IR spectra. These flashes can be found for under $80, and it takes about 15 minutes to remove the front lens, making this a fairly affordable option.

Another great technique for both UV and IR is called "painting with light" and is executed by using long shutter speeds or a bulb setting on the camera. Using a UV, VIS, or IR flashlight to scan back and forth over the subject not only gives the photographer better control of the exposure but can also provide even lighting—more so than by using one or two UV bulbs.

When dealing with any type of bright light or energy source, the crime scene photographer needs to be aware of **safety factors** that affect not only the photographer but also those nearby. When working with visible light, never look directly at the light or point it in a direction that would allow it to shine in the face of a bystander. Damage from staring into visible light can be similar to damage from staring directly into the sun and could ultimately result in serious permanent visual impairment or blindness.

Photographers should also pay special attention to the potential safety hazards and risks of working in the UV and IR portions of the spectrum. Because our eyes are not sensitive to pure UV or IR, we cannot readily "see" this energy. However, that energy can still seriously affect our eyes, and as we cannot see it, we may be unaware of the damage that is taking place.

Eye protection should be used at all times when working with UV or IR energy.

In most cases, the IR is an exception as the source is usually a visible light that is rich in IR. UV energy is of most concern when speaking of potential damage.

Although shortwave UV contains the energy regarded as most harmful to eyes and skin, long-wave UV can also cause damaging effects. Long-wave UV reflectance and luminescence is widely used in crime scene photography; therefore, it is of utmost importance that UV opaque glasses are consistently used. It is a common misconception that ordinary eyeglasses will protect the eye from UV energy. More often than not, eyeglasses are as transparent to UV as they are to visible energy.

Figure 5-14 is an example using the Sylvania Super Saver CFL 60- (13-) watt black light for a UV source, and a standard 40-watt incandescent lightbulb for a visible and IR source. In the foreground, from left to right, are a pair of ordinary eye glasses, a Kodak 18A UV filter, and a pair of UV safety glasses. Figure 5-14 (top) shows the long-wave UV. This image was taken with the Baader BPU2 U-filter (320nm–390nm) barrier filter over the camera lens. Note that both the ordinary eyeglasses and the 18A filter are transparent to the UV and that the UV safety glasses are completely opaque. Figure 5-14 (middle) was taken with a Peca #916 UV/IR blocking filter over the camera lens, allowing only visible energy (400nm–700nm) to pass through the lens. Note that in the visible spectrum, both the ordinary eyeglasses and the UV safety glasses are perfectly clear and that the 18A filter is opaque. In Figure 5-14 (bottom), a Peca #914 IR pass barrier filter is on the lens. Note that both the ordinary eye glasses and the UV safety glasses are transparent, however, the 18A filter is partly transparent in the IR portion of the spectrum. This partial transparency is why the 18A filter was optimal for film which did not reach the IR portion of the spectrum and subsequently worked quite well as a UV pass filter. With the introduction of digital cameras and their extended sensitivity to the infrared, a photographer shooting a UV picture with the 18A filter could not be sure if they were recording UV and/or IR, henceforth, the Baader BPU2 U-filter became the UV filter of choice for digital cameras.

FIGURE 5-14

Top, photographing only UV energy sources, blocking visible and IR; middle, photographing only visible energy sources, blocking UV and IR; bottom, photographing only IR energy sources, blocking UV and visible

From left to right:

(A) Sylvania Super Saver CFL, 60- (13-) watt, 120-volt black light (actually 13 watts, but replaces a 60 watt incandescent bulb)

(B) Bulbrite R-25 Blacklite Bulb, 75-watt, 120-volt black light

(C) Streamlight Twin-Task three-LED, 4.5-volt, 3 C-cell battery UV flash

(D) Portfolia 18-inch Under Cabinet Fluorescent, 15-watt, 120-volt black light

(E) F4T5BLB, 5" Fluorescent, 6-volt, 4 AA-cell battery black light

(F) UVP B-100 Series High-Intensity UV lamp, 160-watt, 120–220 volt black light

FILTERS

One of the more challenging jobs of the crime scene/forensic photographer is to manipulate energy (light) in concert with the sensor to provide an accurate representation of a scene, or to obtain additional evidence that is not readily seen by the naked eye. Enter filters, the third portion of the triad. There are many types of filters that are used in the overall imaging industry; however, most photographic systems and photographers use glass filters. Remember that the triad is composed of energy, sensors, and filters. The purpose of the filter as part of the aforementioned triad is to reduce the spectral range of either the energy source, the sensor, or both to achieve a specific result.

The most common types of filters used in photography are glass substrate **short-pass** filters, **long-pass** filters, and **band-pass** filters. With a short-pass filter, light is transmitted with wavelengths shorter than a certain cut-off wavelength. This means only shorter-wave energy is allowed to reach the sensor—say, 500nm and below—and all longer-wave energy is blocked or cut. With a long-pass filter, light is transmitted with wavelengths longer than a specific cut-on wavelength. This means only longer-wave energy, such as 700nm and up, is allowed to pass, and anything of a shorter wavelength is rejected. A band-pass filter is just what it implies: a filter that allows only light around a specific center wavelength within a certain band while blocking all others. The bands can be a narrow band or a wide band. If the filter passes two discreet bands, or parts of the spectrum at the same time, it is a **dichroic filter**. A relevant example of this is the wide band–pass filter in our everyday cameras, which lets through only visible light and blocks the UV/IR.

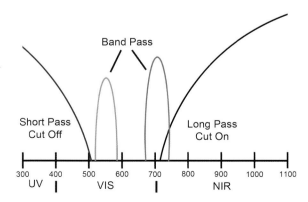

FIGURE 5-15
Sample of various filters spectral response

In order to keep the UV and IR energy from affecting the image, most commercial digital camera manufacturers place a UV/IR blocking filter in front of the digital sensor (with analog systems, coatings are placed on the film) that take advantage of the natural limits of panchromatic film. This filter is used to reduce the spectral range to approximately the visible range, 400nm to 700nm, so that the desired scene looks the same as if we were seeing it with our eyes. In some cases, the digital camera filter is permanent; however, in many cases a qualified technician may be able to remove it. One caveat is that this type of procedure will void most warranties.

If the original filter is removed, the camera can still be used to take ordinary crime scene photographs. In this instance, a screw-on-filter would be placed on the front of the camera lens allowing only the visible energy to pass, thus blocking all UV/IR energy. This arrangement can provide the best of both worlds for an organization with limited funds, allowing use of the same camera for general photography as well as for UV/IR imaging. However, it should be noted that not all blocking filters are the same, and different manufacturers blocking filters and many screw-on filters can produce significantly different results in the image. Therefore, it is best to conduct a little research before purchasing these filters.

There are two additional generic names used for filters worth mentioning, each named for their particular use. The "Excitation" filter is used over the energy source and the "Barrier" filter is used over the sensor. If no other energy is present in a room (i.e., pitch black with no unseen UV/IR), then it does not

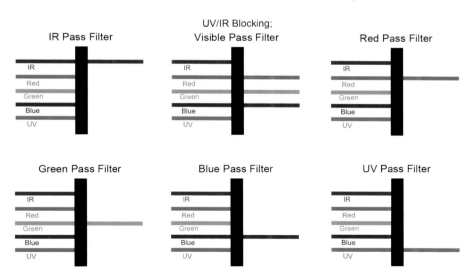

FIGURE 5-16
Graphs illustrating how filters limit and control energy

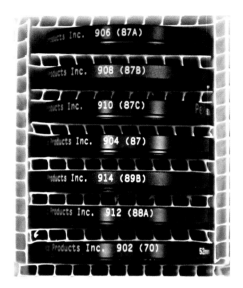

FIGURE 5-17
Seven of the most commonly used IR cut-on filters (bottom to top): Kodak designation 70, 88A, 89B, 87, 87C, 87B, 87A

matter whether an excitation filter is placed over the energy source or a barrier filter is placed over the sensor. The same results will occur due to the spectrum being limited. However, these approaches works only for reflectance. If the photographer is trying to achieve luminescence, then an excitation filter usually must be placed on the energy source, and a barrier filter, in a higher portion of the spectrum, must cover the sensor.

There is an oddity in the way filters are described. When we use a "red filter," based on the name, it sounds like it filters or eliminates red. However, in contrast, the only wavelength that this filter lets pass *is* red, ultimately blocking all other wavelengths.

REFLECTANCE

When energy—such as the visible light produced by the sun, electronic flash, incandescent light, an alternate light source, or other source—leaves its source, it can reach the sensor via various paths, one of those ways being of course direct transmission. Light energy, in most cases, can also be **transmitted**, **reflected**, or **absorbed**. All three of these terms are often combined and simply referred to as a generic term: **reflectance**. This applies to visible energy and energy throughout the spectrum.

Reflectance (as a generic term) includes:

1. Energy that is totally transmitted directly from the source and passing through, or partly through, an object to the sensor. Example: the visible light travels though the air, or a sheet of glass, to reach the sensor. X-ray energy travelling through a body part is a good example of this same process outside of the visible spectrum.
2. Energy that is totally reflected by a surface. Example: all the visible light in the spectrum is reflected from an object, such as a white piece of paper. We perceive, process, and name this condition "white" if it contains the full visible spectrum.
3. Energy that is totally absorbed by a surface. Example: all the visible light in the spectrum is absorbed by an object, such as a black countertop. We perceive, process, and name this condition "black."
4. Energy that is partially reflected and partially absorbed by a surface. Only a specific wavelength of the visible light is reflected, with the remainder being absorbed. Example: red blood on a white floor. This condition is perceived by our eyes or sensor, processed, and named a conventionally agreed-upon name such as "red."

No matter what part of the spectrum we are focusing on, the same three things will happen to the energy when recording an image. The energy is transmitted, absorbed, or reflected at varying degrees, depending on the material the energy is striking and the material through which it passes.

The previous explanation should help solidify the fact that color, such as white, black, red, green, and blue is nothing more than how our mind's eye perceives some portions of the visible spectrum, processing that information to then identify or tag that perception with a conventionally agreed-upon name like puce, coral, garnet, and so on. A camera can mimic human perception; however, it is necessary to use dyes and filters to recreate and record these same, or similar, perceptions (color reproduction). Also, outside of the visible spectrum, there is no such thing as color. That is why when we see photographs taken in the ultraviolet or infrared portions of the spectrum, they are in various shades of gray, unless color has been artificially added. The term used for this is "false color." As color is only perceived in our mind's eye, one might argue that color is a figment of our imagination.

That being said, as we view or record an object in different parts of the spectrum, such as from visible to infrared, an object being photographed may or may not react in the same way to the different parts of the spectrum. As an example, a visible light photograph of a suspect under surveillance may be taken showing him wearing blue jeans and a brown plaid shirt. If photographed in infrared, the jeans and shirt may both appear white, because the dyes used in the clothing partially reflect and partially absorb the light in the visible portion of the spectrum giving us the colors blue and brown. However, in the infrared portion of the spectrum, the dyes are either transparent or reflect light, and what is seen or recorded is the cloth reflecting the infrared, making it appear white or gray. Note that although materials transmit, absorb, or reflect energy throughout the spectrum, they may not have the same reaction in every part of the spectrum.

FIGURE 5-18

Left, unaltered digital camera image, 400nm to 700nm; middle, image with no blocking filter, 350nm to 1100nm; right, image with only IR pass filter (87), 800nm and above

Figure 5-18 shows three simulated surveillance images of a man with a spider on the back of his jacket. The first picture was taken with an unaltered digital camera containing the usual UV/IR blocking filter (spectral range of about 400nm−700nm). The second picture is taken with a camera containing no blocking filter, just the native chip (spectral range of about 350nm−1100nm). Note the difference in the jacket; however, more important, note the shrubs in the background. The third image is taken by the same camera using an

FIGURE 5-19

Left, obliterated mailing label in the visible portion of the spectrum; right, obliterated mailing label in the IR portion of the spectrum

infrared passing 87 filter (spectral range of about 800 and up). If the suspect were described using only the third picture, it would be a completely misleading description.

Another example is when a crime scene photographer comes across a mailing label with black printing that has been obliterated using a black marker. In the visible spectrum, the label is impossible to read and would photograph as black on black. However when photographed in the infrared spectrum under the right conditions, the top black ink will be transparent, revealing the black printing below. In essence, the top black ink, as seen in the infrared, is similar to a sheet of glass in the visible.

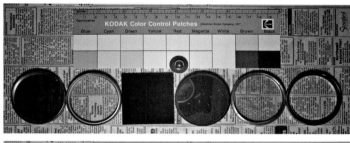

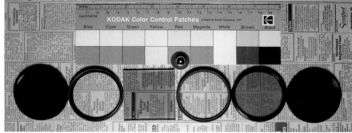

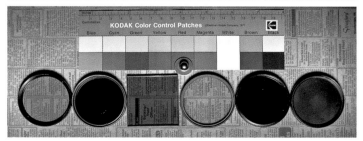

FIGURE 5-20
Top, glass filters imaged in the IR (87 filter) portion of the spectrum, 800nm and up; middle, glass filters imaged in visible light with a UV/IR filter blocking that portion of the spectrum, 400nm to 700nm; bottom, glass filters imaged in the UV (Baader BPU2 U-filter) portion of the spectrum, 320nm to 390nm

Figure 5-20 illustrates how six different pieces of glass (in reality, just glass filters) react in the infrared, visible, and long-wave ultraviolet portions of the spectrum. The six pieces of glass in Figure 5-20 are as follows from left to right:

■ UV pass; VIS/IR block: Peca Products Inc., #900 (18A); (18A is also the Kodak filter designation)
■ VIS/IR pass; UV block: Tiffon Sky 1-A
■ UV/VIS pass; IR block: Blue/Green Corning 4-96 (9782)
■ VIS pass; UV/IR block: Heliopan Digital UV/IR
■ VIS/IR pass; UV block: Tiffon Red 25; (Kodak designation for this filter is also Red 25)
■ IR pass; VIS/UV block: Peca Products Inc., #914 (89B); (89B is also the Kodak designation)

All of these images were photographed with a Fuji S3 UV/IR camera with an approximate spectral range of 350nm to 1100nm.

Figure 5-20 (bottom) illustrates long-wave UV reflectance and was photographed using a Baader BPU2 U-filter over the sensor with a spectral pass of approximately 320nm to 390nm. This filter was designed for astronomical purposes and has therefore gained the nickname "Venus filter." The energy or light for this image was a 365nm LED flashlight using the technique "painting with light" for two minutes. Figure 5-20 (middle) is a visible reflected image with a Peca 916 (Visible) filter over the sensor with a spectral range of 400nm to 750nm. The light source for this image was a 40-watt incandescent lightbulb. Figure 5-20 (top) illustrates near infrared reflectance. It was produced with a Peca 904 (87) filter over the sensor with a spectral range of 750nm and up. The light source for this image was also a 40-watt incandescent lightbulb. It should be noted that incandescent lights provide not only visible light but a tremendous amount of infrared energy. Figure 5-21 is a graphical representation of the above descriptions.

The UV pass, VIS/IR block glass filter (#1) is doing its job by adsorbing, or blocking, both visible and IR energy while sustaining transparency when using UV energy. The VIS/IR pass, UV block glass filter (#2) also appears to be responding well by absorbing the UV and transmitting (passing) the visible and infrared. The UV/VIS pass, IR block glass filter (#3) is a special filter used for visible/IR luminescence; therefore, it is imperative that it absorbs or blocks all IR. The glass transmits only energy in the blue/green and UV portions of the spectrum. The VIS pass, UV/IR block glass filter (#4) is of similar design to a built-in camera filter, supposedly absorbing all UV and IR and transmitting only the visible. This glass filter works well in

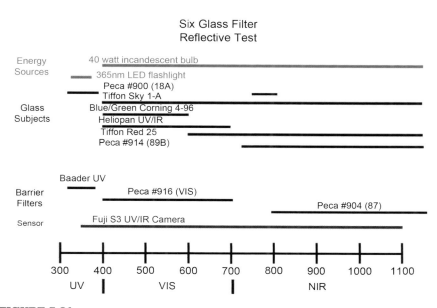

FIGURE 5-21

Illustration of the spectral range of the six glass filters, light sources, and sensor

absorbing the IR; however, it is evident that it does a less-than-adequate job of absorbing the UV. Figure 5-20 (bottom) provides proof that it transmits a considerable amount of UV. The VIS/IR pass, UV block glass filter (red) (#5) works well at transmitting red and IR and absorbing the UV. The IR pass, VIS/UV block glass filter (#6) absorbs both visible and UV while readily transmitting the IR.

The following section provides an example of how one might conduct an exam on writing ink.

Reflection Example

Previous explanation has defined the term "reflectance" generically as the reaction between a light (energy) source and an object. Following is a description of this process:

1. The illuminating energy (light) and sensor are, for the most part, both in the *same* portion of the spectrum.
2. The ink absorbs the light and therefore appears dark relative to the paper, which reflects the light and therefore appears white. This is the most common occurrence. If the ink absorbs only a portion of the light, also reflecting a portion, it may appear colored or gray against the white paper.

3. The ink may transmit the light (like a piece of glass) and therefore become transparent. Such an ink is an "invisible ink," as is used in espionage.

FIGURE 5-22
Top, check in the visible portion of the spectrum; bottom, check in the IR portion of the spectrum

It is important to note that the energy (light) and the sensor (camera) *must* be in the same portion of the spectrum.

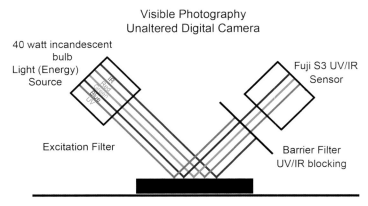

FIGURE 5-23
Illustration of visible reflectance photography

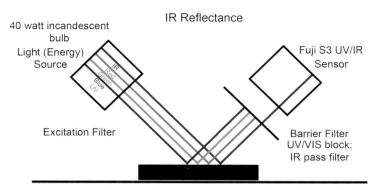

FIGURE 5-24
Illustration of IR reflectance photography

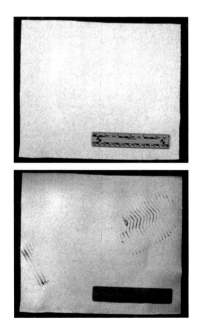

FIGURE 5-25
Top, visible image of shoe print on a paper towel; bottom, UV reflective image of the same paper towel

Most crime scene or forensic photography is done with reflected light in the visible portion of the spectrum. However, it should now be quite evident that a great deal of valuable information may be gained by having the knowledge and skill to produce reflected images in the infrared portion of the spectrum. In most cases, this can be accomplished with the use of

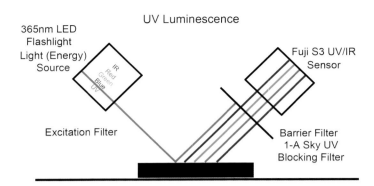

FIGURE 5-26
Illustration of ultraviolet reflectance photography

a camera sensitive to IR, a UV/VIS block/IR pass filter, and an incandescent light source. Although ultraviolet reflectance can be achieved using a UV light and a camera sensitive to UV, most cameras are much more limited in their sensitivity to UV, and the (visible/IR blocking) UV pass filters are expensive. Film may still prove to be a good option for use with a camera containing a UV sensor as it is very sensitive to all wavelengths shorter than approximately 700nm.

LUMINESCENCE

The phenomenon referred to as **luminescence** is another way of using photography to reveal unseen information. "Luminescence," in literal terms, means to glow. We often witness this phenomenon when objects are illuminated with a long-wave UV (black light) source that causes objects to glow. Although we cannot see ultraviolet light with our eyes (we may see a slight blue light that is visible, but the majority of the energy is invisible), the LWUV energy is absorbed by the object, converted, and re-emitted as energy (light), in a longer wavelength of the spectrum. The next longer wavelength other than UV is visible, so we see the object as glowing. Although this instance is perhaps the most relevant to us, this same phenomenon can occur throughout the spectrum.

Luminescence can also be subdivided into the categories of **fluorescence** and **phosphorescence**. The sole difference between fluorescence and phosphorescence is determined by removing the energy source. If the glowing immediately ceases, it is termed fluorescence. If the object continues to glow for a period of time, it is termed phosphorescence. Many objects we see or use daily depend on this principle, such as the fluorescent light. Mercury is heated within the tube of the light to a point at which it emits ultraviolet energy.

Remember that we cannot see ultraviolet energy, so a fluorescent powder coats the inside of the tube, resulting in a glow that is visible to our eyes. When the ultraviolet energy strikes the powder, it is absorbed and re-emitted in the next higher portion of the spectrum: visible light. This light is cool to the touch, as opposed to an incandescent light, which produces light by heating an element. Even though the glass tube and powder absorb most of the ultraviolet light, one should be aware that florescent lights do radiate some ultraviolet light—one reason why many signatures on documents or photographs hanging in office buildings will begin to fade over time, as if they were placed in direct sunlight.

Many signs, children's toys, and novelty products use phosphorescent paints or powders to produce an "afterglow." Some electronics also utilize phosphorescent powders; however, after the energy source is removed, devices such as older televisions and computer monitors that use an electronic beam to illuminate thousands of small colored spots on the front of the screen would not work without this extended emission of light. In the world of crime scene photography, it is not often that we run into many long-lasting phosphorescent materials as evidence.

The basic theory behind this phenomenon is referred to as Stokes Law, named for the individual who first described it in 1852: George Gabriel Stokes. This law basically states that when fluorescence (luminescence) occurs, the wavelength of the emitted energy source (or fluorescent light) is always longer than the excitation energy. There are exceptions to this law, producing what is known as anti-Stokes luminescence; however, that is somewhat beyond the scope and relevance of this discussion.

Following is another writing ink examination example, but this time it illustrates luminescence. The light or energy is blue/green (400nm–600nm) and the camera is recognizing only the infrared portion of the spectrum. In this case, the camera is also sensitive to visible light, so a barrier filter is placed over the lens that absorbs or blocks all visible light and lets pass only infrared. Although only blue-green energy is shining on the ink, when viewed in the infrared portion of the spectrum, the re-emitted infrared energy makes the ink appear to glow.

Luminescence Examples

As noted, the term "luminescence" means to glow. In order to produce luminescence, the following conditions are necessary:

1. Use an illuminating energy (light), and a sensor, that are in *different* portions of the spectrum.
2. Illuminate a material using energy (light) limited to one portion of the spectrum; in this case, we will use blue/green visible light.

3. The illuminating energy is absorbed by the material being studied, such as ink.
4. This absorbed energy is converted and re-emitted from the object in a higher (longer wavelength) portion of the spectrum, such as yellow, red, or infrared.
5. The sensor is filtered or blocked from the original blue/green illuminating energy, allowing only the emitted longer-wave energy to pass.
6. The material is viewed in the (longer) portion of the spectrum as glowing.

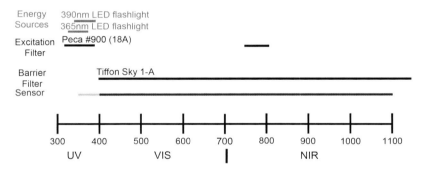

FIGURE 5-27

Illustration of the spectral range of the light source, filter, and sensor for UV luminescence

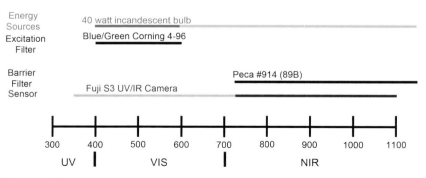

FIGURE 5-28

Illustration of the spectral range of the light source, filter, and sensor for visible (IR) luminescence

It is important to note that unlike in the reflectance example, the energy (light) and sensor (camera) have to be in *different* parts of the spectrum. The sensor must always be in a longer portion of the spectrum (wavelength) than the energy (light) source. This example follows the same process as earlier noted; when objects are illuminated with a long-wave ultraviolet (black light) source, they begin to glow.

There is no one portion of the spectrum that will stimulate luminescence of all materials. Different materials are stimulated by different portions of the spectrum. This is why many commercial crime scene light systems have the ability to "tune" through different narrow bands of wavelengths, perhaps in 50nm increments, in order to detect and record as much of the evidence as possible.

Another oddity is that when most people talk about luminescence they refer to it from the standpoint of the energy source or "excitation" wavelength. For instance, x-ray fluorescence is obtained by x-rays stimulating the subject and the emission energy in a longer wavelength. Ultraviolet fluorescence means that UV is the exciting wavelength being fluoresced into the visible portion of the spectrum or above. Visible florescence is produced by using a blue visible energy source and viewing in the green, yellow, orange, red, or infrared portion of the spectrum. When most photographers discuss "infrared luminescence," the excitation source is not infrared, but blue/green, and therefore should also be referred to as visible or "blue/green" luminescence. However, for purposes of this discussion, we will continue to use the unconventional description of IR luminescence as being visible (blue/green) energy converting to near infrared energy.

Figure 5-29 shows six images of the same piece of cloth with various lights and filters. Note the wide range of reactions from left to right:

- Normal fluorescent room light (visible reflectance)
- Tungsten filament flashlight held obliquely (visible reflectance)
- Long-wave ultraviolet light, with UV adsorbing filter over the camera lens (UVLW luminescence or fluorescence)
- Blue light, with orange filter over the camera lens (blue light luminescence)
- Green light, with red filter over the camera lens (green light luminescence)
- Infrared light, with Kodak #87 IR filter over the lens (IR reflectance)

Alterations such as in Figure 5-30 (top) can be difficult to detect, even with high magnification; however, there is little doubt when imaged in the IR using a blue/green light source, as in Figure 5-30 (bottom). When this demonstrative evidence is present in court, little cross-examination is effective.

FIGURE 5-29

Six images of the same piece of cloth with various lights and filters

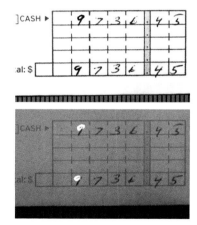

FIGURE 5-30

Top, altered deposit slip in the visible portion of the spectrum; Bottom, the same slip using IR (visible) luminescence

There are instances where an object has been altered and the luminescent ink/material may be underneath the obliterating ink/material. Often, the luminescent ink/material will be bright enough to show through the upper obstruction. This is demonstrated in Figure 5-31, with the top receipt having been imaged with visible light and the same receipt on the bottom having been imaged using IR (visible) luminescence.

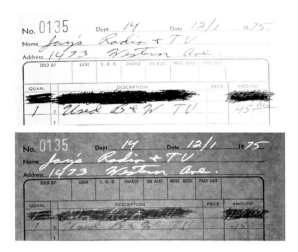

FIGURE 5-31
Top, receipt in visible light; bottom, same receipt imaged using IR (visible) luminescence

Although not specifically covered in this chapter, there are several available powders, dyes, and aerosols that can be utilized to visualize or reveal fingerprints, shoe prints, blood, and other types of evidence. They are usually designed to luminesce by shining a visible blue or green light on the treated evidence, and then viewing or photographing that evidence in the yellow or red portion of the spectrum.

CHAPTER SUMMARY

Mastering crime scene photography and photography in general is a function of one's ability master the manipulation of energy (light) in concert with a sensor. The electromagnetic spectrum is the scale on which we measure that energy, along with the spectral sensitivity of sensors and transmission/absorbance of filters. Once this triad of energy, sensors, and filters is understood and mastered, crime scene photographers have the ability to thoroughly document evidence they can see with the naked eye as well as evidence that is not readily visible.

In this chapter we have explored the spectrum; types of cameras, lenses, and sensors; and various energy sources and filters. The examples and illustrations throughout were provided as a means of demonstration as to how each of these pieces relate to each other and how they tend to form a sort of symbiotic relationship.

The color we see in the visible portion of the spectrum is nothing more than how our minds interpret the electromagnetic energy detected by our eyes. Beyond the visible portion of the spectrum are the ultraviolet and near infrared portions, which have become the new frontier of photography with the advancement of digital imaging technology. Five distinct groups of imaging techniques were explored throughout this chapter:

- LWUVR: Long-wave ultraviolet reflectance
- LWUVL: Long-wave ultraviolet luminescence
- VISIBLE: Visible light reflectance
- NIRR: Near infrared reflectance
- NIRL: Near infrared luminescence

One last example will help better define the different results obtained from these techniques. Figure 5-32 illustrates eight different black writing inks and one pencil. Each box has a set of initials. The same writing instrument was used to write the initials horizontally for one entire row. The same writing instruments were again used to obliterate the initials in the appropriate vertical column. It can be seen how each ink relates to each other in the five different portions of the spectrum as described previously. Note that in the visible, all inks appear black or dark; however, they react much differently when seen in the UV or IR portions of the spectrum. Also note that the pencil is highly reflective of the long-wave UV energy.

Figure 5-33 is a similar illustration, this time demonstrating the reaction of various dyes in small pieces of cloth to the various portions of the spectrum.

Should you like to find out more information regarding these topics, a simple search of the Web will produce hundreds of websites and blogs dealing with the spectrum, UV and other wavelengths.

Discussion Questions

1. What are the three major portions of the spectrum used by crime scene photographers?
2. What parts of the spectrum does the light source and sensor need to be, in order to produce reflectance?
3. What parts of the spectrum does the light source and sensor need to be, in order to produce luminescence?
4. Why do we bother to photograph objects in both the UV and IR portions of the spectrum?
5. When using any strong energy or light source, but particularly UV, what safety precautions should be taken?

Practical Exercises

1. Use your digital camera to view or photograph a television remote pointed directly at the camera as one of the buttons is being pressed. If you can

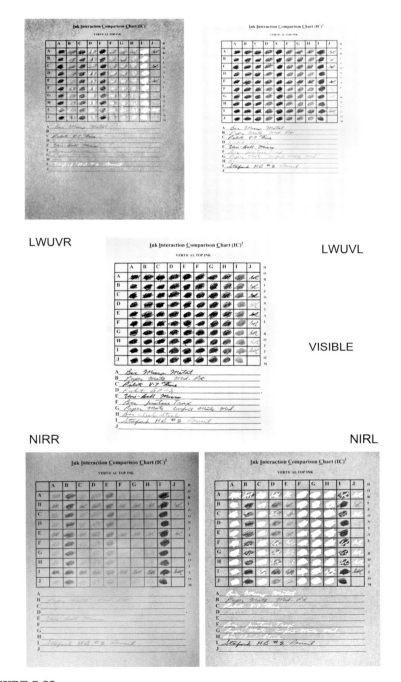

FIGURE 5-32

Eight writing inks and one pencil as seen using reflectance and luminescence in the LWUV, VIS, and NIR

LWUVR

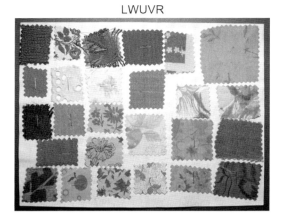

LWUVL

VISIBLE

NIRR

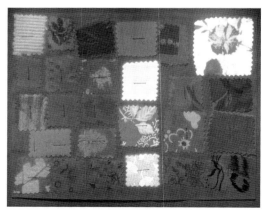

NIRL

FIGURE 5-33

The various dyes in twenty-six pieces of cloth as seen using reflectance and luminescence in the LWUV, VIS, and NIR

photograph the light on the front of the remote, your camera's blocking filter is passing some IR. This shows IR energy (light) directly from the source to the sensor, with only the air acting as a filter.

2. Buy or borrow an infrared passing filter that covers the lens of you camera, perhaps a Kodak equivalent of a #88A or #89B. Use a 60-watt lightbulb and photograph various inks and markers you can find around the house, such as IR reflectance. (By the way, one or two sheets of completely exposed and processed 4×5 color film will make a reasonable IR filter when placed over the lens. You may be able to have a professional photographer who still uses 4×5 color film to expose and process them for you.)

3. Go to a hardware store and buy a 60-watt compact fluorescent lamp (CFL) lightbulb or 18-inch under-cabinet fluorescent black light. Go into a dark room, turn on the light, and see how many things fluoresce. When you turn the light out, do any of the objects still glow, or phosphoresce?

4. Buy and inexpensive UV blocking filter (sky filter) for your camera. Find objects that fluoresce in a dark room and photograph them (UV fluorescence).

Suggested Reading

Dalrymple, B. E. 1983. Visible and Infrared Luminescence in Documents: Excitation by Laser. *Journal of Forensic Sciences* 28:692–696.

David, T. J., & Sobel, M. N. 1994. Recapturing a Five-Month-Old Bite Mark by Means of Reflective Ultraviolet Photography. *Journal of Forensic Sciences* 39:1560–1567.

Eastman Kodak Company. 1972. Ultraviolet & Fluorescence Photography. A Kodak Technical Publication, M-27. Rochester, NY: Eastman Kodak Company.

Eastman Kodak Company. 1973. Medical Infrared Photography. A Kodak Technical Publication, N-1. Rochester, NY: Eastman Kodak Company.

Eastman Kodak Company. 1974. Kodak Infrared Films. A Kodak Technical Publication, N-17. Rochester, NY: Eastman Kodak Company.

Eastman Kodak Company. 1976. Using Photography to Preserve Evidence. A Kodak Technical Publication, M-2. Rochester, NY: Eastman Kodak Company.

Eastman Kodak Company. 1981. Handbook of Kodak Photographic Filters. A Kodak Technical Publication, B-3. Rochester, NY: Eastman Kodak Company.

Eastman Kodak Company. 1990. Applied Infrared Photography. A Kodak Technical Publication, M-28. Rochester, NY: Eastman Kodak Company.

Gibson, H. L. 1978. Photography by Infrared: Its Principles and Applications. New York: John Wiley & Sons.

Harnischmacher, C. 2008. *Digital Infrared Photography*. Santa Barbara, CA: Rocky Nook Inc.

Hilton, O. 1981. New Dimensions in Infrared Luminescence Photography. *Journal of Forensic Sciences* 26:319–324.

Krauss, T. C. 1985. The Forensic Science Use of Reflective Ultraviolet Photography. *Journal of Forensic Sciences* 30:262–268.

Richards, G. B. 1977. The Application of Electronic Video Techniques to Infrared and Ultraviolet Examinations. *Journal of Forensic Sciences* 22(1): 53–60.

Richards, G. B. 2003. Dichroic Filters: Their Use in Questioned Document Examinations. *Journal of the American Society of Questioned Document Examiners* 6(1): 91–96.

Richards, G. B. 2007. Beyond Visible Light. *Evidence Technology Magazine* 5(3): 32–35.

Scientific Working Group Imaging Technology (SWGIT). Overview of SWGIT and the Use of Imaging Technology in the Criminal Justice System. http://www.swgit.org.

Stroebel, L. D., Compton, J., et al. 1986. *Photographic Materials and Processes.* Boston: Focal Press.

Williams, A. R., & Williams, G. G. 1993. The Invisible Image? Part 1: Introduction and Reflected Ultraviolet Techniques. *Journal of Biological Photography* 61:115–132. (or http://www.mediphoto.com.au/articles.html)

Williams, A. R., & Williams, G. G. 1994. The Invisible Image? Part 3: Reflected Infrared Photography. *Journal of Biological Photography* 62:51–68. (or http://www.mediphoto.com.au/articles.html)

CHAPTER 6

Digital Processing of Evidentiary Photography

David "Ski" Witzke

KEY TERMS

Bit
Bitmap
Byte
Camera RAW format
Digital image
Dots per inch (dpi)
Guideline
JPG

Lossless compression
Lossy compression
Mbps
Pixels
Pixels per inch (ppi)
Raster graphics
Requirement

Standard Operating
    Procedure (SOP)
Scientific Working Group
    on Imaging Technology
    (SWGIT)
Tagged Image File Format
    (TIF or TIFF)
Vector graphics

LEARNING OBJECTIVES

Upon completion of this lesson, you will be able to:

- Explain what bit depth has to do with color values in a digital image
- Explain the relationship between resolution and image quality
- Explain the effects of compression on digital images
- Explain the impact of resolution on file size and what a larger file size has to do with uploading and/or downloading image files
- Explain why camera RAW formats are usually preferred by the courts
- Explain why standard operating procedures for digital imaging are required for law enforcement agencies
- Explain why higher resolution produces a better quality image, and why this may not always be true
- Explain why rotating an image in anything other than 90-degree increments is not an acceptable practice for Category 2 images prior to image enhancement
- Explain the differences between dots, pixels, and samples in digital imaging

CONTENTS

303

Introduction to Crime Scene Photography.
Copyright © 2013 Elsevier Inc. All rights reserved.

IN THE BEGINNING

Photography has been used in the criminal justice system since 1839,[1] and the use of imaging technologies is an accepted practice in all forensic sciences, regardless of whether the imaging is performed in a traditional wet chemistry darkroom or in a laboratory equipped only with electronic devices, such as computers, digital cameras, scanners, and/or video capture systems.

In the past 10 to 15 years, we have seen a widespread acceptance of the use of digital imaging technologies in almost every aspect of our lives. Just in terms of cell phones, we have experienced a tremendous increase in the number of users. In 1996, there were only about 38.2 million subscribers. At the end of 2011, there were more than 323 million subscriber connections, which represents over 90 percent of the households in the United States.

At the beginning of 2010, the Worldwide Community of Imaging Associations released its U.S. Photo Industry 2010 forecast report as part of the PMA 2010 trade show. In the report, it was forecast that 22.7 million point-and-shoot cameras and 2.1 million DSLR cameras were expected to be sold in the United States in 2010. It was also reported that approximately 80 percent of U.S. households own digital cameras. Similar to cell phones, only about 10 percent of U.S. households owned a digital camera in 1996.

The PMA report also forecast that the overall market value of digital cameras, printing, and photo publishing in the United States alone would exceed $10 billion in 2010 and that Americans would make approximately 13.9 billion photo prints, with about a third of those prints being made at home.

No wonder it is easier today to capture the moment with the proliferation of high-resolution digital cameras in cell phones by manufacturers such as Apple, LG, Motorola, Samsung, Sony, and others that contain an 8 Megapixel (MP) digital camera. Some phones, such as the iPhone 4s, now also include **high dynamic range (HDR)** capability. This feature captures three photos from a single shot, with each photo using a different value for the exposure level. The photos are then layered together to create a single photo that combines the best parts of each photo into a more balanced photo.

The good news is that more and more people are becoming familiar with and accepting the use of digital technologies. In particular, there is a significant increase in the adoption of digital cameras in the criminal justice community. The bad news is that there is still a very limited knowledge base when it comes to understanding the basics of digital imaging.

---

[1]Charles C. Scott, 1969, *Photographic Evidence, Vol. 1*, 2nd Edition, West Publishing Company (St. Paul, MN. 1969), page 2.

For example, although there is growing desire for higher-resolution digital cameras, there is also a growing level of frustration from users who don't understand that higher resolution means larger image files (file size) that require more storage space (capacity) and more time to upload and/or download.

In this chapter, we will discuss the fundamentals of digital photography and provide you with a better understanding of digital imaging concepts used within the criminal justice community, such as the best practices and guidelines for forensic digital imaging.

THAT REALLY BYTES!

To fully understand the use of digital image processing techniques, you must understand some of the basics of the technology.

According to Wikipedia (http://en.wikipedia.org/wiki/Bit), "a **bit** (a contraction of **binary digit**) is the basic unit of information in computing and telecommunications; it is the amount of information stored by a digital device or other physical system that exists in one of two possible distinct states. These may be the . . . two distinct levels of light intensity." What this means is that when data is stored on a computer, the circuit is either on or off, or it contains a positive charge or a negative charge (i.e., is a one or a zero). In terms of digital imaging, the value can be black or white. By adding additional bits, we can increase the perceived value of a pixel.

For example, if one bit is be black or white and we "add" an additional bit, the combined bits can represent a shade of gray—or a grayscale value. As shown in Figure 6-1, the grayscale value of the single bit would be black. By adding an additional bit, the "combined" grayscale value would be gray.

Typically when we talk about digital images, the value for a specific picture elements (more commonly referred to as a "pixel") can be expressed as 8-bit grayscale or 24-bit color. (In 24-bit color, there are 8 bits for red, 8 bits for green, and 8 bits for blue.)

Represented mathematically, an 8-bit grayscale value would be shown as 2^8. And speaking of math, 2^8 provides a total of 256 different grayscale possibilities. In a color image in which there are 256 different shades of red, 256 different shades of green, and 256 different shades of blue, you would have a total of 16,777,216 possible color combinations—$256 \times 256 \times 256$.

Color values are not always described as **red, green, and blue (RGB)**. Their color values are often described using their counterpart: **c**yan, **m**agenta, **y**ellow, and blac**k** (CMYK—where K denotes black as the letter B is already used for the color acronym RGB). Historically, pixel values are captured using a digital

Bit Position	1
Possible Value	0 1
Bit Value	0

Grayscale value equals black

Bit Position	1	2
Possible Value	0 1	0 1
Bit Value	0	1

Grayscale value equals gray
(black plus white)

Bit Position	1	2	3
Possible Value	0 1	0 1	0 1
Bit Value	0	1	1

Grayscale value equals light gray
(one bit black plus two bits white)

Bit Position	1	2	3	4	5	6	7	8
Possible Value	0 1	0 1	0 1	0 1	0 1	0 1	0 1	0 1
Bit Value	0	1	1	0	0	0	1	0

Grayscale value equals dark gray
(five bits black plus three bits white)

FIGURE 6-1
The combined number of bits determines the shade of gray

camera or a scanner as a combination of RGB values and displayed on a monitor using a combination of RGB values. Pixel values are typically represented in a printed form using a combination of CMYK dots to represent the color value for a single pixel. (We will talk more about dots and pixels later. I don't want to confuse you at this point.)

Because we typically think of images in terms of their "output" or printed value, you may also hear people referring to an image as being in 48-bit color or even 64-bit color.

Today, due to the increased sensitivity (dynamic range) of the camera sensors, the pixel value for a camera sensor (also commonly referred to as a photosite) can be more than just 256 different shades. In fact, a single photosite can distinguish between up to 2^{14} or 16,384 different shades of gray. The image sensors for some cameras are not quite as sensitive and can represent only 2^{12} or 4096 different shades of gray. (Yes, I just said that the image sensors can distinguish between a number of shades of light intensity or *grayscale* value and not color. The color values in an image captured using digital cameras are interpolated, but we will talk more about that process shortly.)

To accommodate the high dynamic range provided by today's capture and display devices, pixel values often require 2 bytes—or 16 bits—to represent the actual color value. A 16-bit RGB image is often referred to as 48-bit color, and its CMYK counterpart is referred to as 64-bit color (or 16 bits for cyan, 16 bits for magenta, 16 bits for yellow, and 16 bits for black).

In computer terms, 8 bits equal 1 byte. Therefore, a single 8-bit grayscale value is stored as a single byte. The color value for a single pixel would require 3 bytes because 1 byte is required for each of the 8 bits for red, 8 bits for blue, and 8 bits for green. For 16-bit grayscale values, two bytes are required for each color value. Figure 6-2 illustrates how the color value for a single pixel could be represented as bits and stored as bytes.

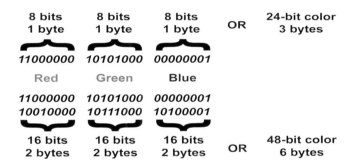

FIGURE 6-2

Each pixel in a digital image consists of a color value for red, green, and blue, where the bits make up the color values and the bits are grouped into bytes for storage on a computer

Another lesson from this exercise is that the more pixels there are in an image, the more bytes are required to store the bit values that make up that image.

As mentioned in the introduction to this chapter, there is a growing desire to capture digital images with better image quality. As demonstrated in Figures 6-3A to 6-3D, image resolution is crucial component of image quality.

The higher the resolution, the better the quality of the image. (This is not always the case, as there are other considerations in play, such as the size of the imaging sensor in the camera, the size of the photosites on the imaging sensor, the light sensitivity (a.k.a. bit depth) of the photosites, the type of lens used on the digital camera, and so forth. We will talk about some of these issues later in this chapter.)

FIGURE 6-3A
The image quality of a fingerprint at 1200 pixels per inch (ppi) when zoomed into the image

FIGURE 6-3B
The image quality of a fingerprint at 600 pixels per inch (ppi); notice the difference in contrast between the fingerprint image at 1200 ppi when zoomed into the image

The problem with higher-resolution images is that they require a significant amount of storage space. For example, an 8 MP digital camera requires 8 million bytes for red, 8 million bytes for green, and 8 million bytes for blue, or a total of 24 million bytes. Like bits, bytes are also grouped for computer storage purposes, as shown in Figure 6-4.

So if you do the math and divide 24 million bytes into kilobytes, and then divide the kilobytes into megabytes, a single picture from an 8 MP digital camera requires approximately 22.9 MB.

Depending upon which source you believe, the most commonly sold high-resolution digital cameras are the Canon EOS 600D (also known as the Canon

FIGURE 6-3C

The image quality of a fingerprint at 300 pixels per inch (ppi); in addition to the visible difference in contrast, it is now easier to visualize the individual pixels when zoomed into the image

FIGURE 6-3D

The image quality of a fingerprint at 150 pixels per inch (ppi); in addition to visualizing the individual pixels, there is a significant degradation of image quality and loss of detail when zoomed into the image

8 Bits = 1 Byte
1024 Bytes = 1 Kilobyte (KB)
1024 Kilobytes = 1 Megabyte (MB)
1024 Megabytes = 1 Gigabyte (GB)
1024 Gigabytes = 1 Terabyte (TB)
1024 Terabytes = 1 Petabyte (PB)
1024 Petabytes = 1 Exabyte (EB)
1024 Exabytes = 1 Zettabyte (ZB)

FIGURE 6-4

Bits are grouped into bytes, and bytes are grouped into kilobytes, megabytes, etc.

EOS Rebel T3i), which is an 18 MP digital SLR camera, or the Nikon D5100, which is a 16.2 MP digital SLR camera. Sony also has a number of cameras that are favorites in the criminal justice community, such as the Sony NEX-7, which is a 24.3 MP digital SLR camera. Regardless of which camera you use, the storage space required for these cameras can be significant depending upon the image file format that you use to store your pictures. We will be discussing this issue in great length in just a moment. For now, suffice it to say that the higher the resolution (more pixels), the more bytes you will need to store the image file. For example, a 12 MP digital camera could require as much as 34.3 MB when storing an 24-bit RGB color image or 68.7 MB if storing a 48-bit (16 bits per color channel) RGB color image. An 18 MP digital camera could require as much as 51.5 MB when storing an 24-bit RGB color image or 103.0 MB if storing a 48-bit (16 bits per color channel) RGB color image. The bottom line is that needing this much storage space for your digital images really bytes! (Sorry, I just couldn't resist.)

Flatbed scanners, like digital cameras, use resolution to adjust image quality. However, flatbed scanners have a variable resolution, which is typically based upon the size of the area captured. For example, you could scan an area that is 1 inch by 1 inch at 1200 pixels per inch (ppi) or you could scan an area that is 6 inches by 6 inches at 1200 ppi. (The 1 inch × 1 inch area at 1200 ppi would produce an image file that is approximately 4.12 MB; the 6 inch × 6 inch area at 1200 ppi would produce an image file that is approximately 148.3 MB.)

Digital cameras, on the other hand, have a fixed resolution regardless of whether you are capturing an image area that is 4 inches × 3 inches or 20 feet × 15 feet. More specifically, a digital image captured using a 12 MP imaging sensor can contain only 12 million pixels regardless of the size of the area being photographed.

DO YOU GIVE A RIP? RASTER GRAPHICS VERSUS VECTOR GRAPHICS

Over the years, there has been a considerable misunderstanding between vector graphics and raster graphics as well as a great deal of confusion about the use of these tools.

From a purely graphical arts point of view, vector graphics—which is based on a mathematical representation of graphical elements using geometrical shapes such as lines, points, curves, polygons, and so on—is a great tool for creating computer-generated graphics (artwork). The use of these mathematical representations allows vector graphics to be enlarged without the degradation typically associated with digital images commonly referred to as **pixilation**.

There are a number of software applications that can be used to create vector-based graphics. In addition, word processing applications such as Microsoft Word often use graphics and fonts that are based on vector graphics so that the fonts can be enlarged without degradation. (Bitmapped fonts are still used frequently, but these fonts often do not have sufficient resolution to avoid the stair-stepping artifacts, also known as aliasing, that are visible when using larger character sizes.)

It should be remembered, however, that all digital images obtained from devices such as digital cameras, flatbed scanners, and digital video cameras are based on the use of a raster format commonly known as a **bitmapped graphic (bitmap)**, which consists of a square grid of picture elements (pixels). Unlike vector graphics, bitmapped (pixel) graphics cannot be enlarged beyond a certain size without degradation (pixilation), depending upon the resolution of the underlying image. (The higher the resolution of the image, the more the image can be enlarged.)

In forensic digital evidentiary imaging, there are times when the use of vector-based imaging tools may be beneficial, such as during the preparation of certain types of court exhibits that are to be enlarged to the size of an average poster. However, a thorough understanding of the advantages and limitations of both technologies as well as the relationships between them is essential. The improper use of these tools can result in images that appear degraded when enlarged.

More specifically, all computer monitors, LCD projectors, and printers are **raster devices**. This means that all vector format graphics must be converted to a raster (pixel) format before they can be displayed or printed on these devices. Some software applications and printers employ the use of a tool (driver) known as a **raster image processor (RIP)** to convert vector graphic images into a raster format for printing as well as enlarging raster (pixel) format images to minimize degradation.

It is easy to convert an image file from a vector format to a bitmap or raster file format, but it is much more difficult to go in the opposite direction, especially if the underlying image is a raster format from a digital camera, flatbed scanner, or video camera, as these devices produce images that are continuous-tone raster (bitmapped) graphics and are impractical to convert into vectors. To process (enhance) digital images, all image editing applications—including Adobe Photoshop—must operate on the individual pixel values that actually make up the digital image file. The goal is to produce high-quality images than can be enlarged quickly and easily and without degradation.

It should also be noted that users typically must save images created from a vector source file as a raster format because different systems (monitors, printers and even software applications such as Adobe Photoshop) have different (and often incompatible) vector formats if they even support vector graphics at all.

In addition, it is rather pointless to use compressed digital images (especially digital images from digital cameras and flatbed scanners that have been compressed using a lossy JPG compression algorithm) in conjunction with vector-based graphics. When a compressed digital image is enlarged, the artifacts created by the JPG compression algorithm can appear quite obvious—even if the graphic overlay does not appear degraded. For example, although the overlaying graphics (such as the lines and letters or numbers) used in the court exhibit may not appear to be degraded when the image is enlarged, the artifacts created during the compression process in the underlying pixel-based digital image can be very apparent. In addition, low-resolution digital images do not enlarge very well either, so even if the overlaying graphics can be enlarged, the underlying digital image will still appear pixilated.

THE SPEED OF LIGHT . . . I MEAN BITS

Another component that plays a major role in the world of digital imaging is speed: the speed of the memory device in the camera, the speed of the connection between the camera and the computer, the speed of the bus in the computer, and the speed of the memory device in the computer. If you are uploading images via the Internet or uploading images to a server, you also have to consider the upload speed of your Internet service provider or the slowest point in the intranet within your network architecture.

Depending upon your computer hardware, you may be using a **Universal Serial Bus (USB)** connection that is either a 2.0 or 3.0 standard. The USB 2.0 standard provides an upload/download speed of 480 million bits (aka megabits) per second (Mbps); USB 3.0 provides a transmission speed of up to 5 gigabits per second (Gbps), which is approximately 10 times faster than USB 2.0. The faster USB speed significantly reduces the time required for data transmission—the time to upload images from your digital camera to your computer.

When you are considering sending image files across the Internet, you must consider both the upload and download speeds provided by your Internet service provider. For example, some standard commercial-grade cable options are:

- Downloads up to 15Mbps, uploads up to 3Mbps
- Downloads up to 20Mbps, uploads up to 4Mbps
- Downloads up to 30Mbps, uploads up to 7Mbps
- Downloads up to 50Mbps, uploads up to 10Mbps

If you are moving images between your computer and a server on your network, you can typically find internal network speeds that operate at a speed of 10 Mbps, 100Mbps or 1Gbps depending upon the types of hubs, routers, and network cables deployed within your environment. The thing that most people forget is that whether you are using an Internet connection or an intranet connection, the highest speed available is limited to the slowest point in the network. For example, your computer could be connected to a 1GB (gigabyte) router but the server is connected to a 10Mbps router, so the fastest speed available when uploading or downloading image to/from the server is limited to the speed of the 10Mbps router.

To calculate what this means as far as performance is concerned, divide the number of Mbps by 10 to convert the number of megabits to megabytes per second. (Technically, it is actually megabits divided by 8 equals the number of megabytes. However, this equation does not account for network overhead and other factors, so being that accurate is not really meaningful in a live environment.)

Based upon the most common cable performance available (downloads up to 30Mbps and uploads up to 7Mbps), it would take approximately 25 seconds to upload a 17MB file. If you were to upload an image file scanned on the flatbed scanner, the typical file size for a scanned 8.5 × 11 inch page size at 300 ppi, the file size would be 24.1MB and would take approximately 35 seconds to upload. For a high-quality scan of an 8.5 × 11 inch page at 600 ppi, the file size would be 96.3MB and would take approximately 2.5 minutes to upload. And not that you would ever consider doing this, but a scan of an 8 × 10 document at 1200 ppi would provide a file size of 329.6MB and would take approximately 7.9 minutes to upload. These times are for uploading just one single image at a time. When uploading multiple images, the times for each image file must be added together for the total upload, and then there are other people on the network that want to upload or download files, too. (How insensitive and inconsiderate, right?)

It is typically not as big of an issue to download a file because the download times are so much faster. For example, using the scenario in the previous example, it would take approximately 8.5 seconds to download a scanned 8.5 × 11 inch page size at 300 ppi; approximately 32.1 seconds to download a scanned 8.5 × 11 inch page size at 600 ppi; and approximately 2 minutes to download a scanned 8 × 12 inch page size at 1200 ppi. Again, these are based on just a single image being downloaded at a time.

In addition to considering the performance at your end, you also have to consider the performance of the server in the equation to calculate upload and download speeds. If you use just a standard, commercial-grade Internet connection, the server would have the same performance issues. But here's where it gets ugly. When images are requested from the server, the server must upload all of the image files to fulfill the request. So if you request multiple images, the server would have to "stack" the requests. Depending upon the upload speed of the connection on the server side, you could be waiting several minutes for your files to be uploaded from the server and then downloaded to your computer.

The bottom line is that image (file) size and storage/upload/download performance are directly related.

TAKING A BITE (MAKE THAT BYTE) OUT OF DIGITAL IMAGING

As discussed earlier, digital images are stored using a combination of bits to represent a single picture element or pixel. As the number of pixel values increase, the number of bytes that are required to store the image also increase. Although data storage is not all that expensive, law enforcement agencies typically have very limited monies for budgetary items such as servers, backup devices, network routers, and so on. As a result, the majority of law enforcement agencies look for ways to reduce the amount of space required for digital images on their servers.

The most common method used to reduce the amount of space required for image storage is to compress the image files using a file format known as JPG or JPEG (which is short for Joint Photographic Experts Group). In theory, "compression" means to encode data using fewer bits than the original encoding would require. Typically, this means resampling the pixel values in the image and storing a reduced number of pixel values. Most JPG algorithms (except algorithms like JPG 2000, which uses "discrete wavelet trans-formation") use lossy compression, which means there is a noticeable loss to the original image quality. (Lossy compression algorithms use mathematical techniques to reduce the file size of a digital image in which the missing information can never be reproduced exactly as it was captured by the imaging device when the compressed image is decompressed.) Lossy also means that once the image quality is lost when the image data from the camera sensor is compressed and saved, the original image quality (data) can never be recovered—and image quality inevitably suffers.

Note: Although JPG 2000 is recognized as a nearly lossless compression algo-rithm, this compression routine requires complex encoders and decoders. Visu-ally, JPG 2000 may produce "ringing artifacts" that often appear as blur or rings near edges in a digital image. Even though JPG 2000 has been published as an ISO standard (ISO/IEC 15444), JPG 2000 is not widely supported in web browsers, but far more importantly, JPG 2000 is not used by digital camera manufacturers.

To display a compressed image on a screen, such as a computer monitor or a television screen, the data that is lost during the compression process must be

FIGURE 6-5
An image with a portion greatly enlarged, in which the individual pixels are shown as little squares

regenerated during the decompression process using a technique that involves trade-offs between efficiency, smoothness, and sharpness. As the size of an image is increased, this process, which can compromise image quality, becomes increasingly more visible, making the image appear "soft" or out of focus. In contrast, reducing the image on the display will appear to improve its smoothness and sharpness.

Apart from displaying an image in a smaller display area, image resampling (subsampling or downsampling) is typically used to create small thumbnail images or images used on web pages and the like. Enlarging an image (upsampling or interpolating) typically is used for full-screen mode or "zooming" an image.

Although compression can be useful (because it helps minimize the consumption of resources, such as computer disk space/server storage capacity or transmission bandwidth), it can also be detrimental in some applications (because the compressed data must be decompressed to be viewed).

FIGURE 6-6
When compressed images are displayed in a small space, the loss of data from the compression process is not readily apparent

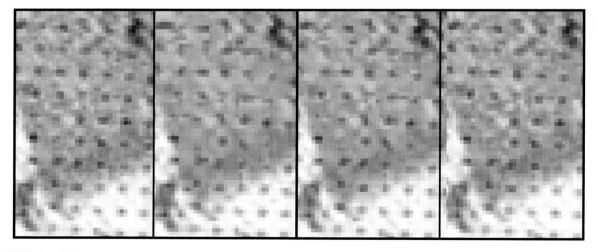

FIGURE 6-7
When compressed images are decompressed and zoomed for purposes of examination, the loss of data, such as color values and blocking of details, from the compression process is readily apparent (As shown in the above image from left to right: non-compressed image, low image quality setting, medium image quality setting and high image quality setting)

During JPG compression, image pixel data (color values) are modified. Minute detail (minor color changes) does not compress well because minor deviations in color values are ignored and the pixel values are not retained. When you open the file and decompress the data to view the image, the pixel values are no longer the same values as they were in the original image.

Note: Although I do not want to repeat myself too much in this chapter, I want to ensure that you fully appreciate the implications of using JPG—lossy—compression. When a digital image is compressed to reduce file size, some of the actual pixel values (and in some cases the pixels themselves) in the image are discarded. Once those data values are lost, they can never be recovered exactly as they were captured. When the image is decompressed, the missing pixel values are replaced with a "reasonable" likeness based upon the decompression algorithm of the software application used to open or display the image. You should not use JPG formats to save enhanced images because additional data is discarded every time the image is resaved. Data is not lost, however, if the image is simply opened for viewing—the loss of data occurs again only when the image has been enhanced and the File Save or Save As function must be used to save the changes made to the image. If no changes were made, there is nothing to save, so no additional loss occurs.

Typically, JPG files are compressed to approximately one-tenth of their original file size. As shown in Figure 6-7, compression may not only destroy ridge detail that is crucial for fingerprint examination and comparison but can also cause color deviations and other "blocking" artifacts that combine ridge detail with background obstructions, thus making it difficult or impossible to evaluate ridge flow and ridge events as well as making it difficult or impossible to eliminate background noise that interferes with the comparison and identification processes.

Some programs, such as Adobe Photoshop and Adobe Photoshop Elements, refer to the level of compression as JPG Quality. A typical compression value might be 10 High Quality or Compression Rate 15. These numbers are relative, have no absolute meaning, and vary from one program to another.

Digital cameras also provide a range of JPG quality selections. High-quality images—large image files—will fill your memory cards very quickly. You could buy additional expensive larger memory cards, or you could compromise by sacrificing image quality for a smaller file size. Unfortunately, the latter is the choice made my many law enforcement agencies, especially for crime scene photographs that are typically referred to as "documentation" and are not considered to have evidentiary (analysis) value.

Today, most digital cameras provide two types of resizing options. One resizing option simply resamples the pixel values from the photosites and stores a reduced number of pixel values. In this case, the pixel values from an imaging sensor in a digital camera that contains 4928 pixels by 3264 pixels (16.1MP) would be compressed based upon the selected image quality value, but when the image is decompressed, the image will once again contain 4928 pixels by 3264 pixels, albeit not with their original pixel values.

Note: This JPG compression process does not modify the number of pixels for a digital image; it alters the color values for some pixels using a mathematical algorithm. As a result, the JPG compression process is complex mathematically and requires considerable CPU processing power to decompress an image for display. In addition, the JPG compression algorithms also contain a number of parameters that may or may not be used or interpreted the same way depending upon which program you use to display compressed images, such as viewing JPG images faster but with less quality (using a browser such as Internet Explorer, Firefox, or Google Chrome), or loading a JPG image more slowly with better quality for image processing (using a program like Adobe Photoshop). The bottom line is that the quality of the decompressed JPG image depends on the details contained within the original image (from the image sensor in the digital camera) as well as on the amount of compression and the method used by the application opening the JPG image.

The second option actually creates a smaller image size that contains fewer pixels using a resampling technique. For example, instead of compressing an image file that contains 4928 pixels by 3264 pixels (16.1MP) that when decompressed contains 4928 pixels by 3264 pixels, the pixel values are downsampled and the modified image resolution contains either 3696 pixels by 2448 pixels (9.0MP) or 2464 pixels by 1632 pixels (4.0MP). Although these images are still compressed, the pixel values are not compressed as much as the full resolution image, but the trade-off is that the decompressed images contain far fewer pixel values than were captured by the imaging sensor in the digital camera.

Your decision for the "correct" compression should be based upon your goal for using the image. For example, if you are going to print an 8 × 10 inch image on paper, your image should contain at least 7.2MP; to print a 5 × 7 inch image on paper, your image should contain at least 3.2MP; to print an 4 × 6 inch image on paper, your image should contain at least 2.2MP. If you are going to view the image only in a 4 × 6 inch area on your monitor, your image should contain only 1 MP—based on the assumption that you are not going to zoom in to view more detail within the image.

Most digital cameras offer three JPG file size choices. When comparing the compressed file size to the uncompressed size, the Fine option will create a compressed image file that is approximately 1/4 the size in bytes; the Normal option will create a compressed image file that is approximately 1/8 the size in bytes; and the Basic option will create a compressed image file that is approximately 1/16 the size in bytes. The best JPG quality (which is also the largest file size) will still suffer from JPG artifacts, but those artifacts are relatively minor (and mostly undetectable) when compared to the smallest file choice, in which the artifacts are very noticeable.

The compression techniques used for most other image file formats, such as TIF or RAW, are lossless, which means that the exact data value for each pixel is fully recoverable. In other words, lossless compression techniques will always return the original pixel value, bit-for-bit.

SOME LIKE THEIR DATA RAW

Although some high-end digital camera manufacturers still offer a TIFF (Tagged Image File Format) format option, most digital camera manufacturers offer a camera RAW format option. Unlike sushi, which is typically uncooked, RAW in this case means simply the original, unprocessed data from the imaging sensor in the digital camera.

There are two primary types of imaging sensors used in digital cameras today, as mentioned in Chapter 5: a CCD (charge-coupled device) imaging sensor or a CMOS (complimentary metal-oxide semiconductor) imaging sensor. Regardless of whether your digital camera uses a CCD or a CMOS imaging sensor, the sensor must convert light into an electronic signal that is broken down into a digital value for each photosite.

In most digital cameras, there is a color filter array that consists of a series of red, green, and blue filters arranged in a pattern commonly referred to as a Bayer pattern. The intensity of the light that strikes the photosite is filtered based upon the overlaying color filter. In other words, the photosite on the imaging sensor collects only one value: a grayscale value that represents the density of the light striking the photosite filtered by a red, green, or blue color filter. The resulting color value for each photosite (pixel) is calculated (interpolated) based on the density of the light striking the specific photosite together with the light density (filtered values) of the eight neighboring photosites that surround that photosite using a variety of demosaicing algorithms.

When capturing images with a digital camera using a JPG or TIF file format option, the color values are processed using the software inside the camera. In addition to interpolating color values, the camera software may also perform a variety of other processes, such as sharpen, noise reduction, auto contrast, auto color balance, and others.

For both TIF and JPG files, there are 3 bytes created for every pixel value in the image. If you have an 8MP digital camera, the uncompressed TIF image size would be approximately 24 million bytes or approximately 22.9MB. The typical compressed JPG image size would be in the range of 2.7MB to approximately 3.4MB, depending upon the detail in the image, the color values in the image, and so on. Also, the bit depth for all JPG and TIF options in a digital camera is limited to 8 bits or 256 shades per color channel.

In contrast, the camera RAW file contains only the original grayscale (light intensity) value from each of the photosites on the imaging sensor. Because the grayscale value requires only a single byte when the image data is written to the memory card in the camera, the file size for an 8MP camera would be approximately 13MB, depending upon whether the imaging sensor has a dynamic range (sensitivity) of 12 bits or 14 bits. As a result, the file is somewhat larger than the JPG image file but is significantly smaller than the uncompressed TIF format.

More importantly, the camera RAW format is totally and completely lossless. In fact, because the camera RAW format includes the actual bit-depth information from the imaging sensor in the digital camera, it is possible to address many photographic issues, such as correcting white balance, hue and saturation, exposure compensation, and so on. About the only problem that cannot be resolved using the RAW data from the imaging sensor is the focusing of the image.

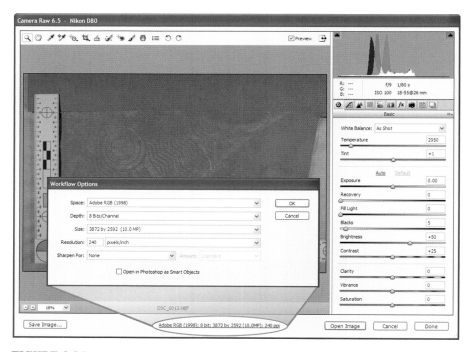

FIGURE 6-8A
Using the Camera RAW converter in Adobe Photoshop, you can adjust bit depth, color space, white balance, image resolution, and much more

The negative issue with camera RAW formats is that all camera RAW formats are proprietary, and must be converted into a standard 8- or 16-bit file format for viewing and/or processing. There is, however, a bit of good news. Because camera RAW file formats are proprietary, they can only be read and cannot be overwritten with a processed copy of the image. Image file formats such as TIF and JPG can be easily manipulated, and the original file can be overwritten with the processed image.

The camera RAW format also provides an additional feature beyond providing data in a secure (protected), totally lossless format. When you open a camera RAW file using a camera RAW file converter as illustrated in Figures 6-8A and 6-8B, you can set the color profile, adjust the image resolution (to include upsampling and downsampling), set the bit depth (to either 8 bits per color channel or 16 bits per color channel) as well as perform basic adjusts such as white balance, brightness, contrast, exposure, and so on. You can also adjust a wide variety of other image settings, such as tonal curve; sharpness (details); hue, saturation, and lightness; shadows, highlights, and gamma settings (split toning); make adjustments for lens distortions; and much more.

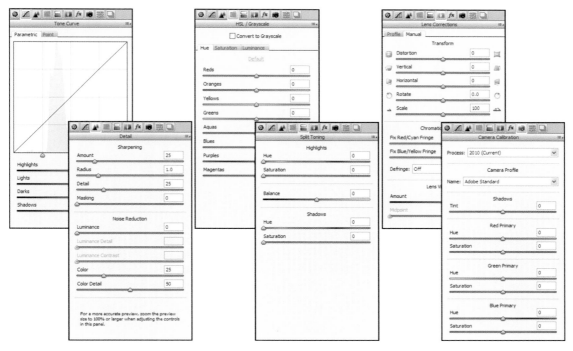

FIGURE 6-8B
You can correct a wide range of photographic issues and override the settings that were set on the camera when the picture was taken

Because the camera RAW file format is a read-only format, any adjustments made using a camera RAW file converter are saved in a an .xmp file commonly referred to as a "sidecar" file. With your changes preserved in this file, you can open the original camera RAW file over and over and start with the same image settings each time you open the original file.

The courts like the camera RAW file format, especially for images that are classified as "evidentiary" photographs. Because the original file cannot be overwritten, the original file can be produced together with the enhanced image during discovery of when the case goes to court to prove that the "content" of the original file was not altered, and that the evidentiary integrity of the image was not compromised.

Note: All camera RAW files must be converted from their propriety file format into an open standard format for processing or even just for printing. Once converted (and processed and/or printed), the converted file must be saved using either a TIF or JPG file format.

GUIDELINES AND STANDARDS

So far we have talked about bits, bytes, resolution, file sizes, and file formats. Now I think it is time we talked about the guidelines and standards that define the policies, procedures, and requirements followed within the criminal justice community. Let's begin with a brief description of some key words that will be used throughout this section.

The first topic that we must address is a thing called a "guideline." A guideline is more of a recommendation or a suggestion that is strongly encouraged to be followed. Most of the guidelines used within the criminal justice system for digital imaging technologies and concepts have been written by SWGIT and SWGDE. The goal of the SWGIT and SWGDE guidelines is to facilitate the adoption of standards and best practices for the capture, storage, processing (enhancement), analysis, transmission, and output of digital images, as well as to provide compatibility between various law enforcement agencies and other entities within the criminal justice system. Without these guidelines, law enforcement agencies might not be able to exchange images with other federal, state, and/or local law enforcement agencies or, even worse, they might not be able to provide images and other documentation that are admissible in the courts.

Note: There are a number of other Scientific Working Groups (SWG) that are also sponsored by the Federal Bureau of Investigation (FBI) that address the use of digital imaging technologies within their specific fields. These groups include the Scientific Working Group for Forensic Document

Examination (SWGDOC), the Scientific Working Group on Friction Ridge Analysis, Study and Technology (SWGFAST), the Scientific Working Group for Shoeprint and Tire Tread Evidence (SWGTREAD), the Scientific Working Group for Firearms and Toolmarks (SWGGUN), the Scientific Working Group on Bloodstain Pattern Analysis (SWGSTAIN), and the Facial Identification Scientific Working Group (FISWG). Each of these SWGs has developed its own guidelines for minimum resolutions for digital images, acceptable file formats, and best practices. In most disciplines, the SWGIT/SWGDE guidelines are used to augment the specific guidelines developed for each respective discipline. For example, SWGIT guidelines recommend that a digital camera with a minimum of 6 MP be used for the forensic documentation and photography of fingerprint impressions at the crime scene, whereas SWGTREAD guidelines recommend that a digital camera with a minimum of 8 MP be used for the forensic documentation and photography of footwear and tire impressions at the crime scene. (At the time of this writing, SWGTREAD is reviewing its guidelines and it is anticipated that the 8 MP requirement will be increased to at least a minimum of 12 or 14 MP based upon the availability and affordability of the latest technology as well as a review of the best practices for the photography of footwear and tire impressions at the crime scene and the and documentation of the analysis and conclusions of footwear and tire impression examination.)

The second topic that we must discuss deals with the issue of standards. A standard is a rule or principle that must be followed, and adherence to that standard forms a basis for judgment and acceptance, such as a judgment of admissibility and acceptance in a court of law. In some instances, a guideline may provide the foundation for a specific standard. For example, the National Institute of Standards and Technology (NIST) standard "NIST Special Publication 500-271 ANSI/NIST-ITL-2007" specifies that 1000 pixels per inch (ppi) at 1:1 is the minimum resolution for capture and transmission of latent print evidence. This standard is strongly adhered to within the latent print community. Failure to adhere to this standard could cause digital images of latent prints not to be used for the analysis, comparison, and identification of latent print impressions found at the crime scene as well as on evidence recovered from a crime scene. In addition, failure to follow this standard could eliminate the ability to search the fingerprint on an automated fingerprint identification system (AFIS).

The International Organization for Standardization (ISO) also develops standards for the criminal justice community. These standards include ISO 17025, which is the standard for the testing and calibration functions performed in the crime laboratory using standard methods, nonstandard methods, and laboratory-developed methods. (There are a number of other standards that are also used for the basis of accreditation, such as ISO 17043, which is the standard for the general requirements for the development and operation of proficiency testing programs in a laboratory.)

Each law enforcement agency is unique and must operate within the boundaries of its jurisdiction as well as the stricture of the judiciary (the system of courts that interprets and applies the law, including the interpretation and application of the rules of evidence, within a local, state, or federal jurisdiction). Therefore, each agency is responsible for publishing its own prescribed procedures also known as a standard operating procedure (SOP) that must be followed routinely for a given situation. For example, a single law enforcement agency would have multiple SOPs that define the standards that must be followed as well as describe the procedures that must be followed within each department.

For example, one SOP would be used to describe the procedures used when photographing a crime scene. This set of procedures could also include the standards that must be followed when photographing individual items of evidence. Alternatively, a separate set of policies and procedures could be defined for a specific unit, such as the Crime Scene Unit, that addresses how each piece of evidence must be documented photographically—both at the scene of the crime as well as in the laboratory—when the evidence is being processed for fingerprints or DNA samples.

In addition, the SOPs for the crime scene investigator as well as the latent print examiner, firearms and tool mark examiner, and footwear and tire tread examiner would include detailed instructions on how to capture, store, and enhance (process) digital images for each respective discipline. In terms of digital processing of evidentiary photographs, the SOPs might include instructions about what procedures to use (as described in the next section in this chapter), when to use those techniques, and so on.

The American Society of Crime Laboratory Directors/Laboratory Accreditation Board (ASCLD/LAB) is a nonprofit corporation that is frequently employed to review and inspect forensic laboratories for compliance with and adherence to standards not only within their own organization but with adherence to standards generally followed throughout the entire criminal justice community for purposes of standardization and accreditation.

The bottom line is that not only does the effectiveness and efficiency of the digital imaging techniques aide in the investigative process, but the acceptance and admissibility of digital evidence often rests with the agency's compliance with the standards and guidelines that are used regularly throughout the criminal justice system.

IMAGE CLASSIFICATIONS

Generally speaking, all of the SWG groups agree that there are two classifications of digital images.

Category 1 images are typically referred to as "documentation" images. More specifically, these images are used to demonstrate (illustrate) what the photographer witnessed or observed, and the images are not "analyzed" by subject matter experts. Digital images that are normally classified as documentation include but are not limited to:

- General crime scene or investigative images
- Surveillance images
- Autopsy images
- Documentation of items of evidence in a laboratory
- Arrest photographs, such as mug shots

Category 2 images are typically referred to as "evidentiary" images. More specifically, these images are used for analysis and comparison by subject matter experts, such as latent print examiner, a medical examiner, a firearms or tool mark examiner, a questioned document examiner, so on and so forth. Digital images that are normally classified as documentation include but are not limited to:

- Latent prints
- Questioned documents
- Impression evidence
- Patterned evidence
- Category 1 images to be subjected to analysis, such as certain types of autopsy images, etc.

The distinction between these categories of images is quite significant. For instance, Category 1 images may be captured using a JPG format, and although it is recommended that the camera have a minimum resolution of 6MP, it is not required. In fact, most law enforcement agencies use commercial, off-the-shelf (COTS) consumer-grade digital cameras for most of their officers (first responders).

Historically, once Category 1 images are taken at the crime scene, they may not be deleted either from the camera or when the images are downloaded from the camera media. The concept behind this guideline is to ensure the sequential integrity of the images (not having numbers missing in a sequence of images) and to avoid the potential for an argument about the possible (intentional or unintentional) destruction of exculpatory evidence (evidence that is considered to be favorable to the individual accused of the crime, such as evidence that demonstrates that the individual is not guilty of or could not have committed the crime of which he or she is charged).

Note: Typically a photo log or a crime scene report is maintained by the person photographing the crime scene, such as a crime scene photographer or a detective. If a photograph is deemed unacceptable, rather than deleting the photograph, an entry is made in the photo log or crime scene report explaining why the image is not acceptable, such as the camera shutter release button was inadvertently tripped, the photograph was taken without a flash or a strobe, and so on.

In addition, the image processing techniques used when enhancing Category 1 images are required to be documented only in the SOPs that describe the basic enhancement processes. Generally speaking, basic image processing techniques are those methods that are used to improve the overall appearance of the image, and a comparably skilled (trained) professional should be able to produce a comparable result without the documentation of specific parameters or settings. Some of the more common techniques that are considered to be basic image processing techniques include:

■ Brightness and contrast adjustment, including dodging and burning
■ Resizing (file interpolation)
■ Cropping
■ Positive to negative inversion
■ Image rotation/inversion
■ Conversion to grayscale
■ White balance
■ Color balancing and/or color correction
■ Basic image sharpening and blurring (pixel averaging)

Note: Although cropping is a commonly used technique, care should be exercised with it. Some defense attorneys argue that by cropping the image, you are changing the context of the image, and that cropping the image can be a material change to the image. Even with Category 1 images, the original image must be maintained to help prove the authenticity of the processed (enhanced) image as well as avoid the earlier argument about the removal (deleting) exculpatory evidence.

To capture Category 2 images, a number of very specific guidelines are in place. For example, the crime scene technician should have a digital camera kit that includes, but is not limited to:

■ A professional SLR digital camera
■ Fixed focal-length macro lenses
■ Dedicated electronic flash capable of off-camera operation
■ Sturdy tripod capable of various angles and positions
■ Variety of light sources (such as flood lights, flashlights, a forensic light source)

- Digital storage media (the media should be formatted/reformatted in the digital camera prior to each use)
- Graduated scaling devices (such as 2-inch or 6-inch photo evidence scales in inches and/or millimeters, photomacrographic scales (4-inch × 4-inch L-shaped ABFO-style scales), L-shaped reversible footwear and tire track photo scales, and a folding footwear and tire track scale)

Note: Due to the requirement to be able to produce a life-size image from a Category 2 digital photograph, a scale must be included in the image when it is captured using a digital camera. By including a scale in the image, you can calibrate the image for 1:1 output. (Don't let the word "output" confuse you. In this case, the word "output" means a hard copy or printed image and *not* the image displayed on the monitor.)

It is recommended that Category 2 images be captured only using a TIF or camera RAW file format. In some instances, the digital image may become the evidence in the case. For example, ASCLD/LAB states that a digital image of evidence that is nonrecoverable (such as a fingerprint impression that was developed on an item of evidence that cannot be permanently preserved as is on the evidence or that could be destroyed by additional processing, handling, or examination) must be handled with the same care, control, and documentation of the chain of custody as the physical evidence itself. An example of an item that is commonly considered unrecoverable is a fingerprint on a piece of paper—such as a check or money order—that was developed using a chemical process known as ninhydrin. In this case, the fingerprint will fade over time, and the only "evidence" of the latent print is the digital image. Another example might be a fingerprint impression that is observed on the breech of a gun that could be damaged or destroyed by additional processing.

In addition, there are additional standards that must be followed for the enhancement (digital processing) of Category 2 images. Besides using basic image enhancement techniques to improve the overall appearance of the image, advanced image enhancement techniques may also be used to improve the overall appearance of the image as well as extract specific information contained in the image (such as tools to remove color information, eliminate background noise, remove patterns, etc.).

There is a more detailed list of techniques—including the sequence or order in which they are applied—that are commonly used to process Category 2 images, but the general procedures used to improve the quality of these images include:

- Tonal range corrections
- Color channel selection and/or multicolor subtraction
- Fourier analysis (pattern identification and extraction)
- Noise reduction

- Advanced image sharpening (such as the Photoshop functions Unsharp Mask and Smart Sharpen)

The use and sequence of all enhancement techniques used in the processing of Category 2 images must be documented for every image. The documentation of the image enhancement process should be sufficiently detailed—including the order (sequence) of the steps and the settings and parameters used—to enable a comparably skilled and comparably trained person to understand the techniques used and to produce a comparable result.

THE BALL IS IN YOUR COURT

Or should I say, I hope the digital image of your ball will be admissible in court. Digital images are powerful, efficient tools for the criminal justice system. The ability to take a picture and view it instantly as well as distribute it immediately can enhance the investigative process significantly as well as augment the presentation of evidence or improve the understanding of testimony in court. However, for forensic digital images to be acceptable and introduced as evidence in a court of law, they must pass four legal tests:

1. Reliability—Does the image accurately represent that which it is alleged to represent?
2. Reproducibility—Is the image enhancement documented thoroughly enough so that a comparable result could be produced from the original image?
3. Security—Can the authenticity (originality) and the integrity (chain of custody) be proven?
4. Discovery—Can the original image (defined in the Best Evidence Rule as the "negative or any print therefrom") be produced for purposes of discovery?

RELIABILITY

The Federal Rules of Evidence provide guidance for the acceptance of digital images; admissibility is based upon compliance with standards that generally can be satisfied by proof that (1) the computer equipment is accepted in the field as standard and competent and was in good working order, (2) qualified computer operators were employed, (3) proper procedures were followed in connection with the input and output of information, (4) a reliable software program was utilized, (5) the equipment was programmed and operated properly, and (6) the exhibit is identified properly as the output in question.

Ultimately, the issue of reliability of digital images depends upon the veracity, integrity, *and* knowledge of the officer or technician who is presenting the evidence. Law enforcement agencies should not be reluctant to stay in step with advances in technology because they are afraid of those in the legal system. Fear about the manipulation of digital images is often exaggerated. (How quickly they have forgotten that traditional film-based photographs were manipulated to alter reality and at worst to fabricate false evidence.)

In 2003, the court in the *State of Florida v. Victor Reyes* case was required to consider the evidentiary value of computer-enhanced digital images with regard to latent evidence. In 1996, Victor Reyes was charged with murder in Broward County, Florida. Originally, latent prints on duct tape were analyzed using traditional film-based photographs and were declared to be of "no value." In 1999, the negatives were scanned digitally and processed using a series of computer enhancement techniques, including a commonly used process known as "burn and dodge." The fingerprints were not only found to be of value, but were identified as prints left by the suspect, Victor Reyes. The State of Florida found that computer-enhanced images did meet the Frye standard for admissibility and the identified latent prints were admitted as evidence in the trial. Victor Reyes was acquitted at trial. Although the jury had no problems with the admissibility of the digital images and accepted the enhancement process, they felt that the existence of the latent prints on the duct tape on the victim's body did not prove that Reyes actually committed the murder. However, this case is significant because defense attorneys realized the importance of challenging digitally generated evidence.

In a posttrial interview with the *Sun Sentinel* Barbara Heyer, the defense attorney for Victor Reyes stated, "The methods cross the line between uncovering evidence and creating it. . . . The computer programs used to enhance the print were too susceptible to being tampered with and do not have enough safeguards to prove that law enforcement is not manipulating the evidence." Heyer further stated, "They take something that is of no value to begin with and start doing this boosting and they turn up something that they claim is someone's print."

The Heyer's belief that the Adobe Photoshop software was used to create fraudulent prints had no basis in fact, and the insinuation that it might have been so used was without a factual basis and was highly prejudicial and unwarranted. In *Cross v. U.S.*, the court stated that the "mere possibility" of tampering was insufficient to prove bad faith. Similarly, in *United States v. Balzano*, the court also approved the trial court's decision to admit duplicate audiotapes on which the defense had alleged that "hypothetically" tampering could have occurred.

Even as late as 2007, there were some courts and legislative bodies that were finally making the move to accept digital imaging. In fact, 2007 signaled the end of an era when the crime laboratories in the State of Wisconsin finally converted from conventional film to digital photography. One of the primary reasons why Wisconsin was the final state to convert to digital imaging was because of Wisconsin Assembly Bill 584, introduced in 2003.

It was reported that a certain Wisconsin legislator (who shall remain nameless) was "angered" by photographic manipulation of a digital image by high school students. In his introduction of Bill 584, he inferred that if students were capable of such malfeasance, then police and others within the criminal justice system must also be capable of such malfeasance. Therefore, the bill was proposed, passed, and became law. This law prohibited "the introduction of a photograph . . . of a person, place, document . . . or event to prove the content . . . if that photograph . . . is created or stored by data in the form of numerical digits."

In 2007, the Wisconsin legislature finally modified this law to allow for the admissibility of digital images; however, the photographer is required to swear under oath as to the authenticity, accuracy, and unaltered state of the original image.

The trend in case law today points to the admissibility of digital photographs as evidence, although there are still many people in the legal community who suggest that digital photographs are subject to abuse and misuse. Their argument is based on the notion that digital photos can be altered—quickly, easily, and effortlessly—not just by changing the color and lighting but by adding or eliminating critical details (content) in the image.

To avoid this discussion (or a potential legal challenge involving the manipulation of a digital image), many law enforcement agencies have started moving toward the use of camera RAW file formats. Although these proprietary files may present their own issues (such as the fact that they must be converted into a standard open file format for extended, long-term storage or for sharing with other law enforcement agencies, the prosecutor's office, the defense attorney, etc.), camera RAW files are read only and cannot be overwritten by a manipulated version of the file. In fact, many people in the criminal justice community refer to camera RAW files as "digital negatives." (It is sad that there are still many people today who are under the false impression that images printed from negatives cannot be easily manipulated. It has not been that long ago that many law enforcement agencies avoided the use of digital imaging technologies solely because they were under the false impression that film negatives provided a more secure and more reliable method for crime scene photography.)

REPRODUCIBILITY

Typically, reproducibility is not a big issue because the History Log function in Adobe Photoshop CS or later can be enabled to record every task performed during the image enhancement process automatically. By selecting the Detailed option under Edit Log Items as shown in Figure 6-9, Photoshop will not only record the function or task performed but will also record the settings and parameters that were used.

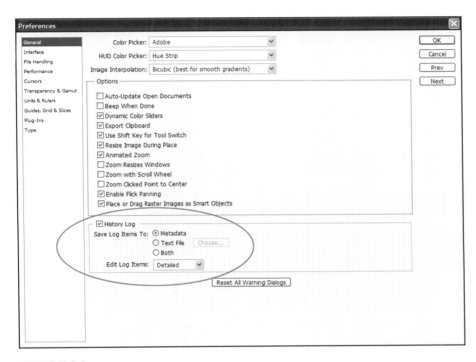

FIGURE 6-9

The History Log function can be enabled in Adobe Photoshop CS or later by choosing Edit from the Photoshop menu bar, then choosing Preferences and clicking in the Options box to the left of the History Log option.

SECURITY

In 2005, David Hrick suggested in his article in *Computer Law Review & Technology Journal* that there is a high level of sensitivity about storing digital files on networked computers (and servers) because such files may be accidentally or intentionally viewed, printed, shared, deleted, and possibly even modified by unauthorized third parties, including computer maintenance personnel."[2] He also stated that courts are concerned because:

1. There are very few information management systems are in place specifically for use with digital images.
2. Without a specific methodology in place to authenticate the digital images, it is difficult to identify which is the "original" and which is the "copy," which reduces or eliminates the contents of the image.
3. The person taking the picture with the digital camera is usually the same person who downloads, processes, and prints the images, rather than

[2]David Hrick, 2005, "The Speed of Normal: Conflicts, Competency, and Confidentiality in the Digital Age Copyright," *Computer Law Review & Technology Journal* (Fall) pp 74 - 99.

a disinterested "professional" (such as a third-party service or a professional print developer).
4. In many cases, there is no "original" that can be used for comparison with the produced image (such as crime scene photos or autopsy photographs for which the original image is often enhanced rather than a working copy of the image), which reduces or eliminates the opportunity to verify that the image has not been altered or that it has been altered using "approved" techniques.

Unfortunately, there are probably as many interpretations of the procedures for protecting the integrity of digital images as there are law enforcement agencies in the United States. Any SOP that is designed to protect the chain of custody should, at a minimum, be able to address the following questions:

1. Who captured the image—when and where?
2. Who has had access to the image between the time it was captured and the time it was introduced in court?
3. Has the original image been altered in any way since it was captured?
4. Who enhanced the image and when?
5. What was done to enhance the image and is it reproducible?
6. Has the enhanced image been altered in any way since it was first enhanced?

DISCOVERY

The Federal Rules of Evidence have long governed the use of film-based photography because of the presumed difficulty of altering conventional photographs without detection. Digital photography has complicated the field of evidentiary photography because of the ease with which digital photos can be altered. However, an advisory group to the Federal Rules of Evidence has determined that changes to the rules are not needed, and that it is sufficient to allow judges the discretion to determine the authenticity of digital images on an individual basis.

That said, Federal Rules of Evidence, Rule 1002, commonly referred to as the "Original Writing Rule," normally required the production of the original document, writing, recording, or photograph. Rule 1003 allows you to produce a "copy" of the original unless:

- A genuine question can be raised as to the authenticity of the original; or
- Under the circumstances it would be unfair (to the defendant) to admit the duplicate instead of the original

If neither the original nor an authenticated copy of the original is available, the courts often turn to Rule 1004, which states that you do not need the original or other copies when:

1. The original was lost or destroyed—unless it can be proven that the proponent destroyed the image in bad faith
2. The original is not obtainable and no original can be obtained because the original is in the possession of the opponent, and they fail to produce the document when they are given notice and asked to do so
3. The controlling issue does not depend solely upon the original document, writing, recording, or photograph

These issues have, however, come under scrutiny recently with more and more law enforcement agencies going paperless in an effort to reduce costs, not only in terms of capture, but also storage and discovery. Some jurisdictions still require hard copies of all records; other jurisdictions prefer electronic copies of reports and images as there is often more data associated with electronic records than hard-copy records.

For example, all electronic files—regardless of whether it is a document, a spreadsheet, or an image—contain data (information) about the file itself. This data is commonly referred to as **metadata**. Generally, metadata defines:

- Means (method) of creation of the file
- Date and time of creation
- Identity of the author (and/or creator) of the data
- Location (the computer or other placement on a network) where the data was created and/or stored

In the case of a digital image, the metadata may also contain:

- Make and model of the camera
- Date and time created
- Date and time modified
- Identity of the author (and/or creator) of the data
- Location (the computer or other placement on a network) where the data was created and/or stored
- Resolution of the capture device (x and y resolutions)
- File format
- Color space
- Bit depth
- Lens information
- Image number
- Serial number (of the camera)
- Approximate focus distance
- Exposure settings
- Aperture
- Metering mode
- Exposure mode/setting

- White balance mode/setting
- Flash mode/setting

While this may appear to be an extensive list, it is only a very small sampling of the data that is available as metadata for a digital image file. Because this data has proven to be invaluable to the courts, the Arizona State Supreme Court ruled in October 2009 that the state's records law covers metadata: "Hidden data (metadata showing electronic file history) embedded in electronic files must be disclosed under the State's rules of disclosure." Several other states have followed Arizona's lead and have ruled that metadata is not only discoverable but also public record.

CASE LAW

Although accreditation currently is not—legally or legislatively—mandated for all forensics laboratories within the criminal justice system, it should be noted that the first step of any accreditation program is a review of the agency's compliance with guidelines and standards commonly accepted by other law enforcement agencies. In fact, failure to follow accepted guidelines and standards can open the door to challenges in the courtroom.[3]

There are only a limited number of cases that have been tried that directly address the admissibility of digital images. In the *Almond v. State* in Georgia, the defense argued that the trial court erred in admitting various photographs taken with a digital camera. The court records showed that the pictures were introduced only after the prosecution properly authenticated them as "fair and truthful representations of what they purported to depict." The Georgia Supreme Court affirmed the lower court's decision that there was no authority for the proposition that the procedure for admitting pictures should be any different when taken by a digital camera.

In *People v. Rodriguez*, the New York Supreme Court, Appellate Division concluded that the trial court "properly exercised its discretion" in admitting images made from bank surveillance videotapes without expert testimony about the digitizing process used in the FBI Laboratory to make still photographs from videotapes because a bank employee responsible for making the original tapes at the bank testified that he compared the original tapes and that what was represented by the photographs was "identical except for speed" (resolving the issue that the images were both relevant and authenticated for admissibility).

There are four other cases that focused on the admissibility of digital image processing. In *State of Washington v. Hayden*, the court held that "because there does not appear to be a significant dispute among qualified experts as to the

---

[3]David Witzke, 2011, "Publish or Perish," *The Forensic Technology Review* 1:26–31.

validity of enhanced digital imaging performed by qualified experts using appropriate software, we conclude that the process is generally accepted in the relevant scientific community."

As discussed earlier, in *State of Florida v. Victor Reyes*, the trial court reviewed and accepted the evidentiary value of computer-enhanced digital images and allowed the digital images to be admissible in the trial.

In *State of California v. Phillip Lee Jackson*, the police department in San Diego, California, used digital image processing on a fingerprint in a double homicide case. The defense asked for a Kelly-Frye hearing, but the court ruled that the Kelly-Frye hearing was unnecessary based on the argument that digital processing is a "readily accepted practice in forensics" and that "new information" was not added to the image.

NOTE: In criminal law, Courts traditionally use one of the standards — Frye, Kelly/Frye or Daubert — to determine the admissibility of scientific evidence. The Frye test refers to a standard for admitting scientific evidence at trial, which is based on a 1923 case, U.S. v. Frye, 293 F. 1013 (D.C. Cir. 1923). Broadly speaking, for the results of a scientific technique to be admissible, the technique must be sufficiently established to have gained general acceptance in its particular field. Some jurisdictions also referred to as the Kelly/Frye test due to a California case, People v. Kelly, 549 P.2d 1240 (Cal. 1976), in which the Supreme Court of the State of California defined what it felt were the main advantages of the Frye standard. In federal courts, a Daubert Hearing — based on Daubert v. Merrill Dow Pharmaceuticals," 509 U.S. 579 (1993) — may be conducted to evaluate the admissibility of defined expert, scientific or technical testimony and/or evidence.

In another California case (*People v. Perez*[4]), the court admitted into evidence at trial digital images of a footwear impression that had been processed using Adobe Photoshop. The defense argued that the digitally enhanced footwear impressions should not have been admitted into evidence because no Kelly-Frye hearing was held, which should have been required because the software and processes used were "new scientific" techniques. The court held that Adobe Photoshop was not a new or novel scientific process and that the evidence was reliable because it did not alter the shoe print images. The court also held that Adobe Photoshop is an easier method for the processing and development of pictures and that digital enhancement is generally accepted by the scientific community as "reliable."

---

[4]*People v. Perez*, No. D039428, 2003 WL 22683442, Cal. Ct. App. 2003, is not a published case. Although unpublished cases are not normally considered as a legal precedent, this case and the *State of California v. Phillip Lee Jackson* case should be very "instructive" regarding the admissibility of digital images in court as well as the use of Adobe Photoshop for digital processing evidentiary photographs.

In *State v. Swinton* in Connecticut, the defendant claimed that the trial court improperly admitted into evidence computer-enhanced images and computer-generated exhibits without an adequate foundation. Specifically, the defendant challenged the admissibility of two pieces of evidence: (1) images of a bite mark on the victim's body that were enhanced using a computer software program known as Lucis, and (2) images created using Adobe Photoshop that showed the defendant's teeth marks superimposed on the images of the bite mark. The defendant argued that the state did not present adequate testimony on the use of Adobe Photoshop for matching the defendant's dentition with the victim's bite mark because the computer-generated exhibits were introduced by an expert with "no more than an elementary familiarity" with the program.

More specifically, Norm Pattis (the attorney for Alfred Swinton in the matter of the State of Connecticut versus Alfred Swinton) appealed the verdict challenging the use of the digital images used in the case and the use of digital imaging technologies. In his appeal, Pattis argued that the state did not present testimony on the adequacy of the use of digital imaging technologies and Adobe Photoshop. In particular, he argued that the expert lacked adequate knowledge about software and computers and lacked even a basic layman's understanding of digital imaging technologies and Adobe Photoshop. Dr. Constantine Karazulas, the forensic odontologist for the State of Connecticut, could not testify as to whether the computer processes that were used to create the overlays were (1) accepted in the field of odontology as standard and competent, (2) whether proper procedures were followed in connection with the input and output of information, (3) whether Adobe Photoshop was reliable for this sort of forensic application, or (4) whether the equipment was programmed and operated correctly. It was argued that Dr. Karazulas—or anyone presenting digital images in court—should have been able to answer these basic questions in his testimony as these have been the "standards" for admissibility since 1979.

In 1979, the Connecticut State Supreme Court in *American Oil Co. v. Valenti* examined the stages in the generation of digital evidence to determine whether the digital evidence was admissible in accordance with the Federal Rules of Evidence. In the Swinton case, the Connecticut State Supreme Court reaffirmed its earlier ruling and took the opportunity to clarify the state's position regarding the six rules regarding admissibility of digital evidence. Since the Swinton case, these rules have commonly been referred to as "the Swinton Six." It should also be noted that Federal Rules of Evidence do not require a detailed, technical understanding of what Photoshop is doing inside the box.

Another expert that testified in the Swinton case, Major Timothy Palmbach, a supervisor for the Division of Scientific Services in the State of Connecticut Department of Public Safety, testified that Adobe Photoshop was "capable of actually altering the photographs." The state did not provide an expert to elaborate on digital imaging technologies used or even clarify the issue of image alteration (enhancement history).

The State argued that the exhibits were merely illustrative evidence, that the exhibits were not scientific evidence, and that the exhibits did not require the testimony of a witness who could explain the inner workings of the equipment that produced it in order to provide an adequate foundation.

In its decision, the Connecticut State Supreme Court concluded that the trial court improperly admitted the images "created" by Adobe Photoshop due to improper foundation provided by the State's experts. The Supreme Court stopped short of specifically listing the experts' lack of knowledge with computer technologies as well as their lack of knowledge, expertise, and experience with Adobe Photoshop.

It is my understanding as of the time of this writing that Norm Pattis may petition the State of Connecticut's Innocence Project to take on the case of Alfred Swinton, alleging that Alfred Swinton was "convicted of murder based on bogus science," and is using the National Academy of Sciences (NAS) report as the basis for his opinion even though Pattis did not challenge the science of forensic odontology during the trial or the appeal.

However, Ray Krone, who has been called the "snaggle-tooth killer" was convicted of murder in 1991 and was sent to death row based on the science of forensic odontology. As in the Swinton case, Krone was convicted based on conclusions drawn from the use of overlays created digitally.

On April 8, 2002, Krone was exonerated and released from prison after DNA evidence proved that he did not murder the victim. The science of forensic odontology is also being called "junk science" as a result of this case and is bringing more attention to the Swinton case.

In the Swinton case, Pattis stated, "Yet the courts are blind to these issues and routinely admit evidence lacking in validity due to the lack of training of judges and lawyers in the basic science and the scientific method."

Over the past few years, the National Association of Criminal Defense Lawyers (NACDL) has published articles in its law and technology journal that challenge the use of digital imaging technologies in general and the use of Adobe Photoshop (processes, standards, and training) specifically as well as challenging the knowledge, skill, training, and expertise of forensic personnel in their use of digital imaging technologies (cameras, scanners, computers, software, printers, etc.).

In early 2011, Senate Judiciary Committee Chairman Patrick Leahy introduced legislation to strengthen and improve the quality of forensic evidence routinely used in the criminal justice system. The stated goal of the legislation was to ensure that the forensic evidence used in criminal cases is of the highest scientific integrity and to ensure application of consistent standards throughout the forensic science community, including standards for the accreditation of forensic science laboratories and the certification of forensic science professionals.

WHAT GOES IN MUST COME OUT . . . SORT OF

One of the most contentious, frustrating, and challenging issues of digital imaging technologies is the understanding of "resolution". Everyone agrees on some level at least that resolution and image quality go hand-in-hand. Unfortunately, most people have no idea what resolution really means or realize that image resolution can be affected by many different components. Plus, a number of challenges have been raised in the courts concerning image quality that have resulted from the lack of understanding of these topics.

In 2004, NACDL published an article that discussed how to challenge the use of digital imaging technologies in the forensic science community. Nearly half of the reasons they provided dealt with the issue of image quality, including resolution (both capture resolution and output resolution) and file formats (lossy compression).

Recently, I spoke with a crime scene investigator who stated that "no matter what I do or what file format I use, every picture I take with my digital camera has a resolution 72 dpi when I open it in Adobe Photoshop." I was a bit surprised by his follow-up question, which was something to the effect of, "is there a problem with my camera or does this really mean that my camera can only take low-resolution images?" He went on to say that he thought he was supposed to have at least 300 ppi, but he was confused because his ink jet printer has a resolution of 4800×2400 dots per inch (dpi). I really confused him when I had him calibrate his "low-resolution" image—the calibrated image had a resolution of 2318 ppi. At that point he was so confused I thought he was going to cry.

To appreciate the image quality argument as it relates to digital imaging technologies, you must understand that there are a number of factors that must be considered:

1. What is the quality of the device used to capture the image (sensitivity—bit depth—of the digital camera, scanner, or video camera)?
2. What is the file format used by the capture device (lossy or lossless)?
3. If it is lossy compression, which type of lossy compression is used (resampling of pixel values or a resample of pixel values together with a reduction in the number of pixels contained within the image file)?

4. What is the resolution of the capture device (including, but not limited to, the number of pixels/megapixels, the type and size of the imaging sensor, the type of lens used—a fixed length macro lens, a wide angle lens, or a zoom lens —and how does that affect the image resolution as it relates to the size of the area captured)?

5. What is the size of the computer screen (17-inch, 24-inch, 27-inch, etc.) and what is the setting for the screen resolution (1024 × 768, 1600 × 1000, 1920 × 1200, etc.)?

6. What is the type (ink jet, laser, or dye sublimation) and resolution (number of dots per inch, number of inks, size of droplet) of the output device, and what type of paper is used (plain, matte, glossy, etc.)?

An entire book could be dedicated to the discussion of image quality, so I will try to keep the discussion brief in this chapter.

PIXELS, DOTS, AND SAMPLES, OH MY

To begin this discussion, let's clarify a couple of terms: ppi, dpi, and spi.

Pixels per inch (ppi) is the number of picture elements (pixels) that are contained within a measurable distance of one inch. This value typically is meaningful when calibrating images for comparison and life-size (1:1) output. In addition, changing the ppi can also resize the image for the desired output size. As shown in Figures 6-10A through 6-10C, a picture taken with a Nikon D700, which has a sensor resolution of 4256 pixels × 2832 pixels (12.0 MP), can have a varying output (the measurable printed document) size just by changing the number of pixels per inch.

Note: When the Resample Image option is disabled (no checkmark in the box), the number of pixels in the actual image file do not change; only the width and height measurements for the document size—the size the picture will be when it is printed—change.

Dots per inch (dpi) is the number of dots that are contained within a measurable distance of one inch. This value typically is used to measure the image quality of an output device, such as a computer screen or a printer. (Dye sublimation printers are the exception to this rule, as these types of printers use a different technology for printing images.) The term "dots" when referring to a computer monitor resolution is the number of red, green, and blue diodes that are used to represent the color value for a single picture element. Similarly, the color dots from a color laser printer (cyan, magenta, yellow, and black) are used in a cluster to represent a single pixel value. For example, it takes a number of cyan, magenta, and yellow dots together as a cluster to represent the color value (of a single pixel) such as teal.

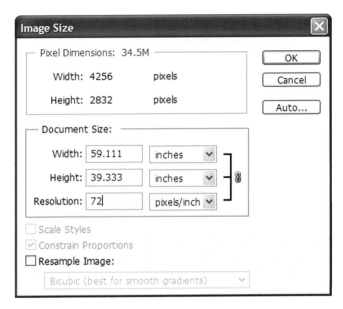

FIGURE 6-10A
Using the digital camera's default resolution of 72 ppi, the image, if printed, would measure 59.11 inches wide by 39.33 inches high; you would need a large-scale printer to print a picture that large

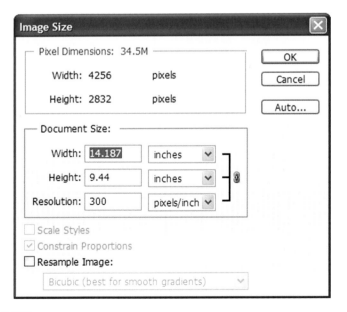

FIGURE 6-10B
By changing the image resolution to 300 ppi, the printed image would measure 14.187 inches wide by 9.44 inches high; again, you would need a large-scale printer to print a picture that large

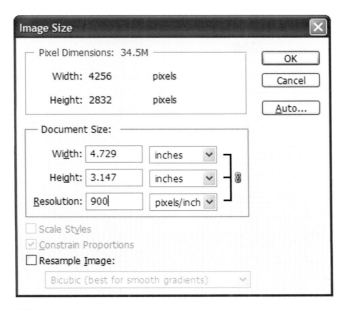

FIGURE 6-10C
By changing the image resolution to 900 ppi, the printed image would measure 4.729 inches wide by 3.147 inches high; you could print a picture of this size on any printer

In the world of dots, a cluster of dots together with the white space that separates them is what determines the color value (hue, saturation, and lightness) that is used to represent a single pixel value. In contrast, pixel values are considered "continuous tone," meaning that there is no white space to separate the pixel values.

So if a color laser printer can print 1200 dpi and the device dot cluster used to represent a single pixel value is 4 dots wide, then the number of pixels that could be represented by the 1200 dots would be 300 pixels (1200/4 = 300).

To calculate the number of device dot clusters for inch jet printers is much more challenging. For example, some high-end ink jet printers have resolutions of 5760 × 1440 dpi, 4800 × 2400 dpi, or 2880 × 1440 dpi. You must also consider the volume of ink that is deposited as a single droplet, which can range from 1.5 picoliters to 4 picoliters. (Please remember that the larger the droplet, the fewer droplets that can be placed in a 1-inch area.) The size of the droplet can have a significant impact on the quality of the output, considering how much the ink spreads out (bleeds) when it hits the paper, depending, of course, upon the type of paper that is used—plain, glossy, matte finish, etc. (For printing forensic evidentiary images that will be used for analysis and comparison, it is recommended that only glossy paper be used.) And to make it even more confusing to calculate the number of dots used to simulate a single pixel value, you could also have 6, 7, 8, 10, 11, or 12 different ink colors depending upon the model of inkjet printer you use. (It really is not your father's inkjet printer any more!)

Samples and samples per inch (spi) is a term that is more appropriate for digital cameras and flatbed scanners in particular. Unfortunately, today most scanner manufacturers label their products—labeling the box in which the scanner is sold, the resolution setting in the software interface, and the detailed specifications—using the image quality measurement of dpi. Although there is a historical significance behind the use of this term, it is no longer appropriate.

The short version is that once upon a time, scanners and printers were available only together as a single unit. In fact, the first true office photocopying machine was introduced by Xerox Corporation in 1958. This device had both a scanner to scan the document and a printer to print the copy. The quality of the output was measured based upon the number of dots that could be placed together to create a reasonable likeness of the original document. In the late 1970s, the first programmable scanner was sold as a separate entity, for the first time separating scanning technology from printing technology. At that time, the red, green, and blue light values were captured using photomultiplier tubes rather than the CCD and CMOS arrays found in flatbed scanners today. The red, green, and blue samples were combined to create a specific color value for each picture element (pixel) in the image. The scanner was no longer dependent upon the number and color of the dots in the printer to determine its image quality. However, no other term had been used to describe picture elements or image quality, so the term "dots" stuck with the scanner to describe its effectiveness. Yet to this very day, scanner resolutions are often labeled as a measure of dpi when it is actually a series of red, green, and blue light samples that are combined to make up the color value for a single pixel.

The bottom line is that the terms "dots per inch" and "pixels per inch" should not be used interchangeably as they represent different types of technologies in digital imaging. The image quality (resolution) of scanners should be described as either samples per inch or pixels per inch because there is a one-to-one relationship between the number of samples and the number of pixels contained in the scanned image file.

CAN YOU SEE IT NOW?

Earlier in this chapter, we discussed the issue of bit depth of the level of sensitivity (shades of gray) that can be captured using a digital camera or a flatbed scanner. We also discussed the loss of image data using JPG (lossy) compression. We concluded that the loss of data might be an acceptable trade-off depending upon the intended use of the image.

As you know, each digital camera has an imaging sensor with a specific number of pixels. So regardless of whether you are capturing an area that is 3 inches × 5 inches, 4 inches × 6 inches, or 13 inches × 19 inches, the image will contain the same number of pixels. In other words, one size fits all. This is why a scale (ruler) is required in all Category 2 images. These images must be calibrated for life-size output as well as to reach conclusions about the size of the object. For example, without calibrating the image, it would be impossible to determine whether the fingerprint in the image were a thumb or a little finger. Without calibrating the image containing a footwear impression, it would be impossible to determine whether the imprint were made by a person wearing a size 9½ shoe or someone wearing a size 15 shoe.

When you are calibrating an image, you are in essence determining how many pixels (photosites) on the digital camera's imaging sensor were used to capture a specific measurable area. For example, if you have a 12MP digital camera with a resolution of 4000 × 3000 pixels and you capture an area that is 4 inches × 3 inches, the resolution of the image would be 1000 ppi.[5]

Using that same camera, you could also capture an area that is 8 inches × 6 inches. Again, simply dividing the number of pixels on the imaging sensor by the size of the area captured, you would have a resolution of 500 ppi.

If you captured an area that is 8 feet × 6 feet, your resolution would be 46 ppi. What is the point of this discussion? There is a direct correlation between image resolution and the size (resolution) of the imaging device and the size of the area of capture. I can't tell you how many times I have been asked to make out the numbers on a license plate when the resolution of the capture device is 800 × 600 pixels (which is an average resolution for a number of video cameras) and the area of coverage is more than 12 feet × 9 feet, providing a resolution of approximately 6 ppi. Although you might be able to zoom in on the image when it is displayed on your monitor to see the specific level of detail, those six squares (pixels) are not going to provide a significant level of detail.

In addition to losing detail by trying to capture too large an area with too small an imaging sensor, you can also loose detail when you try to display a digital image from a high resolution digital camera on your computer screen. For example, if you are going to view an image captured using a Nikon D3X, which has an effective resolution of 24.5MP (6048 × 4032) and your monitor has a screen resolution setting of 1600 × 1000, the resample ratio would be approximately 4 to 1 to fit the entire image onto the screen. The good news is that you have the option to zoom in and see all of the detail contained within

---

[5]For detailed instructions on calibrating a digital image, please refer to *Crime Scene Photography* (2010, 2nd edition) by Edward M. Robinson, published by Academic Press (San Diego, CA), pages 549–556.

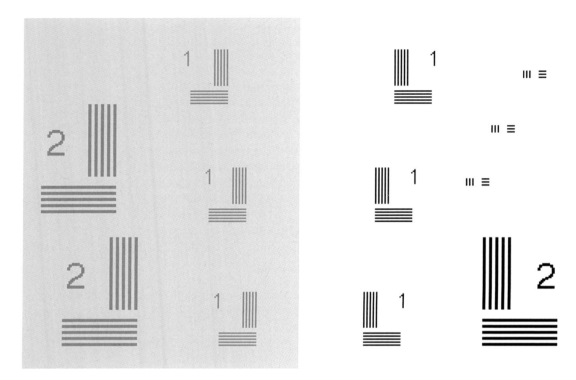

FIGURE 6-11
The conclusion from viewing the zoomed image is that there are five lines vertically and five lines horizontally in each of the numbered line sets

the image; however, you would no longer be able to see the entire image. You would see only a portion of the image.

As shown in Figure 6-11, more detail is visible in the image; however, the entire image cannot be displayed on the screen. In Figure 6-12, more of the image can be seen on the screen, but the resampling rate creates visual artifacts that could change the conclusion derived from the image.

The bottom line is that many people get confused easily by the resolution of their digital image (i.e., the ppi value shown as part of the image size) when they try to compare the size of an object (zoom percent) without considering the implications of their screen resolution setting is as well as the size of their computer screen.

In addition to the issues of viewing the image and understanding the relationship between the pixels in the image (file) and the pixels on the screen, there is another confusing relationship in the ability to visualize image data: the ppi to dpi relationship.

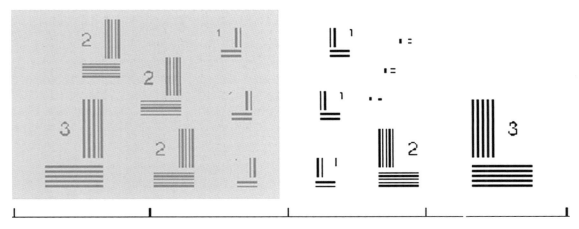

FIGURE 6-12

The conclusion that would be derived from viewing the resampled image is that there are different numbers of lines of varying thicknesses vertically and horizontally in each of the numbered line sets

Previously, I stated that it is extremely challenging if not entirely impossible for the layman to define the exact dot-to-pixel ratio because of the different technologies used by the various types of printers. For example, laser printers use a static charge to write the image onto an imaging (photoreceptor) drum, which collects the dry toner. The toner is then transferred to a sheet of paper and the toner is then fused (melted) onto the paper.

Dye sublimation printers also use heat to melt the dye supplied by a donor film—a long roll of transparent, cellophane film (that resembles plastic kitchen wrap) that looks like sheets of cyan, magenta, yellow, and black colored cellophane stuck together end to end—onto a glossy paper. When the image is printed, the paper is fed through the printer and the first layer of dye is melted onto the paper. The paper is then reset to the beginning and the next color on the film is melted on top of the first layer onto the paper. This process is repeated for each of the colors on the donor film. The amount of dye melted onto the paper for each color determines the color value for the pixel. Like the pixels in the image, the pixels in a dye sublimation printer are continuous tone, and the color values do not use white space to separate the pixels to adjust the lightness of the pixel value. Unfortunately, most dye sublimation printers available today have an output resolution of only about 300 ppi.

Inkjet printers, on the other hand, use a series of nozzles to spray clusters of very small droplets onto the paper. As mentioned earlier, the resolution for inkjet printers varies between different manufacturers as well as different models within the same product line. In addition, there are also variable-size droplets, different numbers and colors of inks, and different types of paper. (Some inkjet printers, such as the Epson Stylus Photo printers, even have variable-size droplets.) Contrast is adjusted by adding or removing white space between the dots in the cluster. As shown in Figure 6-15, the pixel values for the ridge detail in a fingerprint image are represented using a series of color dots.

Unfortunately, the weakest link in the entire digital imaging process is the actual hard copy output. Whether you are using a laser printer, a dye sublimation printer, or an inkjet printer, the pixel values in the digital image file are resampled (much like what happens when an image is compressed) and only a representation of the sampled values are printed.

To print a digital image of a latent print that, according to NIST standards, was captured at a minimum resolution of 1000 pixels per inch on a laser printer, the image would first have to be resampled by the printer driver. In this case, each pixel is represented by a cluster of 16 dots (or spaces for dots) based on a square grid that is 4 dots wide by 4 dots high. If the laser printer has an output resolution of 1200 dpi, then only 300 pixels can be represented by those 1200 dots (1200/4 = 300). This means that the 1000 pixels must be downsampled to only 300 pixels, where each output pixel value consists of the weighted average of approximately $3\frac{1}{3}$ pixels in the actual image file. Just to give you an idea how this works, let's say that you have three pixels: the first is black, the second is white, and the third is black. When averaged together, the number of black values is greater than the number of white values, so the resulting output value would be black. (Compare the detail in Figure 6-11 and Figure 6-13, and you can clearly get a picture of the amount of data that can be lost in the printing process.)

At this point, I must provide you with a word of caution: just because image detail (pixel values) can be lost during the printing process, this does not warrant throwing detail away in the beginning of the digital imaging process. In other words, do not use a lossy (JPG) compression routine when you capture your digital images, thinking that it will not make a difference when you finally output the image because you may have to process (enhance) the image before printing it to suppress background noise, etc.

If you are going to enhance your digital images to remove backgrounds or filter out patterns, you will require the detail provided by each individual pixel

FIGURE 6-13
Color laser printers use a series of cyan, magenta, yellow, and black dots to represent pixel values, and the white space between the dots is used to trick the eye into seeing different intensities (shades) of color

within the image. As shown in Figure 6-16, detail in evidentiary photographs such as latent prints can be lost if a lossy compression format is used to capture the image. As a result, it is impossible to remove backgrounds or even clearly identify the characteristics within the image such as identifying ridge flows and ridge characteristics in a latent fingerprint.

To remove the background pattern from a fingerprint developed on a check such as the image in Figure 6-16, the software must evaluate the intensity (frequency) of each pixel. Repetitive patterns can be removed easily from a digital image without damaging the fingerprint if the frequencies appear in a consistent, continuous manner. Not only has the blocking artifact created by the JPG compression merged the dots into the rest of the background, but the ridge structure of the fingerprint has also been altered by this process.

In addition, Category 2 digital images should not be rotated at any degree of rotation other than 90-degree increments prior to image processing. Rotating images can introduce artifacts, such as creating jagged distortions and color disturbances. As shown in Figure 6-17, these artifacts can be significant and can impair or reduce the analytical value of the image. (These artifacts are significantly more apparent in lower-resolution images than in higher-resolution images.)

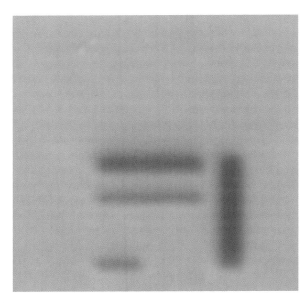

FIGURE 6-14

Dye sublimation printers use the cyan, magenta, yellow, and black dyes on the donor film to create color values that represent the pixel values—if you look closely at this image, you can see the lines created by the heating process

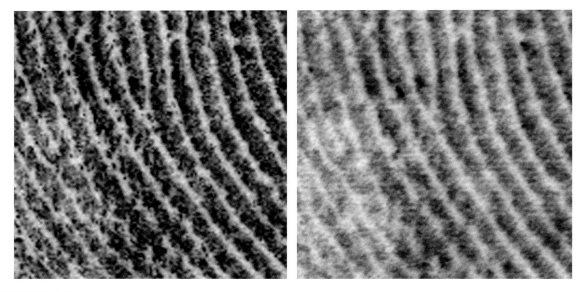

FIGURE 6-15

The ridge detail in the digital image on the left is represented by a series of color dots as shown in the image on the right—if you compare the two images carefully, you can see that some of the minute detail in the digital image on the left does not appear in the printed image on the right

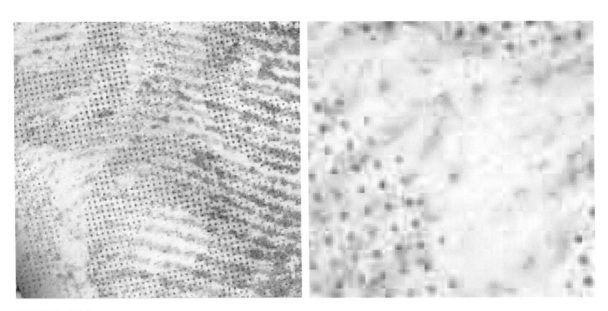

FIGURE 6-16
Although the image on the left does not appear to be affected by the use of a lossy compression capture format, the damage done to the image by the compression algorithm is clearly visible when the image is zoomed, as shown in the image on the right

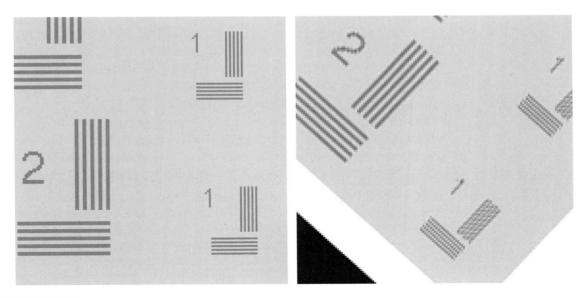

FIGURE 6-17
The image on the left illustrates the set of lines before the image was rotated and the image on the right shows the artifacts of the image rotated at 43 degrees

To maximize image quality as well as improve your chances at removing background noise, it is imperative that evidentiary photographs (Category 2 images) be captured at the highest possible resolution to get the best detail for analysis and comparison. The quality of the captured image will also determine what you can do to enhance the image.

IMAGE PROCESSING GUIDELINES

When you capture an image digitally—whether using a digital camera, a film scanner or a flatbed scanner—it is imperative that you always capture the image in color. This is true if you are capturing a latent lift card (such as a black powder lift) or a ninhydrin print on a check.

Once the image has been captured successfully, there are a number of variables that affect how you process your images for better clarity and visualization of the detail in the image. For example, perhaps you photographed a latent print that was on a plastic baggie that had been processed with cyanoacrylate (superglue) fuming. Using this technique to develop latent prints on nonporous materials, the ridges will appear white. As a result, the image simply needs to be inverted to convert the white ridge detail to black ridges. Similarly, you may have photographed a gray or white power lift that also needs to be inverted to convert the white ridge detail to black ridges.

Perhaps you photographed a latent print that was developed using a ninhydrin process, and the purplish latent print appeared on a check that contained a blue security background or a pink security background or a multicolored gradient security background. Or perhaps the ninhydrin print was on a textured brown paper bag or a smooth brown paper bag.

All of these scenarios are very possible. The bottom line is that you may have to photograph images on an unlimited number of surfaces, including skin, as well as digitally photograph or scan images that have been processed using any number of powders, chemical processes, dye stains, fluorescents, and the like.

You can also have an arsenal of forensic light sources to aid in the visualization and digital capture of latent prints, body fluids, gunshot residue, and so on. Simply stated, all images—even images processed using the same development process (such as ninhydrin) on the same type of surface (such as paper) with the same type of light source—cannot be processed using the exact same technique. Therefore, it is impossible to provide a scenario in which you will always use the same technique to digitally capture every image or use the same technique to enhance every image.

There is, however, a typical order that you can follow when you are processing images, whether of a fingerprint, palm print, shoe print, tire tread, blood stain, tool mark, or whatever else you might encounter. Please be aware that the following steps are offered only as a recommended order and in no way is this intended or implied to be the required order for image processing techniques.

1. Choose the most appropriate device to digitally capture the image (digital camera or flatbed scanner). *Note:* Just because the item is flat is not an indication that it should be scanned. Sometimes it is easier to remove backgrounds when the ambient light picked up by the photographic process provides a higher degree of contrast and makes it easier to visualize the difference between the object of your examination and the background (such as a ridge flow in a fingerprint that appears on top of a color background).

2. Download the electronic files from the digital camera and authenticate the image files following the guidelines described in Section 13, "Best Practices for Maintaining the Integrity of Digital Images and Digital Video," Overview of SWGIT and the Use of Imaging Technology in the Criminal Justice System, Version 1.0, 2007.06.04.

3. Copy (duplicate) the original image file and authenticate the copied file following the guidelines described in Section 13, "Best Practices for Maintaining the Integrity of Digital Images and Digital Video," Overview of SWGIT and the Use of Imaging Technology in the Criminal Justice System, Version 1.0, 2007.06.04. *Caution:* At no time is it permissible to overwrite the original image file! For legal purposes, you must maintain the "original" electronic file, if requested, for discovery and/or court. Any processing performed on the digital image must be performed on a copy of the original.

4. Calibrate (scale) the image for life-size output, including printing as well as exporting to an digital imaging system, such as an AFIS.

5. Evaluate color channels and modes; it may be necessary to adjust color values within the image.
   - Using a color mode such as RGB or CMYK, you can suppress the background by choosing a single color channel.
   - If the background cannot be suppressed using a single channel in either RGB or CMYK, then you may need to adjust individual color values to suppress the background. In other words, a single color channel may be insufficient to remove all of the background color values that interfere with the visualization of the image. Therefore, it may be necessary to adjust individual color values. The following tools can be used in Adobe Photoshop CS3 or later to remove two or more colors and eliminate the background:
     - Image > Adjustments > Hue & Saturation (eliminates two or more color values; used in conjunction with Calculations to eliminate background noise)

- Image > Adjustments > Black & White (Adobe Photoshop CS3/CS4 only)

   In some instances, you may not be able to suppress the background using either of these techniques and you may need to use an advanced image enhancement technique such as Calculations to eliminate backgrounds.

6. After the background noise has been removed, you may want to convert the image to grayscale. (This step also helps reduce file storage requirements, because grayscale images are one-third the size of RGB images.)

   - If a continuous, consistent, and repetitive pattern can be identified within the digital image, you may be able to use a pattern removal filter (such as a Fast Fourier Transform filter). However, this step must be done before any further tonal corrections or contrast adjustments are to avoid making the subject of the analysis, such as the fingerprint or tool mark, the same frequency as the obstructing pattern.

7. Adjust the tonal range and contrast in the image. There are a variety of options for adjusting tonal range and contrast, and you may use one or more of those options together to achieve the desired results. In Photoshop, these options include:

   - Image > Adjustments > Levels (balance tonal range)
   - Image > Adjustments > Curves (extraordinary contrast)
   - Image > Apply Image (multiply, overlay, screen, etc.)
   - Image > Adjustments > Shadow/Highlight (balance tonal range and contrast)
   - Image > Adjustments > Exposure (balance tonal range)
   - Burn and Dodge
   - Image > Adjustments > Brightness/Contrast

8. Once you have achieved the desired tonal range and contrast, you may want to perform a series of functions to eliminate noise that can occur as a result of using a forensic light source with florescent/dye stained latent prints. For instance, you may want to use:

   - Filter > Noise > Dust & Scratches to remove random artifacts introduced through instrumentation, etc.
   - Filter > Noise > Reduce Noise to remove random artifacts—based on edges—introduced through instrumentation, etc.

9. You may also need to eliminate the appearance of blur caused by the digital photographic process or the image enhancement process. Using the Sharpen function, you can create a higher level of contrast between two contrasting pixels positioned side by side or sharpen edges to create the appearance of more contrast by sharpening only edges while preserving the overall smoothness of the image. Alternatively, you could use Unsharp Mask or Smart Sharpen to adjust the contrast of edge detail and produces a lighter and darker contrast on each side of the edge, emphasizing the edge

and creating the illusion of a sharper image. Smart Sharpen is similar to Unsharp Mask but provides significantly more control. Sharpen Edges is also similar to Unsharp Mask because it sharpens areas where significant color changes occur, but the Sharpen Edges function provides significantly less control than Unsharp Mask or Smart Sharpen.

10. Save the enhanced image. *Caution:* Do *not* overwrite the original image! You must retain the original image and be able to provide the original image, if requested.

It is important to maintain a consistent same naming schema to help identify the relationship between the original image and the processed copy of that original.

SUPPLEMENTAL GUIDELINES FOR BRUSH TOOLS (BURN AND DODGE)

When using brush tools, such as burn and dodge, to improve the contrast within an isolated area of a digital image, follow these guidelines to avoid introducing visual artifacts that may obstruct your analysis of the object:

1. Always choose a soft (feathered) round brush.
2. Always choose a brush size that is at least four to five ridges in diameter. Alternatively, you may choose a brush size that is larger than four to five ridges, depending upon the size of the area in which you want to provide additional contrast. *Note:* Generally, you should choose Shadows for the Range when using the Burn tool, and Highlights for the Range when using the Dodge tool.
3. Always drag the brush across the ridges: go across the ridge flow, not with the ridge flow. Alternatively, place the cursor at a single location and click the mouse button one or more times to achieved the desired results.

Feathering Guidelines for Area of Interest Tools (Marquee and Lasso Tools)

It is permissible (and legally acceptable) to use area of interest tools to isolate specific areas within an image and enhance those specific areas. The tools that are typically used to isolate specific areas within the image include the Rectangular and Elliptical Marquee, the Lasso and Polygonal Lasso, and the Magic Wand and Quick Select tools. When isolating specific areas, it is strongly recommended that you "feather" (or blend) the enhancement into the rest of the image to avoid causing visual inconsistencies. Typically, it is not required to feather a selection made using the Magnetic Lasso or the Magic Wand, as those tools are used to select an area of interest based on a difference in edge contrast.

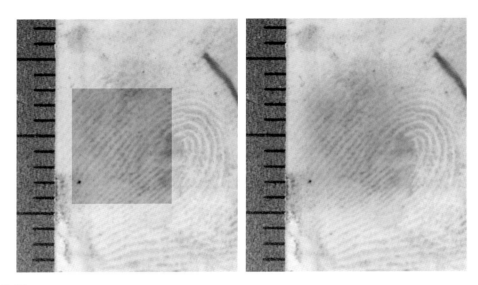

FIGURE 6-18
Both images were enhanced using the exact same marquee selection box and the same settings and parameters—the image on the left illustrates the visual artifacts created when the selection is not feathered; the image on the right illustrates the when the selection is feathered and the enhancement blended into the rest of the image

For high-resolution images, such as latent prints, the amount of blending is based upon the calibrated resolution (ppi) of the image.

- If the calibrated resolution is less than 1500 ppi, multiply the number of hundreds by 3. For example, if the resolution is 1252, multiply the number of hundreds (i.e., 12) by 3, which will give you a feather radius of 36. Enter that value as the Feather Radius in the Feather Selection dialog box.
- If the calibrated resolution is greater than 1500 ppi, multiply the number of hundreds by 4. For example, if the resolution is 1632, multiply the number of hundreds (i.e., 16) by 4, which will give you a feather radius of 64. Enter that value as the Feather Radius in the Feather Selection dialog box.

To keep it simple, I typically round the ppi up to the highest whole number in my head and then use that value to calculate my feather radius. For example, if my resolution is 1232, I simply round the number up to 1300 in my head and then multiply 13 by whatever multiplier I use. Whether you use 3 or 4 is not all that critical. Remembering to feather the selection is far more important to avoid creating artifacts that do not appear in the original image. Not only does it avoid creating artifacts, but it also makes the enhanced image appear more balanced and more natural.

For lower-resolution images, such as footwear impressions or tire tread impressions, the amount of blending is based upon the size of the area selected rather than the calibrated image resolution. Unfortunately, there is not as clear-cut a recommendation for these types of images as there is for smaller items, such as fingerprints, questioned documents, firearms, and the like. When feathering a selection for low-resolution items, a feather radius that is between 50 pixels and 100 pixels is recommended. Use a feather radius that is closer to the top end of the range when blending a selection with a lower resolution and a larger selection; use a feather radius that is closer to the bottom end of the range when blending a selection with a higher resolution and a smaller selection. If an "edge" becomes visible after you have enhanced the selected area, step backward (Control + Alt [or Option] + Z) to undo the last enhancement, then increase the feather radius and repeat the enhancement process.

SUMMARY

Forensic digital imaging is one of the most powerful and effective investigative tools available to the criminal justice community today. Digital imaging technologies have enhanced the way we do crime scene reconstruction, calculate blood spatter trajectories, create photo lineups, create wanted and missing persons fliers, search fingerprints to identify suspects, analyze and compare footwear impressions, annotate and document evidence for DNA analysis, and record and document evidence collected at the crime scene.

Although law enforcement agencies have been using digital imaging technologies to facilitate the rapid investigation of their cases, they have also been using digital technologies to expedite the delivery of evidentiary images to the courts electronically for arraignment of suspects. The ability to get images of sexual assault or domestic violence cases to the prosecutors and judges quickly and efficiently has made a difference not only in the number of cases that have been prosecuted, but also in that the quality of the images has significantly improved the ability to more accurately depict the injuries sustained by victims.

The ability to capture an image digitally and view it instantly as well as share it immediately with other departments, agencies, and the courts can make a huge difference in how quickly a case can be solved and helps law enforcement agencies serve and protect their communities. Investigators can now digitally photograph a fingerprint at the crime scene and send it back to the laboratory where it can be processed and searched on the AFIS system. In fact, the identification of the suspect can even be known before the investigator even leaves the crime scene.

Unfortunately, the ability to capture and enhance an image, such as a fingerprint or footprint, digitally for analysis and comparison or the ability to enhance a questioned document for analysis depends upon the quality of the image as well as the reliability and dependability of the digital imaging process. Having a high-quality image can make a difference as to whether the case is solved, but no matter how good the digital images are or how valuable the digital images were to the investigative process, they must also be acceptable to the courts and pass the four-prong test for admissibility:

1. The images must be reliable.
2. The results must be reproducible.
3. The images must be stored in a secure manner to maintain their authenticity and integrity.
4. The images—both the original and the enhanced image together with their metadata—must be available for discovery and/or court.

To achieve these goals and objectives, law enforcement agencies must—at a minimum—publish and follow standard operating procedures that will help ensure compliance with the guidelines, standards, and best practices and help ensure that the use of digital imaging technologies will continue to make a difference.

Discussion Questions

1. Why should the terms dots per inch (dpi) and pixels per inch (ppi) not be used interchangeably?
2. How does compression impact digital images that must be enhanced, such as removing a background color, patterns, and so on?
3. What are the primary differences between a compressed JPG image and an uncompressed camera RAW image?
4. What is a "side car" file, and how does it affect digital image processing?
5. What is an SOP and what impact does it have on the day-to-day use of digital cameras in the criminal justice community?
6. How are Category 2 images used differently than Category 1 images within the criminal justice community?
7. What are the differences between dots and pixels in relationship to digital images?
8. What affect does the distance of the object being photographed from the lens have to do with image resolution?

Suggested Reading

Blitzer, Herbert, Karen Stein-Ferguson, and Jeffrey Huan. 2008. *Understanding Forensic Digital Imaging*. Academic Press.

Harrington, Richard. 2010. *Understanding Adobe Photoshop CS5*. Peachpit Press.

Kelby, Scott. 2011. *The Adobe Photoshop CS5 Book for Digital Photographers*. New Riders Publishing.

Rand, Glenn, Christopher Broughton, and Amanda Quintenz-Fiedler. 2011. *Capture: Digital Photography Essentials*. Rocky Nook Publishing.

Robinson, Edward M. 2010. *Crime Scene Photography* (2nd Edition). Academic Press.

Scott, Charles C. 1969. *Photographic Evidence* (2nd Edition). West Publishing Company.

CHAPTER 7

Legal Issues Related to Photographs and Digital Images

CONTENTS

LEARNING OBJECTIVES

Upon completion of this chapter, you will be able to:

- Explain the elements for a photograph to be considered a "fair and accurate representation of the scene"
- Explain what is meant by requiring the photograph to be "authentic"
- Explain why all photographs taken at a crime/accident scene may not be admissible in court
- Explain the requirement that a photograph has to be "more probative than prejudicial"
- Explain the difference between a "manipulated" and a "processed" digital image
- Explain how rotations and interpolation change the data within an image's file
- Explain the difference between saving an image as a JPEG file and a TIFF file

Introduction to Crime Scene Photography.

PHOTOGRAPHS AND DIGITAL IMAGES AS EVIDENCE

As crime scene photographers, we have to photograph both the crime scene and the evidence within the crime scene. Just another day capturing images? Hardly! We always have to remember that the images we capture can be used very differently than those captured by other professional photographers. At times, our images can:

- Put people in prison
- Be the evidence that convinces the judge or the jury the death penalty is appropriate

That is quite a burden and responsibility. To do our job properly, our crime scene images must ultimately be admissible in court, just like any other item of evidence. And the judge is the gatekeeper.

Over the years, challenges to the admissibility of photos/images in court have fallen into some reoccurring categories. Our images, as evidence, must be:

- A "fair and accurate representation of the scene"
- Authentic
- Material and relevant
- And they must *not* be overly prejudicial for or against either the defendant or the victim.

As the crime scene photographer is capturing each image, they must constantly keep in mind these criteria by which their images will be judged. Forget these requirements, and the image may not be admissible in court as evidence. In this chapter, we'll look at each of these standards.

A FAIR AND ACCURATE REPRESENTATION OF THE SCENE

To assess the elements of an image related to being a "fair and accurate representation of the scene," it might be useful to ask ourselves how can an image be "unfair" or "inaccurate." There are five elements of this idea.

Exposure

If an image is grossly overexposed or underexposed, it is perfectly understandable that the image may no longer have sufficient detail to be useful to the judge or jury as they deliberate the issues still being contested during the trial.

The judge has the absolute prerogative to decide this issue. Has the image's gross exposure issue made it totally useless for the jury? Is it possible for there to

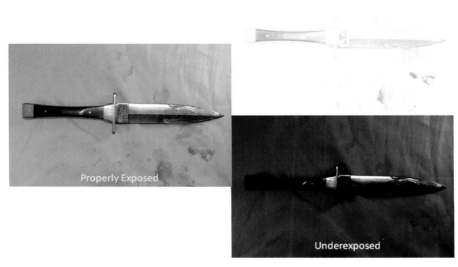

FIGURE 7-1
Grossly overexposed and underexposed images

be some slight value still in the image as it is currently exposed? Or can the image be somehow enhanced or "processed" digitally to see some detail that is currently within the image but just too difficult to see in its current condition? As will be seen later in this chapter, court-acceptable image processing can reveal vast amounts of details currently "hidden" in overexposed and under-exposed images. But if neither the prosecution nor the defense is offering a digitally "processed" image to the judge to be considered for admissibility, and the image under consideration is overexposed or underexposed, the judge may determine that a particular image is inadmissible just because of an exposure problem.

Is there ever a time when an image that is not properly exposed is actually considered the "correct" exposure? Of course, as has been mentioned earlier in this text, when a series of brackets are taken of a particular item of evidence, intentional underexposures and overexposures are collected. This practice is intended to give the examiner or analyst an additional view of details that might have otherwise been overexposed or underexposed in the original image that is considered as a whole as being properly exposed.

There is another time when an underexposed image is the only "correct" exposure? If a witness claims to have recognized a suspect in dim or dark lighting conditions, then returning to the witness's position when he or she saw the suspect must then be followed by capturing an image of the witness's viewpoint under the lighting conditions at the time of the original identification. But camera and flash systems are designed to provide proper exposures. The only way to duplicate the dim lighting conditions of the initial sighting in a photograph is to intentionally begin taking a series of incrementally dimmer and dimmer images. Then, once this series has been captured, you'd need to return to the scene, light it as it was originally, and see which image of the series is closest to the lighting conditions of the scene. In this case, an image such as the example in Figure 7-2 may be the only correct view of a car at night as seen by a witness.

FIGURE 7-2
A witness's possible view of a vehicle at night *(courtesy of I. Walker, GWU MS student)*

Color Accuracy

If the colors of objects within the image do not look as they were seen by those who were present at the crime scene, then the inaccuracy of the colors may be sufficient to have the image excluded from the trial. How can the colors be inaccurate? As mentioned in Chapter 2, colors can be unreliable under two conditions. If the images were captured with the wrong types of light, colored tints may affect the image. Or if the image was printed incorrectly, the colors within the image may not be faithful to the "real" colors that were at the crime scene. When the colors of an object are critical, the solution is to photograph colored objects with the correct lighting and to also insert a color scale in the image so that everyone can be assured that the printing process duplicated the colors originally seen.

FIGURE 7-3
What color is this car? *(courtesy of S. Keppel, GWU MS student)*

Ambient lighting can change the colors seen by witnesses. In the Figures 7-3 and 7-4, using an electronic flash provides the proper colors of the car and jacket. The car is blue, not gray. The jacket is black, not brown.

FIGURE 7-4
What color is this jacket? *(courtesy of S. Keppel, GWU MS student)*

Distance Relationships

The perceived distance between objects can be influenced by both the focal length of the lens and your own viewpoint. In Figure 7-5, where the statue looks further and further away from the photographer, the photographer was actually standing in the same spot for all three images. The top left image was taken with a 100mm lens, the bottom left image was taken with a 50mm lens, and the image on the right was taken with a 28mm lens. You have to be extremely conscious of the effect your choices of focal length have on the relative distance relationships of the scene around you.

FIGURE 7-5
Focal lengths affecting relative distances *(courtesy of J. Buffington and M. Hur, GWU MS students)*

Establishing the correct viewpoint can also affect the perceived distance relationship between an item of evidence and a fixed feature of the scene. Figure 7-6 shows four different possible distances between the knife and the corner. Which is correct? The top three images were composed with a linear viewpoint, taken at different heights. It appears as if the knife is getting closer to the corner. The only accurate distance is captured by the lower image, in which the film plane is parallel to an imaginary line between the knife and corner.

Focus/Depth of Field

An object can appear to be blurred for several reasons. The focus or depth of field can be incorrect, and an object or an area may appear to be out of focus. Figure 7-7 is an example of a DOF inadequate for the size of the area being photographed in the top two images. The top image shows a very short DOF when the focus is on the front pawn and a wide aperture (f/2) is used. The middle image was captured with the same f/2, but this time the last pawn was

FIGURE 7-6
How far is the knife from the corner? *(courtesy of M Blake, GWU MS student)*

the point of exact focus. The lower image was taken with an f/22 and the image was zone focused. This combination results in all the pawns being in focus.

A second kind of blur occurs when the subject is moving and a shutter speed is used that is inadequate to "freeze" their motion.

A third kind of blur is caused when there is inadequate resolution to sharply capture the image, which can also occur during a close examination of an item of evidence if it is enlarged in the hopes of better seeing some critical detail. The enlarging process may be the very action that causes the evidence to lose resolution; if the item of evidence is smaller than necessary in the field of view, many digital pixels are thus being squandered on the surrounding substrate rather than being placed on the evidence in question. This results in the evidence not being able to be enlarged with the proper resolution to see minute details.

In Figure 7-8, a small earring clasp was captured at the proper 1:1 magnification ratio, probably with a macro lens. This setup makes the clasp as large as it can be with the photography equipment normally available to a crime scene

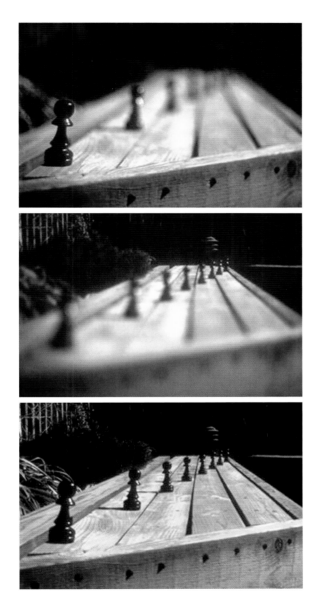

FIGURE 7-7
The DOF varies with f/stop choice and focusing technique

photographer. The clasp was then incorrectly captured with a 1:3 and 1:5 magnification ratio. Both of these images show the clasp smaller than necessary and put more and more of their digital pixels on the substrate. So what? The clasp still looks like the clasp, doesn't it? But see Figure 7-9 which shows the clasp magnified to show the same detail of a small area.

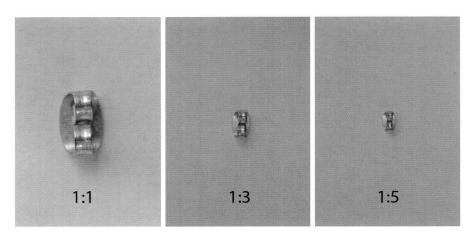

FIGURE 7-8
Differing magnification ratios *(courtesy of S. Kingsbury, GWU MS student)*

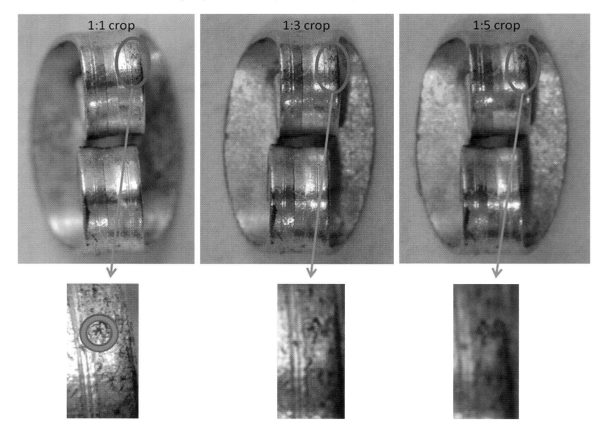

FIGURE 7-9
With inadequate resolution, blur can result *(courtesy of S. Kingsbury, GWU MS student)*

What if the encircled "star" were a jeweler's mark used to identify his jewelry? Only the image on the left has sufficient resolution to show this mark, which could be important to a case.

Size

When the size of an item of evidence is critical, a scale is used so that the image can be enlarged to the appropriate size. But the scale does this properly only if it is placed on the same plane as the evidence being photographed. If the scale is closer to the photographer than the evidence, or farther from the photographer than the evidence, the scale will not be the correct size, and any enlargement of the evidence will be incorrect .

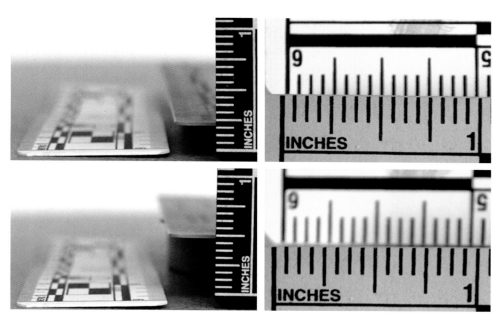

FIGURE 7-10
The size of scales can change *(courtesy of K. Kensie, GWU MS student)*

Figure 7.10 shows two scales that are 1/4 inch apart and 1/2 inch apart. In each case, the scales have clearly changed sizes. And if you look closely, you can see that the scales are also not as sharp as the scale that was the point of focus. It is critical that the crime scene photographer makes an effort to place the scale at the correct position adjacent to the evidence: as high as the evidence is high, or as deep as the evidence is deep.

AUTHENTIC

The second criteria by which images will be judged as being acceptable to be used in court is their **authenticity**. What makes an image "authentic" or "inauthentic"?

"As Found"

One of the first concerns is that our images reflect the crime scene as it was originally found, before anything has been removed from the crime scene or anything has been added to the crime scene. One exception is that the courts seem to understand that before the crime scene photographer arrives at the crime scene, first responders have usually already put out banner guard (the typical "Police Line Do Not Cross" yellow tape) encircling the crime scene. There may also be wooden barricades blocking the streets, and frequently traffic cones and numbered or lettered A-frames have been placed near evidence to remind others not to walk or drive in those areas. The courts don't seem to require all these additions to have been removed before the crime scene photography begins documenting the crime scene.

But what if an item of evidence had been picked up for safety concerns before the crime scene photographer arrives? This action is normally related to officers picking up weapons lying in a public place or any obvious valuables that bystanders may be tempted to run off with. Is it permissible to return this evidence to where it had been within the crime scene so the photographer can photograph the scene as it was first seen by the first responder? The usual recommendation if for the photographer to photograph the scene "as found" by the photographer upon first arrival. The officers who picked up any of the evidence must include that action in their reports and attempt to be specific regarding where they removed it from, but they should not be permitted to replace the evidence into the crime scene. The best compromise frequently suggested is for any officer who feels that he or she must remove an item of evidence from the scene for safety concerns to immediately place a marker where the evidence had been, similar to the way golfers mark their balls on the green before picking them up. Then the crime scene photographers can photograph the marker in place because that marker was within the scene when they arrived.

Manipulations Prohibited

The previous suggestions help assure the courts that the placement of items within the crime scene are "authentic." But what about the image itself? Is the image itself "authentic"? To address this issue, the courts have required that the image itself not be impermissibly altered since it was originally captured. This type of alteration is called a **manipulation**. A permissible alteration, to be discussed shortly, is called a **processed** image.

What is the essence of a "manipulation"? A manipulation is a change to the original image that adds detail to the image that was not originally present or deletes essential detail within the image that was originally present.

What does Figure 7-11 represent? Is the top an original image, or is it what remains after eight of the coins in the bottom image were removed, either physically or digitally? Is the bottom image the original image, or were eight additional coins placed around the original single coin, either physically or digitally? There is a visual clue, if you can see it! Notice the shadow on the bottom side of the single coin. That same shadow is present in all nine coins in the bottom image. If nine coins were lit by a single light source, all their shadows would be slightly different. The bottom image represents the upper coin being digitally copied or cloned and then eight copies being placed around the original single coin.

FIGURE 7-11
Coins copied and added around the original *(courtesy of J. Wreh, GWU MS student)*

In Figure 7-12, the manipulations are perhaps more subtle. In two of the tags, details have been removed and added. In this case, the middle tag is the real tag. In the upper image, the "9" was copied and superimposed over the "U." In the lower image, the letter "P" was changed into the letter "B." Although such manipulations can be done relatively easily with imaging software such as Adobe Photoshop, photographers offering images in court as evidence have to swear that the images are accurate and have not been manipulated.

FIGURE 7-12

Which tag is the original? *(courtesy of J. Wreh, GWU MS student)*

Rotations

The previous few figures are representations of intentional manipulations in which details and been added or deleted by an individual with the intent to deceive the viewer. Can there be "innocent" changes to an image that subject the image to being excluded from court? The answer will depend on the jurisdiction you may be in or the particular judge who will be evaluating the image.

It is probably safe to say that every photographer has at one time or another captured an image and later noticed that the horizon has been inadvertently tilted a bit to the left or right. With a digital camera, this problem is easily fixed. Some cameras and some digital software applications allow the photographer to rotate the image to varying degrees to fix such tilts. But what happens to the image when such rotations are used to correct a tilt?

On most digital cameras, the digital sensor is made up of thousands of square pixels arranged in horizontal and vertical rows and columns. Each individual pixel has captured just one color or one tone from the scene. There are no variations to the color or tone within any pixel—just one color or one tone. What happens when the image is rotated, even just 1 degree?

Figure 7-13 demonstrates the effects of rotating an image. The top two images show a single light-blue pixel being rotated 1 degree to the left. In effect, what this does is put some light-blue detail into each of the four adjacent red pixels. There would then be a bit of red detail in the area that had been totally light blue. How is a pixel to deal with this addition of detail within its square? Because a single pixel can be only one color or tone, each pixel must average its new content until it is just one color or tone.

To demonstrate this issue, an image was enlarged until individual pixels could be seen. Then, four of the original pixels had their colors changed so that the results of rotations would be more obvious. In Figure 7-13, the middle right image labeled "Rotated 1°" shows the surrounding pixels being forced to average the new content that has been placed within their squares. This averaging has produced new colors and tones that were not previously present. In effect, rotating the image has forced the digital software to create details that were not within the original crime scene. Back out of the enlargement, so that the image is its original size, and the scene looks exactly as it did originally, except that the tilt has been corrected. But we all know that this image, although it does not appear to have changed in any significant way, is made up on the pixel level with data that was not originally captured from the crime scene.

You protest that the image looks exactly the same as it did before! Yet in court, one must agree that the image contains details that did not come from the

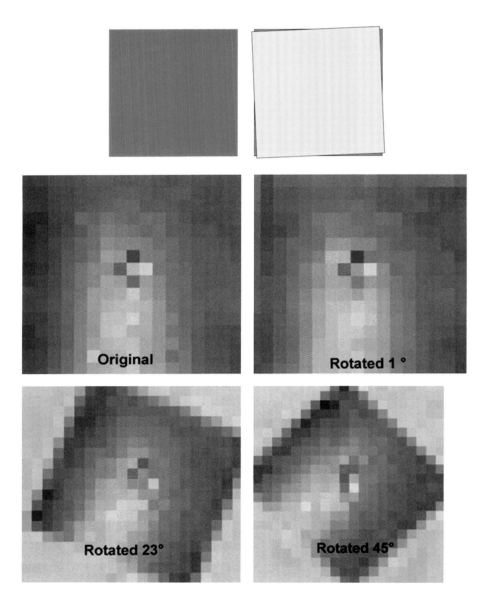

FIGURE 7-13
Rotations put some of their detail into neighboring pixels

crime scene. Is there a compromise solution? Yes, in a way. For all the images that are *not* regarded as examination-quality images, rotations are perfectly acceptable. These images are not going to be the ones that result in a defendant being incarcerated or executed. But the SWGs state that examination-quality images must not be rotated except in increments of 90 degrees, at which angle all the square detail of each pixel remains in square pixels.

Interpolation

There will be times when it is desirable to enlarge an image, and many times this can be done without any negative effects to the image. But there will also be times when an undesired effect will become evident with the image that has been enlarged.

In Figure 7-14, the top image of the cartridge was captured as a JPG image (mentioned in an earlier chapter and discussed more shortly), and the file size would permit a photo-quality print as you see it. Unfortunately, the original

FIGURE 7-14
An image cropped and interpolated to enlarge it

photographer did not fill the frame with the cartridge as recommended in this text. As the trial comes closer, the prosecuting attorney might request that the cartridge be cropped and enlarged for use in court. The crop and enlargement are also shown in Figure 7-14. The reader should be able to notice that the enlargement looks a bit "soft" or out of focus, because the image was enlarged/interpolated beyond its resolution capacity. Every image has a maximum size to which it can be interpolated and the image still retains all its sharpness and detail. Go beyond this size and the image begins to degrade more and more. But even when you can't see the degradation to the image, there is a change to the image on the pixel level, similar to what has been seen previously with rotations.

Each image is made up of a number of horizontal and vertical picture elements (pixels). If an image currently has sufficient resolution for a photo-quality print of 4×6 inches, but you'd prefer to make it an 8×12-inch print, what are you asking the printer to do? The printer must take the current pixel detail and "stretch" it so that the original pixels cover a larger area. How does the printer do this? To simplify the process, it can be said that the current pixels must be "smeared" or "stretched" outward in all directions until they cover the larger desired area. Figure 7-15 shows this effect.

On the left in Figure 7-15, an image was enlarged until individual pixels could be seen, and then various pixels were colored so that the effect would be more noticeable. The right image shows these same pixels after the image was interpolated to increase the image size. As every pixel's detail is moved into its surrounding pixels' areas, each pixel must average all the detail it now has within it to come up with just one color or one tone. In every case, there are now colors and tones that did not come from the crime scene.

All interpolated images will have this change on the pixel level. If they're not interpolated too much, you may not be able to see the effect at all when just viewing the full size image. But there will come a time when, with too much interpolation, the full size image begins to noticeably degrade. This problem is seen as a loss of detail or a blurring of the image.

Lessons learned? Fill the frame so that the primary subject has more pixels covering it, which results in better resolution. When it can be anticipated that the image will be used for examination-quality purposes, avoid capturing it as a JPG image, and no examination-quality image should be interpolated.

RELEVANT AND MATERIAL

Like any other kind of evidence, photographs and digital images must be both relevant and material to be admissible in court. These are specific legal

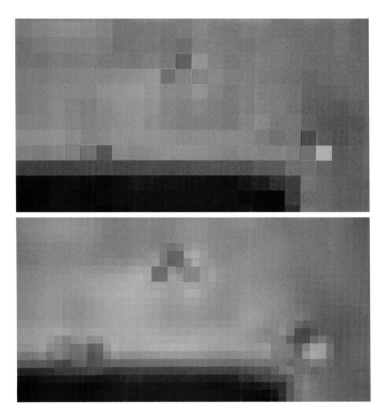

FIGURE 7-15
Interpolation "stretches" the original digital data

terms that to the layman appear to be extremely similar. Being **relevant** means that the evidence tends to prove a matter of fact significant to the case. Being **material** means that the evidence relates to a question still in dispute during the trial and the evidence helps establish the truth or falsity of the contested issue. No legal dictionaries and law books this author has reviewed have offered better distinctions between these two legal terms.

One example might help you understand these terms. At a homicide investigation, officers noticed that the back door of a residence had been broken in. Thinking that this had been the way the suspect entered the residence, we were busy photographing the damage to the door, as viewed from the inside and the outside. As these photographs were being taken, a neighbor came over to report that the victim had previously locked himself out of his home several days prior to the homicide, had broken in through his own door, and had not had the opportunity to fix it. All the damage to the door instantly became irrelevant and immaterial to the homicide investigation.

More Probative than Prejudicial

All evidence offered in a criminal trial is offered to prove or disprove elements of the case. But if an image becomes overly prejudicial to either party of the case, even though it may help prove an element being contested in the trial, the judge may exclude it. How might an image be overly prejudicial? An image might be considered to be too gruesome or gory for the jury to see. The judge might believe that if the jury did see it, they could become so distressed or offended that they might look around for someone to blame, such as the person sitting conveniently nearby in the defendant's chair. The trouble is that this defendant has not yet been determined to be guilty! To protect the defendant against any undue prejudice, the judge might decide to exclude the image. Many agencies have learned to anticipate this possibility and also prepare a black-and-white version of the same image to offer to the judge if the color image is deemed to be too gory for the jury to see. In many cases, the black and white version may be viewed by the jury. The color image in Figure 7-16 is an example. The black and white version might be less prejudicial and therefore admissible.

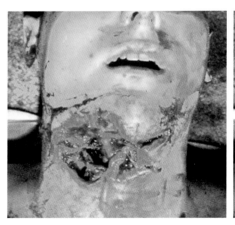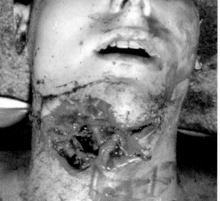

FIGURE 7-16
Color and black-and-white versions of the same image

In addition to unfairly prejudicing the jury against the defendant, an image might unfairly prejudice the jury for or against a victim of a crime. In one case, a victim was battered to the point that hospital treatment was required. When the crime scene photographer was allowed to photograph the victim in the recovery room several days later, the photos of the victim in traction with broken bones was held to be too prejudicial in favor of the victim because in the background, on a table, there was a framed image of the victim in full dress military uniform displaying a chest full of medals. The judge considered this image to be irrelevant to his injuries and likely to prejudice the jury toward sympathy for the victim.

In a rape case, some of the images of the victim's wounds also included some of her tattoos. These were not sweet tattoos of roses or Celtic symbols. They were hardcore tattoos suggesting that the victim belonged to a gang. The judge correctly excluded any of the images that contained any tattoos, as they might have unduly prejudiced the jury against the victim.

LEGAL IMPLICATIONS OF DIGITAL IMAGING

With the increasing use of digital images being offered as evidence during trials, some issues that had not been encountered with film images have been encountered. Because of these differences, standard guidelines and standard operating procedures have been developed to deal with these new issues.

Compression Choices

In the days of film, when the film in a camera body was exposed to light during an exposure, the photographer had choices about the exposure levels of the light and how that light was focused on the film, and this is still the case when using a digital camera. But digital photographers now get to decide how much of the detail from the crime scene actually gets recorded on the memory card in the camera body. Typically, the photographer can preset the camera to record differing amounts of the data that was originally encountered by the digital sensor. Many cameras have the option of saving digital data as RAW or NEF files. RAW in not an acronym for anything; it literally means that all the raw original data is saved in a file. This file is not even an image yet. It has to be processed into an image. But because it has all the digital data that was originally gathered during the image-capturing event, it ultimately gives the photographer (or, typically, the file processor) the most flexibility in processing the file into an image as desired. NEF (Nikon Electronic File) is Nikon's version of a RAW file capture. It also produces an unprocessed file containing all the digital data that the camera's digital sensor is capable of capturing.

Typically, RAW and NEF files are processed into .tif image files. A .tif file is short for TIFF, which stands for Tagged Image File Format. TIFF files are considered a **lossless** compression file format, meaning that all the original digital detail is stored as an image file that does not discard any of the original data. The result is that the file size is very large, and it takes up a lot of space on the camera's memory card and on the computer's hard drive. The plus side is that it produces images with the highest resolution. For this reason, it is recommended to capture all examination-quality images as RAW or NEF files, or as TIFF files, if your camera does not allow a RAW or NEF file options.

A file format more frequently used is the .jpg format. A .jpg file is short for JPEG, which stands for Joint Photographic Experts Group. JPEG files are considered a "lossy" compression format, which discards vast amounts of digital data for the purpose of creating much smaller file sizes. The main purpose for this is to enable more files to be saved on the camera's memory card and on the computer's hard drive. JPEG images can easily be sent over the Internet, as they are so small; most TIFF files are too large to be sent over the Internet.

What makes the JPEG file type so useful is that an image file can frequently have 50 to 80 percent of its digital data discarded and the image still looks like the object photographed. How can this be?

Typically, JPEGs discard digital data in two ways. First, much of the data of an image is very repetitive and similar to other data in that image. For instance, whenever the sky is in the background, much of the sky has the same blue tone. JPEG's job is to determine all the pixels that have the exact same blue tone, keep one of them as a representative for them all, and then discard the remainder. When the image is created, it will take this one tone of blue and use it for where all the others were. Consider an indoor photo in which white walls and a white ceiling are in the background. The JPEG's job is to find one representative white or cream tone, save it, and discard all the others that had the same tone; when the image is created, that one tone is duplicated for all the other missing tones. Huge amounts of digital data can be discarded in this fashion without appreciably degrading the overall image.

JPEG goes further, however. Its next task is to identify very similar adjacent colors and tones and then average them. This step produces multiple colors and tones that have the same values, and then one is retained and the others are again discarded. There are frequently incremental amounts of JPEG formatting that the camera or computer can be set at, such as Max, Hi, Med, and Low. For crime scene photographers, sticking with the Max or Hi options is recommended.

Typically, most images captured at crime scenes can be JPEGed. In fact, capturing RAW, NEF, and TIFF files is recommended only for examination-quality images. The need to archive all the images produced by law enforcement agencies would be unduly burdensome if they all had to be captured as lossless files.

Processing Digital Images

Whereas "manipulating" digital images is prohibited for examination-quality images, "processing" them is permissible. Processing a digital image basically means improvement of the image in ways that allow the details already within the image to be more easily recognized. Changes to the image are being made, but these changes do not add details that were not originally present. And the changes do not discard essential details that were originally present in the image. It just makes it easier to see the details that were there. As some of these changes can be very remarkable, defense attorneys will often dramatically declare that the results have improperly been created to implicate the defendant. To withstand such accusations, some very effective procedures have been developed to ensure that processed images are ultimately acceptable in court as evidence.

Originals Archived/Processing Only Applied to Copies

First, the original image is never processed. A copy of the original image is made, and only the copy is processed. The unprocessed original image is archived and is available to be brought to court if necessary. In this way, a new copy of the original image can be made during the trial, and this new copy can be processed in exactly as the same way the processed image had been, and the judge and jury can then see that the image now implicating the defendant did in fact originate from the unprocessed original.

A History of Processed Images Should Be Maintained

As the first copy of the image is being processed, each step of the processing must be documented. This exact history of processes can then be replicated by any other expert, even the defendant's experts, and the same result will be achieved. This goes for not just the type of processing that was applied to the image but also includes the amount of that processing. What degree of a particular type of processing was applied to the image? This knowledge makes the entire process repeatable by any qualified expert.

Who Did the Processing, and When?

Just like any other type of physical evidence, the chain of custody of the image must be established. It is necessary to establish that impermissible tampering with the evidence has not occurred at any time. Then it is necessary to document who did the actual processing and when this person did the work. It is necessary to establish the original training of this individual to establish that he or she was competent to do the processing in the first place—and not just that the person was at one time competent but also that he or she is presently competent. What kind of subsequent training has he or she completed? Must the person successfully complete annual proficiency tests, for instance?

Examples of Processed Images

Although there are many types of processed images, most often they fall into some common categories. Images can have their contrast adjusted so that details that had been too light or too dark can more easily be seen. Figure 7-17 displays an untreated fingerprint that had been on a metal seatbelt. It is faint, but visible. It is very easy to darken the ridges until they are much easier to see. The lower image is more remarkable. The original image is greatly underexposed. In fact, the original image looks completely black, with no detail visible. Digitally processing this image enables us to see that there was still some remarkable detail present within this dark image. Now, a woman talking on a cell phone can be seen. She has a white jacket and is wearing jeans. Behind her is a fire hydrant and a tree, which might help locate the exact location of the photograph. Rest assured that if this image looks like the defendant, the defense attorney will be screaming that the image was manufactured to implicate his client. However, anyone trained on Photoshop will also be able to make the exact same image appear from the black image on the left.

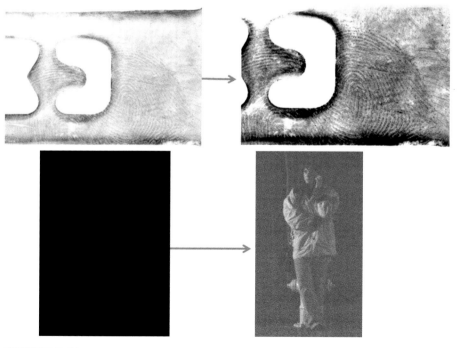

FIGURE 7-17
Contrast adjustments reveal details

Another common type of processing is the removal of multiple colors in the background when they interfere with the visibility of fingerprints on top of them. Figure 7-18 is a good example of this. On the left side of the colored image, a part of the fingerprint is on a black background. The black background has to be lightened; at the same time, the light-toned ridges have to be darkened. Of course, the red and blue background colors have to be removed as well. And the white stripe in the center has to be toned down and the ridges there must be darkened. All of these corrections are very simple to do. The result is a fingerprint that most latent print examiners would love to work with.

FIGURE 7-18
Colors removed and contrast improved

Finally, another magical revelation of a person who had been "hiding" in the dark: Figure 7-19 shows the sequence. On the top left is an image taken with a "normal" lens to show how far away the subject had originally been. In the back center are two white squares. These are interior lights seen through two windows of the building in the background. Just to the right of those two squares is a small light oval, which is a face of person standing in front of the building. At the top right is an image taken with a short telephoto lens, and the bottom left is the same person photographed with a longer telephoto lens. Then it is just a matter of a bit of contrast improvement, and the subject is easily recognized.

FIGURE 7-19
Processing revealing a "hidden" subject

International Association for Identification (IAI): Resolution 97-9: Recognized Digital Imaging as a Scientifically Valid and Proven Technology

Since digital images have become more prevalent in the courtroom, rather than attacking the results of individual images that have been processed, some have tried to attack digital imaging as a whole. After all, if digital imaging can easily create dinosaurs running around islands, how can any of it be trusted as evidence in court? As this chapter is being written, Kodak has filed for bankruptcy. Film will soon go the way of the Polaroid image. Digital imaging will eventually be the only available option.

How is this new digital media to be trusted and accepted in court as evidence? The exact same way that film was admissible in court as evidence. Individuals will testify that their digital images are fair and accurate representations of the crime scene and of the evidence within the scene. And they will testify that their standard operating procedures prohibit improper manipulations to images being offered in court as evidence. When the digital images have to be processed in order to better see all the details that were originally within them, qualified experts will walk the court through a step-by-step sequence of the exact changes they made to copies of the original image. And, if anyone wants to, he or she can start with another copy of the original, follow the same sequence of steps, and arrive at the same result.

Rather than considering digital imaging as a radical change from the film images we had long grown accustomed to, the International Association for Identification determined in 1997 that digital imaging is a scientifically valid and proven technology, which is a natural extension of film imaging.

CHAPTER SUMMARY

Rather than being feared, digital imaging is to be embraced. The courts already have. Digital images are constantly being accepted into court cases as evidence. Processed images are being accepted into court as valid types of evidence. Although digital technology can create remarkable and fanciful images, qualified experts are ready to put their integrity on the line and testify that no improprieties were taken with the processing used to produce the images being offered as evidence in court.

It was pointed out how photographs intended to be offered in court as evidence have certain standards by which they will be evaluated. They have to fairly and accurately represent the scene as it was originally found. They have to be authentic, not recreations of the original scene, unless they are clearly documented as being recreations. They have to be relevant and material, just like any other evidence introduced in the course of the trial. And they cannot unduly bias the juror against either subject in the proceeding by appealing to the emotions of the juror.

Discussion Questions

1. How would the color accuracy of photographs be established?
2. Which lens best assures the accuracy of distance relationships?
3. Is it permissible to return evidence that has already been collected to the crime scene to photograph it approximately where it was originally found?
4. "All photographs taken at the original crime/accident scene will be admissible as evidence later in court." Comment on this statement.
5. If a suspect has been charged with a mutilation homicide, photographs of body parts of the victim in the defendant's residence may not be admissible at trial, even though they are strong evidence of the defendant's guilt. Why? How might it be argued that these photographs should be admissible?
6. In what situations is it permissible to admit an underexposed photograph as evidence in court?

7. Can a person stopped as a possible suspect in a crime legally refuse to have his photograph taken to be shown to a witness who cannot respond to the area of the stop?

8. Define "relevant" and "material."

Suggested Readings

Berg, E. 2000. "Legal Ramifications of Digital Imaging in Law Enforcement." *Forensic Science Communication* 2(4).

Blitzer, H. L., and Jacobia, J. 2002. *Forensic Digital Imaging and Photography*. San Diego: Academic Press.

Eastman Kodak Company. 1999. Digital Imagery in the Courtroom. http://www.ictlex.net/index.php/1999/10/05/digital-imagery-in-the-courtroom.

EPIC (Evidence Photographers International Council). 1999. Outline for Standard Crime Scene Photography. Honesdale, PA: The Council.

Mello, K. 2002. *Photography and Digital Imaging in Law Enforcement*. Jacksonville, FL: Institute of Police Technology and Management.

Nickell, J. 1994. *A Handbook for Photographic Investigation*. Lexington: University Press of Kentucky.

Redsicker, D. R. 1994. *The Practical Methodology of Forensic Photography*, Boca Raton, FL: CRC Press.

Glossary

18 percent gray card An 18 percent gray card is the standard. There are many shades of gray. A gray card that reflects precisely 18 percent of the light that strikes it is the standard. This particular shade of gray is used because the real world, considering its light shades and dark shades and the various colors found in a "normal" scene, typically reflects 18 percent of the light that strikes it.

Absorption Energy that is neither reflected or transmitted by a surface but assimilated into the surface.

Accurate To be admissible in court as evidence, an image or photograph has to be a "fair and accurate representation of the scene." If the image is inaccurate or does not fairly depict the scene of object as it was originally found, it may be inadmissible.

Analog Data represented as a continuously variable quantity.

Aperture Priority exposure mode (AV) The photographer manually sets the f/stop desired, and the camera will automatically set the corresponding shutter speed required to properly expose the photograph for the reflected light coming into the camera.

Aperture Priority mode Currently, this is the best way to proper expose large dimly lit crime scenes. Although not a flash technique, it does provide extra light for a large scene when the ambient light levels are not sufficient.

Aperture The size of the/diaphragm opening.

Authentic Photographs taken at crime/accident scenes should portray the scene as it was originally found, before any alterations.

Automatic flash exposure mode The sensor eye on the flash unit measures the amount of light reflected from the scene, and when it has determined that enough light has been reflected towards it for a proper exposure, these units can actually cut short the flash duration to prevent overexposure.

Automatic focusing By depressing the shutter button halfway, the camera will automatically focus on an item in the center of the viewfinder.

Barrel distortion A wide-angle lens effect in which straight lines at the edges of an image appear bowed outward.

Barrier filter A filter placed in front of a sensor that allows only specific wavelengths to pass.

Bit A basic unit of information used in computing and telecommunications to define one of two possible states: either a 1 or a 0; also referred to as an on switch or an off switch. A group of bits can be used to describe a data (information) value in a digital device or other physical system as well describe a specific color (grayscale) value. For example, 8 bits are used to store 1 byte of information in a computer system, whereas the term "8-bit gray-scale" is used to describe the 256 values of gray from pure black to pure white.

Bitmap A rasterized graphic format commonly known as a bitmapped graphic, which consists of a square grid of picture elements (pixels).

Bracketing The act of intentionally taking multiple exposures of the same subject from the same point of view at different exposure levels.

Burning and dodging In the days of processing film, photographic paper was white until subjected to light. Adding light to the photographic paper darkened it; withholding light from the photographic paper kept it a lighter tone. After the "normal" exposure of the entire print, selected areas previously overexposed can be subjected to additional light while the rest of the image is masked so it does not receive additional light. This is called **burning**. The effect is that previously overexposed areas of the image now look properly exposed. During the "normal" exposure of the entire print, the areas previously underexposed can be masked for a part of the normal exposure. This is called **dodging**. The effect is that previously underexposed areas of the image now look properly exposed.

Byte A measurement used to describe a data value in computing; consists of 8 bits.

Camera RAW format One of the methods used for storing the unprocessed (RAW) data from the imaging sensor in a digital camera.

Close-up filters A set of three filters with different individual magnifications that can be stacked for additional magnification ratios, usually from 1: 6 to about 1:2. These filters can be added to a lens to allow closer focusing and magnification of the subject.

Close-up photographs All items of evidence have close-up photographs taken of them. These are images that attempt to fill the frame with the item of evidence.

Cut-off filter Filters that pass shorter wavelengths of energy until a specific wavelength is reached.

Cut-on filter Filters that reject shorter wavelengths of energy until a specific wavelength is reached.

Dedicated/TTL flash exposure mode Rather than relying on a sensor eye on the front of the flash unit, a dedicated flash's light output is controlled by the light meter in the camera body. Then, the light coming in through the lens (TTL) is metered and the light emitted by the flash is adjusted for the distance of the subject.

Depth of field (DOF) The variable area from foreground to background that appears to be in sharp focus to the eye. The variables that can affect the DOF are the focal length selection, lens choice, and camera-to-subject distance.

Depth of field scale This scale is frequently shown as pairs of f/stop numbers on either side of the focusing point on the lens. Sometimes they are shown as pairs of colored lines on either side of the focusing point on the lens. They allow the photographer to know the precise depth of field range when either hyperfocal focusing or zone focusing. Unfortunately, many newer lenses do not have this feature.

Diaphragm A set of blades that can be opened to let more light through the lens or closed down to restrict the light entering the camera.

Digital Data represented as discreet values such as numbers.

Digital image The process of creating an electronic recording in a two-dimensional form of a physical object such as a person, place, or thing.

Digital noise/dark noise When a digital sensor is exposed for long time intervals in dim situations, the result is often a "grainy" appearance, in which individual pixels are not recording colors and light levels accurately. Rather than smooth evenly toned surfaces, the "noisy" digital image appears speckled with odd random colors. This is also the result of using "faster" digital ISO equivalents to attempt to cope with dim crime scenes.

Dirty snow If the reflective light meter is relied upon when taking images of snowy scenes, the result will be "dirty snow"—dark or underexposed snow. This applies to all light-toned subjects. When the composition is predominantly light toned, the light meter tends to underexpose them.

Dots per inch (dpi) The number of dots that can be placed within a 1-inch area by an inkjet printer or laser printer. The number of dots is based on the number of inks, the varying sizes of droplets, and the number of nozzles per print head in the printer.

Electromagnetic spectrum (spectrum or EMS) A continuum that encompasses the entire range of electromagnetic radiation. The range consists of radiation in the form of waves and is usually measured in wavelength or frequency. A common unit of measurement for much of the spectrum is in nanometers (nm) where $1nm = 1$ billionth of a meter. Gamma rays, which have the shortest wavelength and highest frequency, are at one end of the spectrum that continues through x-rays, ultraviolet rays, visible light, infrared rays, microwaves, and radio waves, which have the longest wavelength and lowest frequency.

Examination-quality photographs Special types of close-up images. They are taken when it can be anticipated that the image of an item of evidence will be used for comparison purposes or to allow an examiner or analyst to extract information from the image, which usually involves putting the camera on a tripod, having the film plane parallel to the evidence, having the scale on the same plane as the evidence, using the smallest f/stops, and bracketing the exposure.

Excitation filter A filter placed in front of a energy source that allows only specific wavelengths to pass.

Exposure compensation To bracket in one of the automatic exposure modes, this dial/button is set to the appropriate exposure desired, usually ranging from −2 to +2 stops.

Exposure latitude Daylight color film has an inherent inability to properly expose items within wide extremes of light. The positive aspect of exposure latitude is to realize that daylight color film can have exposure errors corrected in the wet-chemistry darkroom.

Exposure stops An exposure change from an image with a proper exposure is normally expressed as a change that either halves or doubles the overall lighting from the original exposure.

Extension tubes A supplemental lens, inserted between the camera body and the lens, that moves the prime lens elements farther from the film plane, resulting in magnification. Extension tubes of different sizes provide different magnifications.

Exterior overall photos Photographing all four sides of a building in which a crime occurred and documenting the general conditions of the exterior of the scene and how the specific crime scene relates to the surrounding area.

Exterior overalls If the crime occurred within a building, each side of the building is photographed in the hope that this complete overview will ultimately show the point of entry and point of exit of the suspect(s) when these are not known.

F-16 Sunny Day Rule Recommends both an f/stop setting and a corresponding shutter speed for most outdoor photographic situations.

F/stop A fraction relating the size of the aperture opening to the lens currently being used.

Fair and accurate representation of the scene This is a flexible legal standard in the United States that is in effect based on common sense. The basic standard is that the photograph must be accurate enough so that the average person who views the photograph would not be misled about what the original object depicted in the photograph actually looks like.

Fill-in flash A flash technique to ensure that a scene including both bright sunlit areas and dark shadows will have both areas properly exposed in one photograph. The sun is metered to properly expose the sunlit areas of the scene. Flash is used to properly expose the shady areas. The flash is balanced for the exposure necessary to properly expose the sunlit area and is set to be exactly one stop less bright than the flash.

Fixed features Evidence is shown in relationship to fixed features of the crime scene. These are features that cannot be moved, such as doors, windows, corners and electrical outlets, trees, light poles, and so on. They are features that are likely to still be there if a return to the scene were possible.

Fluorescence Luminescence or glowing created by a material absorbing a specific wavelength of energy from a source and immediately ceasing upon the removal of that energy source.

Focal length the distance in millimeters (mm) between the optical center of a lens and the sensor when the camera is focused on infinity (∞).

Focal length multiplier Medium-priced and less expensive digital SLR cameras use digital sensors that are smaller than a film's negative. The effect is that the smaller digital sensor captures less detail than the film negative would have. Another way to look at this is that the smaller digital sensor produces a "crop" of the full-size image. This crop can be thought of as a reduced field of view, or an image captured by a longer focal length lens. Therefore, a 50mm lens used on a digital camera with a 1.5 focal length multiplier captures what a 75mm lens would have captured had the camera been a film camera or a digital camera with a film-sized digital sensor.

Focus Setting the camera so that a particular object or a particular area is photographed so that it is sharp or in focus. Setting the camera so that light coming in through the lens converges to a precise point on the sensor.

Full-body panorama These begin with a midrange photo of the body and a fixed feature. They include images of the body from both sides, from both ends, a full-face image, and an overhead image. After being measured in its original position, the body is rolled over onto a clean surface and the sequence of close-ups is repeated.

Graininess As images are enlarged, the film's silver halide crystals, which make up the image, begin to separate and may become individually visible. Rather than a composite image being seen, the individual silver halide crystals become evident. These appear as grains of sand. Digital cameras have the equivalent; rather than silver halide crystals making up the image, the digital sensor has individual pixels. If an image is enlarged too much, the image will appear to become pixilated; individual pixels become evident as the image loses definition.

Guide number A means to determine a flash's relative output power. It can also be used to determine the f/stop to properly expose an object at a particular distance by using the formula GN/ distance = f/stop.

Guideline A suggested (recommended) process or procedure to be followed under specific conditions. Guidelines are generally expressed using terms such as *may*, *can*, or *should*.

Hard shadows Shadows produced by holding the flash at an oblique angle. These shadows are very dark—so dark that details within the shadow areas cannot be seen.

Hyperfocal focusing The method to maximize the depth of field when infinity must also be in focus. Take a meter reading to determine the f/stop required for the exposure, then align the infinity symbol on the focusing ring with the corresponding f/stop on the depth-of-field scale.

Identification Aspects of the body that may help to ultimately identify the body are photographed. These include identification papers, scars, marks, tattoos, and the like.

Interior overalls If the crime occurred within a particular room, the paths from the exterior doors to that room are photographed, if known. Then, each room containing major aspects of the crime are also photographed. This usually includes images of all the walls of the room featuring fixed features of the room.

Interpolation Increasing the original resolution of an image by having the computer software expand the original pixels of the image. The software will then "create" new pixels to insert between the original real pixels. The result is a new larger image that looks indistinguishable from the original smaller image. The difference is that the new image contains digital data that did not come from the original crime scene; those new pixels were created by computer software.

Inverse square law The intensity of light diminishes by the inverse square of the distance change. If the distance light travels is doubled, that distance, 2, is inverted to become 1/2. 1/2 squared ($1/2 \times 1/2$) is 1/4. As the distance light travels is doubled, its intensity is quartered.

Isosceles triangle The best camera orientation for a midrange photograph: the photographer will be at one point of the triangle and the evidence and the fixed feature of the scene will be at the end of the two equal length sides of the triangle.

Joint Photographic Experts Group (JPG, JPEG) An image format in which the image file size has been reduced—typically sacrificing image quality—so that the image does not require as much storage space or require as much time to upload and/or download.

Labeled scale When scales are used to help determine the size of an item of evidence, a label is also included to provide more information about the image such as the incident number, the date/time, the address/location, and the photographer's name/initials/badge number/ID number. In addition, it frequently includes the evidence number that is being assigned to a particular item of evidence. Also, the name of the subject being photographed can be added.

Lens distortion When taking midrange photographs, lens distortion should be avoided by primarily using the "normal" focal length for the camera being used. Wide-angle focal lengths tend to elongate the perceived foreground to background distance, making the scene appear larger than it really was. Telephoto focal lengths tend to compact the perceived foreground to background distance, making the scene appear smaller than it really was.

Lens flare If the sun is in front of the photographer, direct sunlight can enter the lens, bounce around the various lens elements, and result in unwanted multicolored geometric shapes.

Long-wave ultraviolet (LWUV) The portion of the spectrum from approximately 300nm through 400nm.

Lossless compression TIFF (Tagged Image File Format) compressions reorder the digital data into a smaller file size without deleting any pixels data at all.

Lossy compression JPEGs result in lossy compressions. In order to store more images, some of the data of each image file is discarded to make a smaller file size. Once this digital data is eliminated by a JPEG format, the data can never be retrieved again. It is permanently lost.

Luminescence To glow. Energy of one wavelength strikes a material and is absorbed, converted, and re-emitted as a longer wavelength.

Macro lenses Designed to provide magnifications of up to 1: 1, where the true size of the object is captured at life size on the sensor.

Magnification with a 1:1 ratio An item of evidence is life-sized on the sensor.

Manipulations Involves either the addition of details that weren't in the original image or the deletion of essential details that were in the original image.

Manual exposure mode (M) The photographer is responsible for manually setting the f/stop and the shutter speed.

Manual flash mode The full power of the flash is used each time the flash is fired. Because the flash is used to photograph objects at different distances, the only way to alter exposures is to change f/stops.

Manual focusing Rotating the manual focusing ring to ensure that a particular object or area is in focus.

Material evidence Evidence that is important to the case; it cannot be too remotely connected to the facts at hand.

Megabits per second (Mbps) An abbreviation commonly used to express the speed, also referred to as bandwidth, in telecommunications, measured in millions of bits per second or megabits per second. To calculate what this means as far as performance is concerned, divide the number of Mbps by 10 to convert the number of megabits per second to megabytes per second. (Technically, the number of megabits would be divided by 8 to determine the actual number of megabytes; however, this does not account for network overhead and the like.) When checking network performance, you must identify both the download and upload speeds. For example, a standard (home) commercial-grade cable option would be downloads up to 15Mbps and uploads up to

3Mbps; uploading a file could take as much as five times longer to upload (send) a file than it would to download (receive) the same file.

Midrange photographs Each item of evidence is photographed showing its spatial relationship to a fixed feature of the crime scene to give the viewer a sense of this distance.

Natural perspective To the extent possible, most photographs should be taken with the photographer standing at their full height so that the images look as they would appear if the viewer were standing alongside of the photographer when the image was taken.

Near infrared (NIR or IR) energy or light The portion of the spectrum from approximately 700nm through 1000nm.

Negative dust print A dust print in which the shoe walking across a dusty surface removed dust and now the shoe print is a clean area on a dusty floor.

Neutral density filter One type of filter that can block some of the light coming in through the lens. These filters can be considered "sunglasses" for the lens.

"Normal" Lens A 50mm lens portrays the scene in exactly the same way as the eye saw it. A distant object viewed through a 35mm camera with a 50mm lens looks the same distance away as when we directly look at it. A near object viewed through a 35 mm camera with a 50mm lens looks to be the same distance from us as when we look directly at it. And the relative distance between the near and far objects looks the same to the eye as when viewed through a 35mm camera with a 50mm lens on it.

"Normal" room The common living room or bedroom. It is about 10×12 feet in dimension, has white ceilings about 9 or 10 feet high, and has light-colored walls rather than walls painted with any other color.

Oblique flash Electronic flash that can be removed from the camera's hot-shoe but still attached with a PC cord. It can then be held at the side of 3D evidence in order to produce shadows within the texture or pattern of the evidence. These shadows allow the details of the evidence to be seen rather than being washed out by direct flash.

Overall photographs Images depicting the approach to the crime scene, the area around the crime scene, and the path of exit the suspect(s) used if known. This gives the viewer a feel for the neighborhood of the crime scene.

Perspective distortion The angle of view can make the perceived distance between an item of evidence and a fixed feature appear to be closer than they really are. This includes linear and diagonal points of view. The points of view that avoid perception distortion are the film plane parallel or the isosceles triangle points of view.

Phosphorescence Luminescence or glowing created by a material absorbing a specific wavelength of energy from a source and continuing to glow after the removal of that energy source.

Photo identifier A form containing information to document a series of photos: (1) case number, (2) address or location, (3) date and time, and (4) name/initials/badge number/ID number of photographer.

Photo memo form As each image is captured, details about it are logged on this form, such as the ISO, f/stop, shutter speed, focal length, light used, and description of the shot.

Pincushion distortion Usually a result of using a telephoto lens, an image may show straight lines at the edge of the image bowed slightly inward.

Pixels (picture element) The smallest component of a digital image.

Pixels per inch (ppi) A measurement used to describe the number of picture elements (pixels) that are contained within a measurable distance of 1 inch.

Polarizing filter (polarizer) This filter blocks polarized light, removes reflections from glass and water, helps ensure accurate colors are obtained, makes skid marks more evident, and helps darken an otherwise over-exposed sky.

Positive dust print A dust print in which the details of the shoe print have been deposited on a surface with dust.

Post-mortem interval (PMI) Aspects of the crime scene and the body that can help determine the time since death are photographed. This includes decomposition changes, signs of insect infestation, crime scene markers, and other aspects.

Prefocus Most photographers first determine their distance from the subject to be photographed, then focus the camera for that distance. Prefocusing entails first focusing the camera for a particular size of object, then moving the camera towards the object until it come into focus. This is the optimal focusing technique for small evidence.

Prejudicial Evidence that is otherwise relevant and material to the case may not be admissible in court if the evidence is judged to adversely prejudice the jury against the defendant. If the judge believes such photos would upset the jurors to the point that they might lose their objectivity and forget that the defendant has not yet been found guilty, the images may be excluded from the trial.

Processing Taking the detail that is in the original image and making it easier to see.

Program exposure mode (P) The camera sets both the f/stop and the shutter speed automatically based on the amount of reflected light coming into the camera.

Raster graphics An image format commonly known as a bitmapped graphic (bitmap), which consists of a square grid of picture elements (pixels).

RAW A RAW (not an acronym for anything) file, to be precise, is not yet an image: it is an unprocessed file. The RAW file will have to be brought in to a RAW converter program, where decisions will then have to be made on everything about the image. The RAW format gives the photographer the most control over what the finalized image will look like.

Reflectance Energy that is redirected by a surface.

Reflective light meter 35mm SLR cameras typically have reflective light meters built into them, designed to meter/measure the amount of light reflected from the scene through the lens into the camera.

Relevant Relevant evidence is any evidence that tends to prove or disprove any disputed fact in the case.

Remote flash cord An electronic cord, frequently coiled, that allows a remote flash to remain electronically connected to a camera so that the flash will fire when the camera shutter button is depressed. It also allows the camera to inform the flash unit of the ISO selection, the f/stop selection, and the focal length of the lens being used.

Repeatable If an image has been processed to make otherwise difficult to see detail easier to see, the entire step-by-step sequence should be able to be repeated by any other qualified expert. This is why a history of each processing step is maintained.

Requirement A process or procedure that is mandatory for compliance within a set of standards and is generally phrased using the words *will* or *must*.

Resolution Although this term is frequently understood to mean the number of megapixels a digital camera offers, it really means the ability of the sensor to distinguish black and white line pairs as they become thinner and closer together. If the separate black and white lines can no longer be distinguished, they appear to merge into gray.

Rule of Thirds To maximize the depth of field when focusing on medium-sized areas, focus at a distance point midway between the top and bottom of the viewfinder. Geometrically, this technique is approximately the same as focusing one-third of the way into the length of the scene.

Scales on the same plane The scale should be placed at the same plane as the evidence being focused on—as high as the evidence is off the ground or as deep as the evidence is impressed into a surface.

Scientific Working Group on Imaging Technology (SWGIT) An organization whose goal is to help facilitate the adoption of standards and best practices for the capture, storage, processing (enhancement), analysis, transmission, and output of digital images as well as to provide compatibility between various law enforcement agencies and other entities within the criminal justice system.

Sensor Any device that detects, responds, and processes stimulus.

Shadow control Shadows can sometimes be distractions, and in smaller scenes they can be eliminated by blocking the sun in the areas in question, or by repositioning the flash head.

Shortwave UV The portion of the electromagnetic spectrum from approximately 200nm through 300nm.

Shutter When the shutter button is depressed, the shutter opens for a predetermined amount of time to allow light coming in through the lens to strike the film for different amounts of time.

Shutter Priority exposure mode (TV) The photographer sets the shutter speed desired, and the camera automatically sets the corresponding aperture required to properly expose the photograph based on the light reflected into the camera.

Single-Lens Reflex (SLR) First, the image viewed by the photographer through the viewfinder and the light striking the film both come from a single lens. Second, to accomplish this dual role, the light coming from the lens is reflected (reflex) by a series of mirrors to the viewfinder. During the actual image capture, a movable mirror is flipped up to allow the same light to strike the film.

Snow print wax Used with shoe and tire tracks in snow, provides contrast for photography as the white subject matter makes it difficult to see pattern and details within the imprints.

Soft shadows When a reflector is used with oblique flash, the light from the flash strikes the impression and continues past it until the light strikes the reflector. The light then bounces back toward the impression, lighting areas previously covered by "hard" shadows. The reflected light isn't strong enough to wash out the shadows, but it is strong enough to light details within the shadow area. Shadows are called "soft" shadows when details within them can be seen.

Standard Operating Procedure (SOP) A set of prescribed procedures that must be followed routinely for a given situation.

SWGFAST The Scientific Working Group on Friction Ridge Analysis, Study, and Technology. Experts developing guidelines for the use of digital photography when related to capturing friction ridge images.

SWGIT The Scientific Working Group on Imaging Technologies, "created to provide leadership to the law enforcement community by developing guidelines for good practices for the use of imaging technologies within the criminal justice system."

SWGs Scientific Working Groups.

SWGTREAD The Scientific Working Group for Shoeprint and Tire Tread Evidence. Experts developing guidelines for the use of digital photography when related to capturing shoeprint and tire track images.

Sync speed The shutter speed to use whenever an electronic flash is also used. The shutter speed that has the shutter completely open when the flash fires.

Tagged Image File Format (TIF or TIFF) An uncompressed file format used for storing digital images.

Telephoto lenses Lenses with focal lengths greater than 50mm.

Theory of reciprocity The same exposure may be obtained from a variety of different exposure settings. A smaller aperture may be used as long as a longer corresponding shutter speed is used. A wider aperture may be selected as long as a corresponding shorter shutter speed is used. ISO settings work the same way. These three exposure variables can be changes to arrive at the same exposure level while different "effects" are controlled by the photographer. For example, an exposure combination with faster shutter speeds freezes motion better; with smaller apertures, the photographer can increase the depth of field of the image, the area from foreground to background that appears to be in focus.

Transmission Energy that is conducted through a surface, material, or object.

TTL Through-the-Lens. (See *Dedicated/TTL flash exposure mode*.)

Ultraviolet (UV) energy or light The portion of the spectrum from approximately 200nm through 400nm.

UV filter A filter that blocks the UV (ultraviolet) light transmitted by the sky so that the sky will not look overexposed. It also serves to protect the outer element of the camera lens.

Vector graphics An image format based on a mathematical representation of graphical elements using geometrical shapes such as lines, points, curves, polygons, and so on; commonly used for creating computer-generated graphics (artwork). The use of these mathematical representations allows vector graphic images to be enlarged without the degradation typically associated with digital images commonly referred to as pixilation.

Visible (VIS) energy or light The portion of the spectrum from approximately 400nm through 700nm.

Wagon wheel ellipse Shows graphically how different wheel spokes will seem to be different lengths, depending on the viewpoint of the photographer. The only wheel spokes that represent the true distance diameter of the wheel are the spokes aligned from the far left to the far right.

White balance Instead of relying on color corrections in a wet-chemistry darkroom when there may be objectionable tints that result from exposing the scene with the wrong type of lighting, the photographer using a digital camera can set the white balance on the digital camera so that it is appropriate for the light in which the image is being taken. This ensures that the colors in the image are properly recorded.

Wide-angle lenses Lenses with a focal length shorter than 50mm.

Wounds/bruising/injuries Each injury has a midrange photograph captured with a fixed feature of the body in view. Then a series of close-up images are captured.

Zone focusing The technique to maximize the DOF for an area when infinity is not in the background. A focusing technique to ensure a particular area of the scene is included in the camera's depth-of-field range. If the lens has a depth-of-field scale, the rear distance needing to be in focus is aligned with the f/stop on the depth-of-field scale required for a proper exposure. Comparing the depth-of-field scale to the distance scale shows the resulting depth-of-field range.

Index

Page numbers with "f" denote figures